# AFTER THE BOSTON HERESY CASE

BY

## GARY POTTER

CATHOLIC TREASURES BOOKS
Monrovia, CA

ISBN: 0-9620994-6-5

Library of Congress Catalog Card Number: 93-079287

Printed and bound in the United States of America

On the Cover: Map of Harvard Square detailing the building which housed St. Benedict Center at Bow and Arrow Streets, copyrighted and used with the permission of Harvard Square Business Association.

CATHOLIC TREASURES
Box 5034
135 W. Foothill Blvd., Suite A
Monrovia, CA 91016

1995

I am deeply honored to have been asked by Gary Potter to write the Preface for this book. Had I both the time and the talent I should like to have written it myself. Shortly after my ordination in 1975 I had the privilege of meeting Father Leonard Feeney for the first time. My last visit with him was three years later, and less than a month before his death. From nearly the first moment of that first encounter I knew that my life was going to be linked, in one way or another, to Saint Benedict Center and its doctrinal crusade, not to mention the accompanying stigma. With the permission of my bishop, I served as chaplain to the sisters of St. Ann's house for several years, and worked with Bishop Timothy Harrington and Father Lawrence Deery in the early stages of trying to bring about the canonical regularization of those followers of Father Feeney who wished to take advantage of "official recognition". While my contribution to this effort was infinitesimal, I am nevertheless proud to have played some role in it, albeit a negligible one. Though I was called back to my diocese six years ago, my heart remains inextricably entwined with Saint Benedict Center, and with the truly remarkable men and women there who have dedicated their lives to the cause of truth.

During this latter half of the twentieth century there have been few names which have sparked such discussion, controversy, and polemics among Catholics in this country as has that of the late Father Leonard Feeney.

Interestingly, one of the few agenda items—perhaps the ONLY one—upon which there is consensus of agreement between mainline liberal, conservative, and traditional Catholics is the condemnation of Father Feeney. It is truly an amazing sight to behold articulate (and supposedly knowledgeable) spokesman and "spokespersons" vying to excel one another in their anathemas, diatribes, and just plain infantile name-calling when it comes to Father Feeney and his so-called "Feeneyites". Some of the epithets which spring to mind include: FANATIC, CULT-GURU, HATE-MONGER, RENEGADE, and even HERETIC (never mind that the sole objective of Father Feeney's efforts was to prevent souls from falling into the one heresy which alone undermines the entire deposit of the Catholic Faith).

Sadly, few—if any—of Father Feeney's modern-day critics and/or detractors knew him personally, or ever heard him speak. Some of these commentators are simply uninformed, others are misinformed, and still others disinformed. Whichever the case may be, such writings hold one thing in common, namely that their authors fail to reflect correctly the fullness of Father Feeney's teachings on the thrice-defined dogma: EXTRA ECCLESIAM NULLA SALUS.

After more than forty years from his bogus "excommunication" (which, even if it were valid, was for disobedience, not for erroneous teaching), and a decade and a-half from his death, Father Feeney's name is far from being the obscure footnote in history which many Churchmen had hoped it would be. "Man proposes; God disposes", observed the great St. Augustine, and although illness and age laid Father Feeney to rest in 1978, the doctrinal crusade he inadvertently launched in the 1940's has continued unabated. In fact, in the wake of the current tidal wave of ecumenical hysteria, and the resultant scandals provoked by ecclesiastics from the highest to the lowest echelons, the crusade is growing in strength and numbers. As a part of this renewal of interest in the person and teachings of Father Feeney, serious Catholic thinkers are gradually beginning to review and reconsider the background and events leading up to what has become known as the "Boston Heresy Case".

What was the henious offense for which Leonard Feeney has been accused, tried, convicted, sentenced, and morally executed? It was the unspeakable crime of upholding an infallible dogma of the Church; it was for insisting that black can not at the same time be white; it was for refusing to sacrifice the literal word of Divine Revelation on the altar of theological opinion; it was for demanding that the hungry multitudes be fed not with the gruel of sentimentalism, but with the nourishing meat of truth. Would that God would swell His Church's priestly ranks today with such "criminals"!

Of course, this book is not a biographical work in the commonly understood sense of that word, and it profiles the lives of several persons aside from Father Feeney, most notably Catherine Goddard Clarke. Mrs. Clarke (who will hereafter be referred to by her religious name of Sister Catherine) was the remarkable and indefatigable foundress of Saint Benedict Center. Gifted with a fine intellect, she was disarmingly gracious—as the saying goes, "every inch a lady." Though largely hidden from the public eye, it was Sister Catherine's indomitable spirit and tireless efforts which seemed to keep things going. She was a red-haired dynamo from which the Center members, and even Father Feeney himself, would draw energy from what must have seemed an inexhaustible supply.

However, it is Father Feeney's name which will always be connected with the "Boston Heresy Case", and it is his story which receives the lion's share of biographical treatment in this book.

Mr. Potter successfully synopsizes Saint Benedict Center's early history, along the way introducing us to other key figures involved, and deftly guides us through the intricate chain of events which precipitated what the Irish would euphemistically refer to as "the troubles".

From his hind-sight advantage, the author demonstrates how clearly Father Feeney and Sister Catherine were able to foresee the tragic and inevitable consequences of theological liberalism and Americanism. As the story unfolds, more than a few readers will be surprised to learn that the doctrinal position of Saint Benedict Center was in no way at variance with the constant teaching of the Catholic Church and the declarations of numerous popes down to and including Pius XII.

Of special note is the author's careful examination and exposition of the facts concerning the 1949 Letter of the Holy Office to the Archbishop of Boston and the 1953 Decree of Excommunication. The former, loudly and widely touted as being the Church's official declaration on the doctrinal position of Father Feeney, is seen for what it really is: the UNOFFICIAL opinion of one man, Cardinal Marchetti-Selvaggiani, whose signature it bears.

As regards the latter document, Mr. Potter refers to it as "dubious". I would go a step further and insist that the blatant invalidity of this decree could be detected by a first-year student of Canon Law. That any competent theologian could take this document seriously boggles the imagination.

The Holy Ses *did* eventually make known its mind on this matter (though Father Feeney's name nor that of Saint Benedict Center were mentioned) by way of the Papal Encyclical, *Humani Generis*, which WAS an official document: properly signed, properly sealed, and canonically published. What Pope Pius XII had to say on the subject was an almost verbatim quote from a press release given by Father Feeney when he was silenced.

Few Catholics nowadays know anything about the Church's teaching prior to the Second Vatican Council. Today it is: "Vatican II says...", pronounced as though this non-defining pastoral council was the Magisterium's ultimate word on all things religious, overshadowing and superseding every other conciliar and papal teaching. In the homey idiom of the late Will Rogers: "Folks, it just ain't so."

Apropos of the above, the reader will appreciate this book's masterful and eye-opening examination of Vatican II's "Declaration on Religious Liberty", which is presented in the light of the Church's previous, unambiguous, and sometimes infallible teachings on the subject (as all the documents of Vatican II must be understood).

Before concluding my remarks for this Preface, I would like to express my admiration for Mr. Potter's treatment of the protagonists in the story of the "Boston Heresy Case", especially those most closely associated with Saint Benedict Center. I, for one (and I may be the only one), am profoundly grateful that the author resists the temptation of sculpting "plaster saints" for the edification of his readers. What Catholics need today to edify them are flesh and blood models with sinew and bone—especially backbone. We need the example of men and women who, for all their gifts, virtues, and heroism were capable of making mistakes, sometimes failed, and occasionally fell short of the perfection toward which we are all supposed to be striving.

In considering whether—and if so, to what extent—in the course of the Center's history there occurred mistakes in judgment and action, this book makes no attempt of "covering up" or "white-washing" the facts, which would be indefensible. Nor is the reader offered anemic and unconvincing excuses. Rather, the author makes a straight-forward and scrupulously honest effort to assess certain words and deeds within the context of their times and the events which surrounded them.

One of the most revealing parts of this book is that which deals with the subject of Father Feeney's "reconciliation" and the current status of the various branches of Saint Benedict Center. Readers may very well (and with more than a little justification) wonder whether, in the final analysis, it was a matter of Father Feeney being reconciled to the Church or visa-versa.

In giving us this book, Mr. Potter makes a unique and invaluable contribution to the current list of books treating the subject of the Church's teaching about salvation. In an era when our Catholic people and prospective converts are being force-fed on a starvation diet of watered-down doctrine and junk-food liturgy, the author has provided a banquet for the heart and soul.

To Mr. Potter, I will merely say thank you for feeding God's hungry people, and to the reader, bon appétit.

Father Dennis P. Smith
St. Patrick Cathedral, Fort Worth, Texas
Feast of the Immaculate Conception
December 8, 1994

This book is not a complete history of its subject. A bigger volume would be needed to tell the complete history. To be sure, all the chief facts of the story are here related, but the book is more about discovery. That is, it is the result of a search—a search for the truth concerning one of this century's most notable religious controversies. That is why it is called, *After the Boston Heresy Case*. It could only be written when its author, the writer speaking to you now, had gone after the truth concerning the case and the supposed excommunication of its principal figure, Rev. Leonard J. Feeney, S.J. (later, M.I.C.M.).

To speak of going after the truth, as I just did, is to be quite literal. There is widespread misunderstanding and even misrepresentation of the facts of the case. To penetrate them, researches were conducted in books, libraries and archives, and there had to be travel to speak with persons who were part of the story of St. Benedict Center, who knew Fr. Feeney and the remarkable Catherine Goddard Clarke. Thus there was a trip to California to sit with the man who was closer to Fr. Feeney for a longer time than any other still living. But California is my native state. Despite its having radically changed in some ways during past recent decades, I know it.

By contrast, New England, to which I also traveled, is more foreign to me than most of Europe. I suspect it will remain so, no matter how often I visit. Its insularity would seem to guarantee that.

Of Boston and its environs, in particular, there is a more insular feeling than is to be felt in many actual islands. As a Catholic journalist, I had grown accustomed long before preparing this book to the distance Boston keeps between itself and the rest of the nation. For instance, when regularly writing news stories a few years ago for the conservative Catholic weekly newspaper, *The Wanderer*, I was never able to develop "contacts" in the town.

Truly, Bostonians seem possessed of concerns different from everybody else's. You can see it in their politics. Consider how Massachusetts, led by Boston, was the only state to vote for George McGovern back in 1972. I shall not dwell on the men I have seen Boston send to Washington, D.C., during the years I have lived and worked in the nation's capital: the Kennedys, Tip O'Neill, Robert Drinan, Barney Frank, etc., etc. The place has been *extremely* liberal for a long time.

The popular expression, "banned in Boston," might suggest it would be otherwise. However the expression came into being, I arrived at a for-sure conclusion after discovering the facts of the so-called Boston Heresy Case and briefly revisiting the city and its neighborhood for this book: There could be no more likely setting for the case than Boston.

If this book is about discovery, it is not simply discovery of the facts concerning the case. Before even seeking them, something else was learned. It had to do with my own religious beliefs.

To understand this discovery, it needs to be known that the idea of looking into the so-called Boston Heresy Case and supposed excommunication of Fr. Feeney, and writing something about them, came to mind early in my career as a Catholic journalist. In other words, it was about a quarter-century ago, or nearly 20 years after the case was the subject of newspaper headlines throughout the U.S. and around the world.

The case and the supposed excommunication suggested themselves as wanting to be written about for the reason that 20 years after their being in the headlines, they obviously still mattered to many Catholics. It was not merely that they were still being discussed. One even encountered families which had been, and remained, divided over the question of whether there had been a true heresy and a real excommunication.

If the idea to write about the question returned to me several more times over the years after it first arose, circumstances never seemed to allow for the work. It could be said that I did look into the case, however. That is insofar as the time came—it was about five years ago—when I investigated the "heresy" itself, the one for which Fr. Feeney was said to have been "excommunicated." This was really the first step in my search for the truth concerning the case, although I did not at the time think of it that way.

In any event, it deeply intrigued me to learn that the "heresy" was a teaching of the Church not presented to me when I came into her as a convert after Vatican II, but which in truth always had been, and thus must always remain, *de fide*. That is to speak of a teaching "of the Faith" to which a person must assent in order to be fully a Catholic.

This particular teaching is expressed in a formula of the Church's official language, Latin: *extra ecclesiam nulla salus*. The formula is usually translated: Outside the Church there is no salvation.

Once the teaching became known to me, not simply was I dumbfounded that it had fallen into such obscurity that it could take more than two decades for even a "professional Catholic" like myself to learn about it. I also grasped that it was truly the reason for becoming a member of the Church even if I was uninstructed in it when I received conditional baptism. Why, after all, embrace the Faith or, having embraced it, stay a Catholic (at least in the kind of serious way that has led very many to martyrdom) if the Church is merely the "best" or "most efficient" vehicle for getting to Heaven? "Best" for whom? Me in 1965, but not a Korean Buddhist a century before? "Efficient" when? In Paris in 1250, but not in multicultural New York City with the Third Millennium about to dawn?

In a word, I may have felt it desirable to join the Church because she was venerable and seemed to have a certain purchase on truth—a purchase strong enough to make her, at 2,000 years, the most venerable institution on earth—but I had learned the real reason was because there was no other means (provided I availed myself of them) for me ever to see the face of God. Under the circumstances, I felt very fortunate to have joined the Church, even though it was not consciously for the right reason.

The teaching, once I grasped it, necessarily became for me a belief to which had to be related all else I held as a member of the Universal Body of Christ, the Church. "All else" now included the understanding that without the teaching, *extra ecclesiam nulla salus*, the Catholic Church's precepts would really be no more than another offering in the national pluralism's famous "marketplace of ideas."

Of course, to speak of that understanding and my religious beliefs in general is to speak of myself primarily as a Catholic. As a journalist, other writing kept standing in the way of my turning my attention to the so-called Boston Heresy Case, but I was resolved that one day it would not. The main reason for my resolution may be easily stated.

It was grotesque to me that a *de fide* teaching of the Church was so obscured that upholding it could be construed as "heretical" even as most U.S. Catholics remained ignorant of a genuine heresy and the role it continues to play in their lives, despite the fact that this genuine one (it is formally known as the heresy of Americanism) was once papally condemned in an indisputable way—as indisputable as the "excommunication" of Fr. Feeney for upholding the teaching, *extra ecclesiam nulla salus*, is far from being.

The sense of that absurdity is the keener now that my search for truth concerning the Boston Heresy Case has revealed—it will be shown in these pages—that Fr. Feeney was not excommunicated, if excommunicated he truly was, for doctrinal reasons. None such were cited in the questionable Decree of Excommunication published in the *Acta Apostolicae Sedis* on February 16, 1953.

In other words, *Fr. Feeney was really never charged with heresy by Church authorities*. Further, the decree "excommunicating" him was dubious to say the least. Its character became more so in my eyes upon the discovery that when Fr. Feeney in 1972 was officially "reconciled" to the Church—How do you become "reconciled" if you have never truly been apart?—he was not required to recant anything he had ever written or said.

It was the same when 29 members of the religious order he co-founded with Catherine Goddard Clarke, the Slaves of the Immaculate Heart of Mary (*Mancipia Immaculati Cordis Mariae*, in Latin), were "reconciled" shortly after. It remained the case in February, 1988, when 14 sisters of Fr. Feeney's order were "regularized" (the term which had come by then to replace "reconciled").

In regard to the 14 M.I.C.M. sisters, there is at hand an official letter, one written on May 4, 1988, by the Judicial Vicar for the Diocese of Worcester, Massachusetts, to the Secretary for Ministerial Personnel of the neighboring Archdiocese of Boston. "In our discussion with the Congregation [for the Doctrine of the Faith]," it says in part, "it seemed rather clear that proponents of a strict interpretation of the doctrine [*extra ecclesiam nulla salus*] should be given the same latitude for teaching and discussion as those who would hold more liberal views."

The judicial vicar's letter went on to state that when its members were "regularized," the "community in no manner abandoned Father Feeney's teachings. Consequently the sisters do a good deal more than keep the memory of Father Feeney. They now actively proclaim his teachings as they did before the regularization."

No consideration will be given just now to the implications of the willingness of the Congregation for the Doctrine of the Faith to allow the proclamation of the "strict interpretation of the doctrine" *and* discussion of the teaching of those who hold "more liberal views." However, it should be noted at this juncture that the judicial vicar's letter also affirms that "the Congregation for the Doctrine of the Faith holds the doctrine [*extra ecclesiam nulla salus*] to have been defined and consequently definitive." The judicial vicar's English construction is awkward, but his sentence makes its point.

His letter will be examined again later in these pages, but it should be further observed at this time that the judicial vicar could write authoritatively because it was in the diocese of which he was an official that the sisters resided and were, as he put it, "regularized." Today, their convent, St. Ann's House in Still River, Massachusetts, is the official Tridentine Mass Center for the Diocese of Worcester. Thus, the sisters' exquisite chapel is (at this writing) one of but nine locations in the U.S. where the historical Mass is publicly celebrated every day of the week with episcopal approbation.

The likelihood that Fr. Feeney never was truly "excommunicated" became stronger in my mind when I learned that on at least one occasion and before numerous witnesses, a prince of the Church, Boston's late Archbishop Humberto Cardinal Medeiros, actually went down on his knees before the priest and asked his blessing. (Some M.I.C.M. religious remember this happening more than once.)

Yet, the facts of the Boston Heresy Case lead inescapably to the conclusion that despite its not being cited by the February, 1953, document, it was on account of Fr. Feeney's upholding the *de fide* teaching, *extra ecclesiam nulla salus*, that action was taken against him. He obviously believed that. The record, which is extensive, shows his striving during all the period when the controversy surrounding him was at its height to win a Church hearing where the doctrinal question could be aired. Such a hearing never took place.

The point is that action was taken, but without the *de fide* teaching, *extra ecclesiam nulla salus*, figuring in it officially—to the extent the "excommunication" of Fr. Feeney was official. The action was taken—there is no way to avoid concluding this when all the circumstances and facts are known—because Churchmen, probably in Rome as well as Boston, found Fr. Feeney's upholding the teaching to be inopportune. The disobedience referred to by the decree of February, 1953, was the grounds —provided by Fr. Feeney, it could be said—for taking action.

(The term "inopportune," just employed to describe Fr. Feeney's upholding the teaching, *extra ecclesiam nulla salus,* is a famous one in modern Church history. At Vatican Council I, a general council now thoroughly obscured by the aftermath of Vatican II, most of the bishops opposed to a dogmatic definition of papal infallibility—they included the majority of U.S. bishops—were known as "inopportunists." I.e., they claimed to believe in papal infallibility, but argued it was "inopportune" in 1870 to define it solemnly as Church teaching.)

Reference was made a few lines ago to Boston Churchmen. Numerous of them were involved in the Boston Heresy Case and "excommunication" of Fr. Feeney, as also his expulsion from the Society of Jesus (also on grounds of disobedience), but the two who counted most were Archbishop Richard Cushing and his auxiliary bishop (also a future cardinal) John Wright.

Although Cardinal Cushing was still on the scene when I began my career in Catholic journalism—this was at *Triumph* magazine in 1966—I never had contact with him or any member of his household, and I do not believe anyone else at the magazine ever did. My chief knowledge of him has been that he was close to the Kennedy family. Beginning my researches for this book, I recalled, for instance, that he said the Requiem Mass at St. Matthew's Cathedral in Washington, D.C., for John F. Kennedy after the President's assassination, and I also remembered that when Jacqueline Kennedy Onassis married Aristotle Onassis in a Greek Orthodox ceremony, His Eminence was very loud in asserting that the lady remained a Catholic in good standing. Remembering that, I cannot say I was very surprised when I learned while preparing this book that His Eminence had a sister he dearly loved who was married to a non-Catholic gentleman. (The gentleman, Mr. Richard Pearlstein, adopted the name Pierce—without changing his religion.)

As for Cardinal Wright, the first U.S. American ever to serve in the papal curia, I did know him. Our acquaintance is memorialized in another book of mine, *In Reaction.* Not merely was he quite close to *Triumph,* he was supportive of my career in its early stages, subscribing to every periodical for which I wrote or that I edited.

It is a matter of extreme regret to me that during the years of my acquaintance with Cardinal Wright I knew so little of the Boston Heresy Case that I was totally ignorant of his role in it. I would have asked him questions about it. I believe he would have given me answers—some kind of answers.

Whatever they would have been, Cardinal Wright, as a member of the curia, did help arrange for Fr. Feeney's "reconciliation." He also penned a letter of condolence when Fr. Feeney died in 1978.

Other persons besides the two Boston Churchmen and, of course, Fr. Feeney will figure in these pages because they figured in the Boston Heresy Case and all that followed, but none except Fr. Feeney himself had a role in developments more significant than Catherine Goddard Clarke.

In regard to her, a purely personal note here wants to be sounded. That is, I feel compelled to say that Catherine Clarke, or Sister Catherine as she was eventually known, came during my search for the truth concerning the Boston Heresy Case to interest me even more than Fr. Feeney in some respects. Perhaps the reader can understand why if some things are briefly told about her.

Wife and mother, as well as director of St. Benedict Center, when with Fr. Feeney she founded the Slaves of the Immaculate Heart of Mary, she would become the first female in the United States since St. Elizabeth Ann Seton still to be raising children while serving as the superior of a religious order. Even as she tended her family and administered the order—seeing to practical affairs was very much her task, while the spiritual direction of the brothers and sisters was Fr. Feeney's—she somehow found the time and energy to write three full-length books and to conduct the researches necessary for a stream of articles and lectures on numerous subjects which also issued from her pen. Her dedication and self-discipline were such that not until nearly the end did the Hodgkins Disease which killed her at age 68 in 1968 cause her to slacken her pace.

The thought suggests itself that a woman like Sr. Catherine could have struck persons who knew her as hard and coldly efficient, somewhat like many of the women in more recent times who have aimed to incorporate homemaking and a successful career in one life. Yet, from those who knew Sr. Catherine, the adjective most often heard attached to her name is "charming."

There are others. One M.I.C.M. religious describes her as "more canonizable" than Fr. Feeney. "You couldn't talk with her without coming away burning with zeal," this person says.

No real slight to Fr. Feeney could be intended by such a description, not when it is heard from a committed "Feeneyite" (the label, clearly meant as derogatory, stuck on M.I.C.M. religious—and often anyone who upholds *extra ecclesiam nulla salus*—for the past 40 years). But Leonard Feeney was a poet, a genuine one with volumes of published verse to show it, and poets—anybody who has known a genuine one will attest to it—can be less than completely congenial company on occasion. They can be moody. If the poet is Irish, and perhaps especially if he also has Spanish blood, he may fall into a mood fairly often. Sr. Catherine, it seems, never did. She was always charming.

To have referred already to Leonard Feeney as a poet opens the way to touching on another matter which may as well be dealt with now. It has been suggested or flatly stated in published materials that Fr. Feeney had a "drinking problem." There was also mention of the "problem" in a 1991 Boston television documentary about Fr. Feeney and St. Benedict Center. My own conclusion is that he could have had a taste for drink, and when being a poet was mainly what he was, some alcohol may have helped lubricate his pen, as it has those of many others. It remains, however deep his taste for drink, he literally lacked the stomach for much of it, nearly half that organ having been surgically removed when he was still a young man. Beyond that, it is very difficult to see how he could have written so many books, prepared and delivered so many lectures, heard so many confessions, converted so many to the Faith and otherwise done all that he did for so many years if he was lost in alcohol. As for persons who imagine as evidence of drink the ferocity with which he could excoriate enemies of the Faith, enemies found in the Church's very midst as well as those entirely outside her, they fail to understand the depth of his Catholic belief. It appears to have been total. It was certainly sufficient for him to preach to crowds that included men calling for his death.

The actual physical danger he eventually faced on account of his teaching raises another matter which will also have to be addressed later, especially when we come to the years Fr. Feeney spent preaching every Sunday afternoon in Boston Common and during which St. Benedict Center published *The Point*. Was he, as often charged, an anti-Semite? Did he hate Jews?

There was an occasion in the Common one Sunday, an occasion still vividly recalled by persons who were present, when a Jewish heckler cried out, pointing to the crucifix held aloft by an M.I.C.M. brother, "Take your Jesus down off the Cross and we'll crucify Him again!" Fr. Feeney, in the heat of that moment, responded, "You hate Him and I hate you!"

Frankly, I see no reason to hear in the words more than they say. They do not say Fr. Feeney hated the heckler because he was Jewish. All they say is that Fr. Feeney just then was not ready to feel love for someone expressing hatred, violent hatred, of his God. My thought, knowing as much as I have come to know about Fr. Feeney, is that *anyone* crying out as did the heckler would have met the same response. And again, in his response there was nothing to suggest that Fr. Feeney would hate the man for who or what he was. His feeling, certainly sharply expressed, arose in response to the hatred proclaimed. Effect flowed from cause: *Because* you hate Christ, *inasmuch* as you hate Him, this is how I feel about you.

(Fr. Feeney, it might also be reported at this juncture, is known personally to have converted at least 13 Jews to the Faith, several of them

New York City cabdrivers, during his years as a priest. The traditional teaching of the Church, as expressed, for instance, in a famous passage in the writing of St. Peter Julian Eymard [canonized in 1962 even as Vatican II began], is that "the greatest charity we can do a man is to lead him to the true Church, outside which there is no salvation." In Christianity, charity is another name for love.)

One further note as concerns Fr. Feeney's alleged anti-Semitism: St. Benedict Center, founded and directed by Sr. Catherine and of which Father became the leading light, had after World War II numerous students who were veterans of that conflict. They were able to attend its classes—it was accredited as an educational institution—thanks to the G.I. Bill. Some of them, as well as others, quit Harvard University in order to do so. (The center was located in Cambridge, Mass., a few moments' walk from the Harvard campus.) That they and some who were not on the G.I. Bill quit Harvard for the center was a principal contributing cause, along with Fr. Feeney's championship of the teaching, *extra ecclesiam nulla salus*, of action being taken against the priest and the center. So it can be easily believed when the facts of the Boston Heresy Case are considered in the light of the history of the Church in the U.S. and the circumstances prevailing at the end of the 1940s. No fact leads to this conclusion more surely than that some of the students who quit Harvard for the center— they were not ones on the G.I. Bill—were from among some of the nation's richest and most powerful Protestant families. Worse, they were among the 200 young persons who actually converted to the Faith at the center during the years of its existence in Cambridge. Their conversion was no way for the Catholic Church to prove, as her bishops were claiming, that all she desired was a position of equality with other religious faiths in the U.S., and the families let Archbishop Cushing know exactly that.

However, the more immediate point which here wants to be made as regards Fr. Feeney's alleged anti-Semitism is that veterans of the recent fight against Naziism would hardly have been inclined to attend classes where Nazi-type ideas were expounded. Indeed, as we shall see, the veterans who quit Harvard for the center did so largely because they perceived that it was at Harvard they were having foisted on them the kind of ideas which provided the philosophical underpinning of Naziism—and other of the "isms" in which the 20th century has abounded. They were looking for truth, not an ideology (of which anti-Semitism is simply one more). They believed they heard the truth proclaimed in the proclamation of *extra ecclesiam nulla salus*. (This is not to say the young veterans might not have also felt outrage like Fr. Feeney's if they heard someone call for crucifying Christ again.)

Some of the main facts concerning the so-called Boston Heresy Case and supposed excommunication of Fr. Feeney now having been outlined, it remains to be explained why this book has finally been written a quarter-century after its author first thought to write on the subject.

Truth to tell, I should have preferred to delay the writing for a still longer time. Why would that have been desirable?

For one thing, the full confidence of some "Feeneyites" has not been won. These are brothers and sisters who could have shed light on key questions, but whose cause has been so maligned by most journalists over the years that they could not quite open up even to one who came to them with traditional, rather than merely conservative, Catholic credentials. Thus, no conclusive answer can be offered in these pages as to why Fr. Feeney did not present himself in the capital of Christianity, Rome, when he was summoned, thereby providing the proximate grounds of his "excommunication." Was he in fact ready at one moment to make the trip, but then discouraged from it, as some conjecture, by Sr. Catherine? Does anybody still living really know?

Did Fr. Feeney, feeling the need of a priest to be under obedience to someone, make a vow to Sr. Catherine after he was cast out by the Jesuits and "excommunicated"? Again, some suggest that possibility, but it is another question which cannot here be answered.

As for Sr. Catherine, the "Feeneyites'" protectiveness of her memory is extraordinary. That is with the exception of a couple of persons to whom I spoke. Some of what they said suggested that they thought Sister's influence on Fr. Feeney was too great, but even they would not provide real answers, if they had them, to certain questions. (That Sr. Catherine undeniably exercised a strong influence on Fr. Feeney is seen by the present writer as additional proof that she was a remarkable woman. After all, priests of his generation, and he probably more than most—even among the then "elite" Jesuits—were not much given to deferring to any lay person in anything, and especially not to a female. Such priests knew who they were and thus were still capable of addressing an adult as "my son," "my child," and so on. Fr. Feeney's awareness of the dignity of his office is illustrated by the way he expelled the young Robert F. Kennedy from St. Benedict Center.)

In any event, as to this book being written with no further delay, the writing was decided by a series of unrelated incidents during the first six months of 1992. For instance, having invited questions from a Philadelphia audience which had just heard me deliver a talk on the heresy of Americanism—this was in May—the first one I received, from a young man in the back of the room, was this: "Do you think the excommunication of Fr. Leonard Feeney was an example of Americanism in action?"

I was stunned. I had made no mention of the "excommunicated" priest in my talk. My questioner was not born until many years after the "excommunication." How much could he know about it? Why was he interested?

Doubtless at least a partial answer to the last question: Bro Leonard Mary, M.I.C.M. (formerly Fred Farrell), a member of Fr. Feeney's order who lives in California and the very one here earlier identified as the person still living who was probably closest to Father for the longest time, estimates that over the years the eight branches of St. Benedict Center which now exist have between them distributed 500,000 pieces of "Feeneyite" literature. So many seeds have probably begun to bear fruit, perhaps especially among remaining Catholic youth wanting to hear, and listening for, some sound from the Church other than a very uncertain trumpet. The point is, if they are interested in the case of Fr. Feeney, should not the truth about it be uncovered and told to them?

That was the question I put to myself that evening in Philadelphia. I asked it especially on account of another incident, one that had taken place in March. Another young man—he was close to a well-known traditional Catholic group, but not a member of it—was driving me to a meeting in Northern Virginia sponsored by the organization. Apropos of nothing we were saying at the moment, but perhaps because of things he had seen me recently write for *The Remnant*, the St. Paul-based fortnightly that by then had been an outlet for me for a couple of years, he suddenly asked if I was a "Feeneyite" (it was the word he used).

I asked him what he meant by the term.

"Well," he responded, "do you think Koreans a hundred years ago couldn't go to Heaven because they weren't Catholic?"

I considered what answer to give. Finally, I said that I was less concerned about the salvation of Koreans a hundred years ago than that of fellow Americans today. That remains my position.

The question in Philadelphia and the conversation in the car in Northern Virginia were among a half-dozen incidents which led to the decision that this book be written without further delay. I shall relate one more, the one that clinched things.

It took place in June. It amounted to my being verbally assailed by a priest, one who says Mass no way except according to the principal historical rite of the Western Church, the so-called Tridentine. In a word, the priest was a "traditional" one. Overhearing me in conversation with other persons defend the teaching, *extra ecclesiam nulla salus*—I also allowed I was thinking of undertaking a book like this—he joined the company, listened for a few moments, made a statement about Fr. Feeney being "excommunicated" because he was "guilty of heresy," and then declared to me in front of everybody: "You have not read enough theology! You do a great deal of damage because you have not read enough theology!"

A couple of months later, by which time I was doing research for this book, I received from the priest a written apology for his "rudeness" (his word), but at the moment of the occurrence I thought of all the clerics, including theologians and other "experts," who contend that the faithful have no right to the celebration of the historical Mass and that therefore no priest should be allowed to say it.

With that thought came another. It was that no other Mass but the historical one was being said in the Western Church in 1962, the year Vatican II began, and it did not prevent the ecclesiastical disarray we have known during the three decades since. As far as that went, I said to myself, no other Mass was being celebrated in 1500. It did not stop thousands of bishops and priests leading millions, including entire nations, out of the Church and into the heresies of Luther, Calvin, Zwingli and Henry VIII.

In other words, the priest who assailed me for not reading "enough" theology might himself be in a theological minority on account of his belief that the historical Mass makes for better worship than the Mass of Pope Paul VI, but it really did not matter. The truth is that celebration of the historical Mass, by itself and no matter how punctiliously it is done, will not necessarily keep anybody Catholic. Rather, celebrant and worshippers alike must *believe*—as the apostate clerics of the 16th century clearly did not.

That is to say, in order for a man to be fully Catholic and remain so, or for a non-Catholic to become one for a truly compelling reason—these were thoughts racing through my mind that evening in June, 1992—there had to exist belief that assistance at Mass is *necessary*, that reception of the sacraments there confected is *necessary*, even as is the Sacrament of Penance if it is needed for the reception. Why necessary?

There was the main question. There had to be some special reason for being Catholic. After all, if it were a matter simply of believing everything stated in the Nicene Creed, there are sects whose members recite it every Sunday even as do Catholics. Do those members not therefore believe the same things as Catholics, or think they do? However, the sects lack priests and the sacraments priests alone can confect. The Orthodox have them, but they lack Peter, the rock on whom Christ built His Church.

Evidently, I concluded, it is belief in the necessity of the sacraments and Peter which uniquely makes a man Catholic and will keep him one, but to what are they necessary? I saw no answer except one. It was to be drawn from the teaching upheld by Fr. Feeney and which I had learned to be *de fide*: They are necessary for the man's salvation. Yet, Fr. Feeney is thought by countless persons to have been "excommunicated" for upholding the teaching, and many who know vaguely that he was eventually "reconciled" suppose he must have recanted in order for the "reconciliation" to take place. I already knew enough to know these persons to be wrong. Now it was time, I decided, to learn the details and to write the pages which follow.

The decision taken and the work now accomplished, I can quote at this juncture something said to me by Bro. Thomas Augustine, M.I.C.M., when I interviewed him during my researches for the book. (Brother is the superior of an "unregularized" branch of St. Benedict Center in Still River.) His position can be contrasted to the one taken by the "traditional" priest who will celebrate nothing but the historical Mass and who assailed me for defending the teaching, *extra ecclesiam nulla salus*.

"How can we be outside the Church?" Brother asked. "For the sake of their salvation we seek to convert people and to move fallen-away Catholics to return to the sacraments. Where are they going to go except to the mainstream Church? They can't all come to our chapel [where the historical Mass is celebrated]."

The externals of liturgical observance evidently are more important to some "traditional" Catholics than doctrine. To some, they may be the only thing that is important, but the "Feeneyites" are not among them.

The reference to there now being different branches of St. Benedict Center, a couple of them "regularized" and others not, provides an opening to tell what more is not in this book.

One thing which is not is a very detailed account of how there have come to be different branches of the center, one in Richmond, New Hampshire, three in Still River, two an hour's drive from Still River in Petersham, Massachusetts, one in Vienna, Ohio, and one called St. Benedict Center West in Los Angeles. (All except the ones in Petersham and Vienna were visited for this book, and I met and talked at length with two sisters from the Vienna community at a conference in Chicago where I was speaking and which they attended.)

The chief reason why the separation into different branches will not be treated at great length is that this book is written from the perspective of the Faith. That is, a typical reporter or any other non-believer could look at the center's eight existing branches and see as many "factions" divided by personal as well as some other differences. I submit that when viewed through the eyes of the Faith, what can be seen is eight religious foundations which have come into existence thanks to the teaching and labors of Fr. Feeney and Sr. Catherine, and this at a time, as is well known, when most religious orders are shrinking and religious vocations drying up.

It becomes even easier to see the situation in such a way if some Church history is known. Then, for instance, the turbulent early years of the Franciscans will be recalled. It will also be recollected how the great St. Alphonsus Liguori was rejected as superior by all the members of the order he founded, the Redemptorists, save by one lay brother.

There is an additional reason not to dwell very much on the division of St. Benedict Center into eight branches. In every one of them I visited, and also from the Vienna sisters, I heard some degree of regret expressed that greater cooperation between the different branches does not exist. For me to write too much of the divisions could delay or thwart cooperation by opening old wounds which have at least closed, if they are not already completely healed. Why run the risk?

Another subject which will not here be addressed at length, although it will not be completely ignored, is the position Fr. Feeney eventually came to hold in regard to the Sacrament of Baptism. This is for the reason that he did not fully develop his position until after Archbishop Cushing interdicted St. Benedict Center and he was expelled by the Jesuits and supposedly excommunicated. The subject of baptism of water, and of the so-called baptisms of desire and blood, certainly figures in Father's most significant book, *Bread of Life*, but it had no role at all in the controversy surrounding him when it was at its height.

Another matter needs to be touched upon in this Introduction: sources. As a journalist, I try to get facts right and report them accurately. Persons familiar with my work over the years can attest that I regularly confess errors in print when I discover them, or when they are brought to my attention. That is when I am writing for periodicals. You cannot do that when it comes to a book. A book is a more permanent thing than a newspaper or magazine, and much more than something merely spoken. (Doubtless this is why the Church, in her wisdom, refrains from assessing the orthodoxy of her children according to what they merely speak. She especially looks at their writing, especially in books.)

It is prayed that nothing but orthodoxy marks these pages. However, that is not right now the point. We are talking about sources.

Many persons who know something or even a great deal about the so-called Boston Heresy Case and its aftermath, including persons who were interviewed for this book, are sure their view or understanding of the facts and events is the true one, the best one, the most accurate one. They may find that what is here related does not correspond, or not entirely, to their view. To them, I shall have "got it wrong," and they may say so to whoever will listen. I shall be sorry for that. On the other hand, if I do actually get something wrong, objectively speaking, I hope these sources will let me know so the error can be corrected for any possible future edition of the book.

Still speaking of sources, the question of footnotes must arise. I decided to do without them for this book. Instead, attributions, whether from a printed source or an interview, will be given in the text itself whenever it is required or appropriate, as with the remark of Bro. Thomas Augustine quoted a few paragraphs ago.

However, attributions will not be given when it is not possible or appropriate. It obviously is not appropriate if a source has asked to go unidentified. In some instances an attribution will not be given because I judge it should not. That has already happened, as when I did not identify the M.I.C.M. religious who characterized Sr. Catherine as "more canonizable" than Fr. Feeney.

As for attributions being impossible, there will be instances where none can be given because the quotation has been passed down among "Feeneyites" as received knowledge or a kind of folklore. I.e., no one now living can say he or she heard the thing said, nor can it be told exactly who may have done, but everybody agrees it was said.

An example: It is recounted that when Fr. Feeney and Catherine Clarke met for the very first time, there was the following exchange.

Fr. Feeney: "No Catholic should go to Harvard. "

Sr. Catherine: "*Nobody* should go to Harvard."

Doubtless nobody should, and Sr. Catherine's delightful remark could be an excellent way to segue into the body of our book, except that one final thing asks to be said before these introductory pages come to an end.

I believe readers of books are entitled to know it in advance if some over-all or directing idea infuses the particular volume they have in their hands. I certainly have had such an idea in mind while preparing this book. It has to do with what came after the so-called Boston Heresy Case and supposed excommunication of Fr. Feeney. It can be explained in terms of the Americanist triumph at Vatican II recently so-well described by Michael Davies in his book, *The Second Vatican Council and Religious Liberty*. I do not believe Americanism in the person of John Courtney Murray could have succeeded, or succeeded as readily as it did, had Leonard Feeney not been squashed a decade before—and squashed he was.

Definitely, Fr. Feeney could hot have been so thoroughly silenced had he not in a sense cooperated. For instance, after Archbishop Cushing's interdict, it was St. Benedict Center itself (at Fr. Feeney's direction) which "cooperated" by keeping its doors closed to an inquiring public. It was somewhat the same after publication of the dubious decree of excommunication in 1953. Who can doubt that the day after publication a real heretic would have had himself photographed by the newspapers receiving Holy Communion? Doubtless this is exactly why Church authorities have not tried such a tactic on real heretics in the age of the mass media. Also, Fr. Feeney (and the Slaves of the Immaculate Heart of Mary) clung to the teaching, *extra ecclesiam nulla salus*, but what one word other than squashed can better explain the reality of two generations of Catholics believing that he was "excommunicated" for doing so?

Considering the "cooperation" they gave to their own silencing, the priest, Fr. Feeney, and the members of the order he co-founded, must have believed all along that sooner or later they and the teaching to which they clung would be rescued from obscurity. That is, they must have believed the memory of their work would be rescued, and the teaching again proclaimed. Perhaps this book is a sign that their belief was not misplaced.

14

The scene on Boston Common was exciting enough every Sunday afternoon that young Marine First Lieutenant Francis J. Kelly, then stationed on the aircraft carrier U.S.S. Wasp, more than once used part of his weekend shore leave to watch and listen. Now a retired colonel living in the suburbs of Washington, D.C., Kelly says, "I don't think I fully appreciated what I saw—that it was really something historic. It was more a show to me."

It may have been no more than that to him and most of the very many thousands who turned out over the years for the weekly spectacle on the Common, the large park in downtown Boston on which fronts the Massachusetts State House. To others, including those screaming epithets at the principal speaker, it was clearly serious business. The mounted police who always surrounded the speaker's platform were there to see that the business did not turn deadly.

Search contemporary press accounts of the Sunday afternoons as you will, no description except as "hecklers" can be found of those who screamed the epithets and against whom the police protected the speaker. The adjectives become more colored only when the press accounts turn to the speaker and his associates. Here, for instance, is a description of the Sunday afternoons in the park that appeared in a feature article in *Life* magazine in 1953:

"Every Sunday afternoon, rain or shine, for more than two years a peculiar and frightening demonstration has been repeated on the normally staid and peaceful public Common of Boston, Mass. It begins with a procession of stern, black-suited young men and women who march silently onto the Common, sing a few hymns and then begin giving wild and defamatory speeches. Finally their leader speaks, poring out a stream of invective particularly aimed at Roman Catholic Archbishop Cushing of Boston, at Protestants, Jews and the 'filthy, adulterous' people who have come to the Common to heckle him. The speaker is Leonard Feeney, a one-time Jesuit priest and seminary teacher."

On another occasion *Life* referred to Fr. Feeney as the "hate priest." It was in one of numerous articles *Life* and its sister publication, *Time*, devoted to Fr. Feeney in the late forties and early fifties. The articles are interesting to see today because Clare Booth Luce, wife of *Time* and *Life's* publisher Henry Luce, had once been an admirer and friend of Fr. Feeney. She even wrote articles for *From the Housetops*, publication of St. Benedict Center, the school near Harvard University where Fr. Feeney lectured and of which he was spiritual director. Archbishop Cushing also contributed articles to the journal. When the archbishop subsequently interdicted the center, forbidding Catholics to go there or to have dealings with Fr. Feeney, Mrs. Luce phoned the priest and volunteered to help in the situation any way she could. That was in 1949. By 1953 she was only one of many former celebrity friends of Fr. Feeney who had decided they could no longer be friendly.

Leonard Feeney was born on February 15, 1897, in Lynn, Massachusetts. It was also in Lynn that he grew up until at age 17 he went off to prepare to become a Jesuit. To someone after the truth about Fr. Feeney and the so-called Boston Heresy Case, it is a minor but interesting discovery to learn that down the street from the Feeney family home was the house where Mary Baker Eddy lived when she wrote her "bible," *Science and Health with a Key to the Scriptures.*

Leonard was one of four children, himself, two other boys who also grew up to become priests, and one sister. Leonard was the first-born. His mother, to whom he would always be exceptionally close, was 18 when he was born.

Her name was Delia Agnes and she was Irish. The father was named Thomas Butler Feeney. Predominately Irish, he also had Spanish blood. It gave him, as it did Leonard, a dark complexion and dark eyes. In her book, *The Loyolas and the Cabots,* Catherine Goddard Clarke relates that when Fr. Feeney would go marketing in the Italian section of Boston, storekeepers frequently took him for another *paisano.* He was that Mediterranean in look.

In one of his own works, *Survival Till Seventeen,* a collection of "light" essays of the kind which made him, along with his verse, nationally famous years before he became controversial, Leonard Feeney writes lovingly of his parents' first meeting. It was on a summer's evening at a seaside-cottage gathering of young persons. "There was the gaity and song appropriate to a group of merry exiles dwelling in a Puritan stronghold by the beaches of the North Shore. There was ginger ale for the girls, which makes them giggle, and beer for the young men, which makes them bothersome. My mother in her light blue dress and delicate manners easily prevailed, and my father was taken captive by the little streamer dangling from her hat."

Thomas Butler Feeney went into the insurance business and became a good provider to his family. They lived comfortably. Unfortunately, neither as a child nor a grown man did Leonard Feeney, slight of build but filled with intense, nervous energy, enjoy robust health. As a boy he was frequently ill. No doubt that, as well as his being the first-born, helped account for his being so close to his mother.

Sickly as he was, something else marked Leonard Feeney apparently even as a child. It was more than a gift for putting together words. It was a native ability or quality that enabled him to be "on," like an actor. One concludes he possessed this ability from press accounts of his lectures, speeches and readings, as well as from talk with those who knew him and are still living.

There is a downside to possessing such an ability. When the actor is no longer "on," when the energy is turned off or spent, he can crash pretty hard, and Leonard Feeney, in a passage of writing having to do with himself and other members of his family, acknowledged that perhaps due to their Spanish blood "our Celtic light heartedness is chastened, and sometimes completely shut off, by bursts of mysterious and exotic loneliness, occasionally verging on despair."

It had to be a source of pride to the family, Catholic and (mainly) Irish as they were (and because it was a time when persons could and did speak of the Jesuits as "elite"), that by age 17 Leonard Feeney not merely found a vocation for the priesthood. He was accepted as a novice by the Society of Jesus.

He left Lynn to spend his novitiate at St. Andrew-on-Hudson in Hyde Park, N.Y. There is an existing photo of him with his parents, taken, one supposes, during a visit the father and mother made to Hyde Park. Young Leonard stands between them in his cassock, smiling radiantly, but it is easy to conjecture that there must have been moments during the period of his novitiate, especially at first, when he did not feel all that happy. Most young men away from home for the first time in their lives have such moments.

It was also during his period at St. Andrew that half his stomach was surgically removed. Research for the present book did not uncover the precise nature of his ailment, but that the surgery took place is certain.

After St. Andrew, Leonard Feeney was sent to the Jesuits' famed Woodstock College in Maryland. From there he went for teaching experience to a high school run by the Society in Buffalo, New York. He was 24 by that time.

After his stint teaching at the high school, he spent a period at Holy Cross College in Worcester, Massachusetts, before returning to Woodstock for theology.

During the over-all 14 years he spent in priestly formation, two things were happening besides his studies that would be important in Leonard Feeney's life. He was forming friendships that would endure for decades— until his expulsion from the Society of Jesus. He also was writing poetry.

In 1927 he went to the Jesuits' House of Studies for the New England Province in Weston, Massachusetts, to complete the academic requirements for the priesthood, and on January 20, 1928, at Weston, he was ordained. Before then, in 1927, his first collection of verse, *In Towns and Little Towns,* saw publication.

Rev. Leonard Feeney would soon be sent to England to do graduate work at Oxford University, but before the thread of his life is here again taken up, it is worth recalling that in his day priests at their ordination still took the *Oath Against Modernism* prescribed by Pope St. Pius X early in this century. Many Catholics today have heard of the oath, but do not know of what it consisted. It said in part:

"I sincerely accept the doctrinal teaching which has come down from the Apostles through the faithful Fathers in the same sense and meaning to our own day. Therefore I wholly and entirely reject the false invention of the evolution of dogmas, whereby they pass from one meaning to a meaning other than that formerly held by the Church."

Leonard Feeney did not realize it at the time, but he would later allow that his Jesuit teachers—decades before Vatican II—had inculcated him with more than one "evolved" teaching. So successfully did he assimilate all that he was taught, the day would come when he was hailed by a Jesuit provincial as "the greatest theologian we have in the United States by far"

Judging from his book, *London is a Place,* the two years Leonard Feeney spent in England and Wales, with a year at Oxford, must have been among the best of his life.

At Oxford he occupied rooms which were those of Gerard Manley Hopkins, 19th-century convert, Jesuit priest and poet, in his student days. (The coincidence was somewhat droll, as will be seen.) He also had as a professor the redoubtable Lord David Cecil. Redoubtable as he was, Lord Cecil reported at the time, "I am getting more from my association with Leonard Feeney than he could possibly get from me."

By 1931 Fr. Feeney was back in the United States. He began teaching at Boston College. He was also continuing to write. His second collection of verse, *Riddle and Reverie,* was published by Macmillan in 1933. The next year saw publication, by Sheed and Ward, of *Fish on Friday*, a collection of essays. It became a best-seller. Another book of poems, *Boundaries*, was published by Macmillan in 1935. It was followed the next year by *Song for a Listener*. A biography of Mother Seton appeared in 1938. A few years after that (1944), Sheed and Ward published *The Leonard Feeney Omnibus (Survival Till Seventeen* originally appeared as part of this volume). *Your Second Childhood*, published by Bruce, came out soon after the *Omnibus*.

To complete the list of Fr. Feeney' s books, he brought out *London is a Place* in 1951. *Bread of Life*, a collection of his lectures, was published by St. Benedict Center in 1952.

Merely to list the titles and dates of his books cannot convey the range of Fr. Feeney's work, nor the impact it had on Catholics and the general public alike. Patrick J. Buchanan, commentator and 1992 candidate for the Republican presidential nomination, remembers in his autobiography, *Right from the Beginning*, that the textbooks used at his parochial school in Washington, D.C., included poetry by the priest. (He also remembers that after the "excommunication," the sisters at the school pasted blank pieces of paper over the poems.)

His impact really began to be felt after June, 1936, when Fr. Feeney was named literary editor of the Jesuits' magazine, *America*, and moved to Manhattan for the job. He lived in the same Society-owned building where the magazine was put out, remaining there until October, 1940, when he returned to New England.

As with his years in England and Wales, the period he spent living in New York City left him with many memories. T.S. Eliot, Noel Coward, Fulton Sheen, Sinclair Lewis, Dorothy Thompson and Jacques Maritain were among the celebrated personages he met and who met him. However, the young men and women who would hear his stories a few years later at St. Benedict Center learned more about the friends Fr. Feeney made among the city's dock-workers, janitors, waiters and cabdrivers (especially the cabdrivers) than the ones he had among the celebrated. Many of the ordinary New Yorkers who were brought by chance into contact with Fr. Feeney were subsequently brought by the grace of God into the Church— no doubt thereby proving that there is no such thing as a chance meeting. The converts included several Jewish cabdrivers, enough of them that the priest used to joke about having a vocation to cabbies.

Still, when all is said and done, it had to be some of his contacts among the celebrated who opened the way for Fr. Feeney to do much of what he did. That included, besides the publication of his books and his work at *America*, an endless stream of invited lectures and talks delivered at colleges, communion breakfasts, from the pulpit of St. Patrick's Cathedral, and other platforms.

The thirties were of course the heyday of radio, and there was a special hour on Sunday evenings that was especially Catholic. It was *The Catholic Hour*. Millions listened to it. Often it was to Fr. Leonard Feeney. Here is some of what the "hate priest" had to say one Sunday evening on the program:

"You came from nowhere, brought here by God's omnipotence, especially chosen for existence because He loved you, and now that you are, you will ever be. God does not expect you to be different than He made you, either. All He asks in return for the greater gift of creation is that you be yourself. 'Will you be John Jones or Mary Smith for Me?' God asks each one of us. 'Will you be big or small, young or old, good-looking or not, with many talents or few, just as I planned you? If you will, and will bear the burden of being yourself for a few years on this earth for Me, then I shall be your God for all eternity. I shall be your Father, your Friend, your Protector. I shall always interpret you with sympathy and understanding. Others may think they know how wicked you are for they see in your sins what has been consented to; but I shall always remember what has been resisted, and the struggles you have made to keep at least something in you fine and innocent and pure. I shall be your Defender against your enemies and no one will dare to speak unkindly of you without having to settle a score with Me. I shall be the faithful Watcher at your bedside when you are ill, or tired, or uninteresting. For you will never be uninteresting to Me, never a bother, never a bore. You will always be my creature, infinitely fascinating, whom I made out of nothing for my own celestial purposes. You will always be my loved one, always my child."

If that was how Fr. Feeney talked on the air, his New York friends probably thought of him for the humor he expressed in private. It found particular expression in punning. That is recalled by Sister Mary Clare, superior of one of the branches of St. Benedict Center in Petersham, Mass., in the graceful introduction she wrote for the memorial edition of *Survival Till Seventeen* published by St. Bede's Publications in 1980.

"His wit was natural, spontaneous, and lavish," she says of Fr. Feeney. "He was introduced to a Mr. Case and quipped, 'I hope your first name is Justin.' He accosted a florist named John D. Lyons and said the John should be changed to Dan. He preferred a long-established oil company to a new one, he said, 'because there's no fuel like an old fuel.' He thought he ought to bow his head whenever he used the word 'exegesis' lest he be accused of profanity. He heard that a hen had won a prize for hatching almost 200 eggs in one year, and remarked that the hen deserved the Pulletser Prize. Unaware that he had a personality essentially individual, he wrote: 'If one is a Catholic, one cannot think without being cosmical and without being comical either, because the Faith links all realities together and fills the world with surprises.'"

His humor and a gift for mimicry made him an amiable companion. In public, whether on the platform as a lecturer or in the pulpit as a preacher, he was spellbinding by all accounts. Rev. Avery Dulles, S.J., who was an early associate of St. Benedict Center, eulogized Fr. Feeney in an obituary written for *America* after the priest's death in 1978. This was a quarter-century after the men had parted ways.

"Never have I known a speaker with such a sense of collective psychology," Dulles wrote. "Totally aware of the reactions of every person in the room, he would focus his attention especially on those who seemed hostile, indifferent, or distracted. When at length he had the entire audience reacting as a unit, he would launch into the main body of his talk, leading them from insight to insight, from emotion to emotion, until all were carried away, as if by an invisible force permeating the atmosphere."

In the same obituary, Fr. Dulles said that "there are certain texts from the Bible that I can never read without hearing, in my imagination, the voice and intonation of Leonard Feeney."

Sr. Mary Clare says, "Father Feeney was at his best with the Greek New Testament in his hands. He felt that Holy Scripture was full of inexhaustible treasures for those who were simple and innocent of heart. Combining evangelical ardor with Catholic charm, he insisted on the primacy of the Gospels; and soon bookstores around Harvard Square started running out of Bibles. With resourcefulness and originality he explained the Gospel narratives, pacing up and down, and translating them as he went along."

She gives an example of the sort of thing he was capable of saying. He was commenting on the story of the Gerasenes: "When a Man can come into a town and, without apologizing, send 1,000 pigs into the sea and have the townspeople beg Him to leave, and He doesn't have to give a weak, cowardly explanation, I know that I have Authority on my hands."

He made certain points often enough that those who knew him will today preface their quotation of him with the words, "Fr. Feeney used to say." For instance, "Fr. Feeney used to say, 'If you are childlike of heart, you know two things about the world: that it isn't God, and that it couldn't be without a God. But it takes humility to know God. Pride likes to destroy Him. An atheist is a proud, academic snob who snubs all the minds of history who have seen order where he says there is none. He loves to be infinite enough to destroy Infinity.'"

Another quality of the priest, all agree, was fearlessness. It was not only on Boston Common that he showed it. As Sr. Mary Clare describes him, "He was never afraid to hit hard at error in high places." A story about him is often told to illustrate that.

It concerns a Harvard student who attempted suicide. Another student sent for Fr. Feeney to come minister to the young man soon after the attempt. The priest found on the scene a very august personage, a Harvard dean. "Dreadfully unfortunate!" this gentleman murmured. Fr. Feeney snapped, "What do you expect him to do when you teach him he's a bunch of electrons descended from a monkey?"

The priest loathed studied, insincere politeness. "Its credentials in academic circles (which vouch for its kindred behavior everywhere) are the subdued voice, the indefinite reference, the qualified statement, the sustained smile."

But we have already begun to tell about Fr. Feeney in the years after he returned to Massachusetts from New York and had become active at St. Benedict Center. To do so is to anticipate ourselves. The point that wants to be made now is that by the time he turned 40 years old in 1937, Leonard Feeney was being called "an American Chesterton."

Research for the present book did not succeed in tracing back the comparison to the first critic or reviewer who made it, but it peppers much of these past decades' published material on Fr. Feeney and St. Benedict Center, and it is easy to see, on the basis of the priest's own writing, why and how the comparison was made. Chesterton was also of course a wonderful conversationalist, like Leonard Feeney, but no one ever talked about him as a spellbinder on the speaking platform, as ordinarily is the case with the priest.

What Fr. Feeney may have thought of the comparison of himself to the great G.K.C. cannot be said. In *London is a Place* he professes to be scandalized (it is his word) that even after Chesterton had written *Orthodoxy* it still took him 16 years to come into the Church. Fr. Feeney also writes:

"Anyone looking for the Babe of Bethlehem at Christmas time— either by way of regal wisdom or rural simplicity, as a king following a star, as a shepherd listening to a song—had better avoid the books of G.K. Chesterton. There is altogether too much of Christianity in them, and altogether too little of Christ. If I may reverse a proverb of Omar Khayyam, Chesterton was one who 'took the credit and let the cash go.'"

We are not used to hearing criticism like that, or any criticism at all, of G.K. Chesterton. It is the same with respect to Cardinal Newman, of whom Fr. Feeney writes (also in *London is a Place*): "John Henry Newman was constantly praised for the clarity of his English prose and the limpid lucidity of his style. That he possesses these qualities, no one can deny. But this is the cold clarity of clear water in a fish bowl, in which one looks in vain for the fish."

In just this one book, *London is a Place*, Fr. Feeney does not hesitate to disturb our received view of numerous other literary luminaries besides Chesterton and Newman. (The latter comes under criticism for more than his writing. There was the matter of his being an "inopportunist" at Vatican I, as also his having written of the Immaculate Conception of the Blessed Virgin Mary that "her case is essentially the same as St. John the Baptist, save for a difference of six months." That, Fr. Feeney observes, "is precisely the difference this dogma demands.")

Of Msgr. Ronald Knox he says, "One is in doubt at times as to whether he wants England to come back to the Church, or the Church to come back to England." Evelyn Waugh is dismissed in a couple of lines (he "whitened his sepulchre with the life of a saint"). Regarding T.S. Eliot: "I once sat opposite T.S. Eliot at a dinner, where he made a sincere effort at being sincere, and a modest effort at being modest, all during the meal."

Of all the eminent figures about whom Fr. Feeney expresses at least some degree of reservation (the list will here be left incomplete, and he did like Belloc), none did he treat more scathingly than his brother poet and predecessor in the Society of Jesus, Gerard Manley Hopkins, the very one whose old rooms at Oxford eventually became his. He quotes Hopkins' *Tom's Garland* and comments: "This is tortured expression, if there ever was any. It is neither prose nor poetry. It is not even English."

What is going on here? The question demands being asked because, to speak only of Hopkins, Fr. Feeney would lecture on him at St. Benedict Center, and the lectures, one gathers, were not contemptuous of their subject. He also had good things to say about Chesterton, different from what he said in *London is a Place.* So why did he write as he wrote there?

In part, a certain irrepressibility probably made it difficult for him not to use a good line or voice a sharp thought when one came to him. Beyond that, the criticisms he makes are not entirely ill-founded—You probably do find more of Christianity than of Christ in Chesterton, but where else do you find as much Christianity anymore?—and it is not a bad thing to have someone willing to disturb our received views. It can—it should—cause us to sharpen our own thinking. In the end, however, what one senses—this is the real reason we have dwelt on *London is a Place* and the opinions expressed in it—is the Irish temperament at its most exasperating (to everyone except an Irishman). What we see in this book, let it here be suggested, is a love of argument for argument's sake, a love strong enough to make a man start an argument, if need be, in order to have one. If most of those who knew Fr. Feeney do not see this side of him, and they probably do not, it is probably because most of them are Irish.

There is another side they do not see, or do not want to see, or certainly do not want to talk about very much, but anyone else can see it in the priest's writing—at least in the early editions of some writing. When it comes to the *de fide* teaching in whose defense he became most famous, *extra ecclesiam nulls salus,* Fr. Feeney's position was not always as the world eventually knew it. This must be acknowledged because if the present lines move one person to read Fr. Feeney himself, as it is hoped they will, he will discover it. He will, that is, unless he reads editions revised during Fr. Feeney's lifetime and with his approval. The expurgated passages show up in the editions apt to be found in reference libraries. For instance, in a piece in his 1934 best-seller, *Fish on Friday,* he writes about meeting and very much liking two American YWCA ladies on a train in Europe. He calls them "Good Christians." "I am so very sure," he says, "that my Good Christians will go safely to Heaven when they die (for God loves us for our effort and forgives our ignorance) that, if I shall have managed to get there myself, there will not have been any need for saying goodbye."

Supposing the YWCA ladies read Fr. Feeney' s words when they first saw print, and then supposing they also read, or read about, what he was saying a decade later, you are bound to wonder what they thought. No doubt they asked, "What could have happened to that Catholic priest? He was so *nice.*"

The answer to their question is in part that before the decade passed, Leonard Feeney had decided that being "nice" might be nice, but what was really needed from a priest was an ability and willingness to answer forthrightly the kind of questions which can be asked by a man whose wife has betrayed him, or whose children have deeply disappointed him, or who has lost everything in a bad financial investment, or whose doctor has told him not to expect to live more than six months. What is it all about, Father? Why does God allow something like this? Has life any meaning? What is it?

Real men want real answers, not "nice" ones, at such a time. They can win salvation or lose their soul according to the ones they receive. However, in 1938, Fr. Feeney was still writing in the same vein as in *Fish on Friday*. This was in his biography of Mother Seton, *Elizabeth Seton: An American Woman*.

Apropos the death of the saint's dear sister-in-law, Rebecca, Fr. Feeney says: "The Catholic Faith has, of course, a merciful place in its own Kingdom for those who die in invincible ignorance of the Truth. It attaches them 'to the soul of the Church' and grants them the Beatific Vision much more generously than might be supposed. Nor does it even hold that those who die outside the Faith are necessarily lost....That Rebecca Seton's soul went shortly, if not immediately, to the contemplation of the Beatific Vision no one who has any Christian sensibilities will deny."

Fr. Feeney also writes of Richard Bayley, the saint's Protestant father: "In the high place he holds with her now in Heaven..."

How can talk like that—Again, these passages were expurgated in the revised editions of his works—be harmonized with what Fr. Feeney later preached?

It cannot be harmonized. How, then, explain it?

The explanation is that he wrote as he did in *Fish on Friday* and *An American Woman* because that was as he was taught by his Jesuit masters during the 14 years of his priestly formation. It was their inculcation of "evolved" dogma, contrary to the *Oath Against Modernism*, that caused him to write as he did. If the result of the inculcation was such that the Jesuits were ready for a time to hail him as "the greatest theologian we have in the United States," by 1947 he was ready to shake off the influence. That was the year he decided nothing but a constant preaching of the *de fide* doctrine, *extra ecclesiam nulla salus,* could make America Catholic, and that failure to uphold the teaching already accounted for as many Catholics leaving the Church through the back door as there were converts coming in the front (the high rate of defection is an often-ignored fact about the pre-conciliar Church in the U.S.). What was needed, Fr. Feeney had decided, was a steadfast defense of the teaching, perhaps even a pugnacious one—one which maybe could only be mounted by an Irishman (albeit with Spanish blood) who loved an argument.

That observed, what is to be said of the ultimate objective? Allusion was made to it a few lines ago: "To make America Catholic." It was clearly Fr. Feeney's purpose. There will be plenty in the following pages to attest to that. The question now arises, were there no Catholics besides Fr. Feeney and his associates at St. Benedict Center who dreamed of a

Catholic America? Were they—are they—an aberration?

The truth is that there was once no other kind of Catholic in the land. Another truth is that other Catholics, notably certain bishops who would later play commanding roles in the history of the Church in the U.S., sought harder to Americanize the Church than to baptize America.

Before we turn our attention to the so-called Boston Heresy Case we shall look back briefly at the lives and work of men who would have been as one with Fr. Feeney, men who came to this land expressly to make it Catholic, and who arrived—many of them—long before the Puritan Pilgrims arrived in Massachusetts and established Plymouth Plantation. We shall also want to consider the Americanizers and what they were about.

Chapter Two

There was a time when America was Catholic. That is to say, there was no Christian presence in the vast territory of North America which is now the United States except the Catholic one. Even as late as the beginning of the 19th century three-quarters of the territory—all the land west of the Mississippi—remained Catholic. Before we consider developments which led eventually to the conditions prevailing at the time of Fr. Feeney' s "excommunication"—conditions which virtually dictated that action would be taken against him and which still prevail today—let us recall the Catholic America which earlier was.

The event which today marks in the minds of most Americans the beginning of their history was the landing in 1620 of the so-called Pilgrim Fathers at a place they named Plymouth on the coast of what is now Massachusetts. However, nearly a century before then, in 1528, a Spanish Franciscan priest, Fr. Juan Juarez, was designated Bishop of Florida.

That was but 15 years after Florida was discovered by Juan Ponce de Leon on Easter Sunday, 1513, and no more than 36 after Christopher Columbus, sailing under the flag of Catholic Spain, made his first voyage to the New World and planted the cross on its shores. (In Spanish, Easter Sunday was known as Pascua Florida, Flowery Easter, which is how the land discovered and named by Ponce de Leon is still called Florida.)

Bishop Juarez died in his diocese the year of his appointment. If he was killed by Indians, as were many in his party (we do not know how, or exactly when, he died), he would be the first American martyr. However, of the 116 American martyrs whose names over the years have been submitted to Rome for canonization, the title of American protomartyr is bestowed on Fr. Juan de Padilla, another Franciscan. A chaplain attached to the 1541-42 expedition of Francisco Vazquez de Coronado deep into the American heartland, Fr. de Padilla was slain by Indians at a spot in today's Kansas which is practically the geographical center of the continental U.S.

Three more martyrs: Fr. Luis Cancer, Fr. Diego Tolosa and Hermano Fuentes, all Dominicans. They were murdered by Indians soon after going ashore on the Feast of the Ascension, 1549, near Tampa Bay. The bay had been discovered 10 years before, in 1539, by Hernando de Soto, and was named by him Espiritu Santo, Holy Spirit, because the discovery took place on Pentecost. (From Florida, De Soto would go on to explore lands we now know as Georgia, the Carolinas, Tennessee, Alabama, Mississippi, Louisiana, Arkansas, Oklahoma and Texas. At one point his path nearly crossed that of Coronado.)

The Spanish explorations of Florida would lead to the founding, on September 8, 1565, of the first city in what is now the U.S. This was St. Augustine, named that by its founder, Admiral Pedro Menendez de Aviles, because he sighted the peninsula on which it stands on the feast day of the great saint.

Accompanying the admiral were 12 Franciscan priests and four Jesuits. They would be followed by an army of missionaries who set out to evangelize Georgia, Alabama and Mississippi, and later the Carolinas and Virginia, as well as Florida, from their base in St. Augustine.

To speak of an army of missionaries is not to exaggerate. In all, from the end of the 15th century until 1822 Spain sent to America 16,000 missionaries who were members of religious orders. Also active as missionaries were countless diocesan priests and religious who were born in Spanish territories in the Western Hemisphere.

If their work of evangelization was initially blessed, it soon enough suffered because of the incursion of Protestants. The first on the scene were Huguenots to whom it was seldom sufficient to destroy the Catholic settlements they attacked and overran. It was common for them to put to the sword the Catholic missionaries and native converts who fell into their hands.

It was the same story with the English after they began settling coastal areas north of Florida. For instance, in 1704 the English governor of South Carolina, Moore, led a military expedition against Apalachee Mission in Florida. Capturing three Franciscan priests, he executed them along with 800 Catholic Indians. He also forced into slavery another 1,400 Indians who were living at Apalachee.

Nearly a century before then and far to the northwest, in today's New Mexico, Pedro de Peralta in 1609 founded a city which he named Royal City of the Holy Faith of St. Francis, and which soon became known simply as Holy Faith, Santa Fe. Peralta built on one side of the town's central plaza, in the manner typical of Spanish capitals, a Governor's Palace, a long one-story edifice of adobe and log beams. Serving well into this century as the residence of New Mexico's governors, it still stands.

More important to the work of planting the Faith within our shores, and once again typical of Spanish settlements, 11 churches or missions had been built in and around Santa Fe by 1617, and in 1625 there were 43 churches serving 34,000 Catholic Indians.

The existence in the early 17th century of a thriving center like Santa Fe wants to be known not simply because it predates the arrival at Plymouth in 1620 of the Pilgrims and their first encounter with some Indians. There is also a widespread notion today that America west of the Mississippi, the whole territory that was Spanish and French and therefore Catholic as late as 1800, was a wilderness untouched by civilization until English-speaking Protestants settled in it during the 19th century. The existence of a center like Santa Fe shows the notion to be false.

If the Hugenots and English Protestants impeded the Spanish missionaries' work of evangelization, it also has to be admitted that these heroes of the Faith were not always as successful in bringing it and its civilizing influence to the native population as they were at Santa Fe. There was much about Christianity and Christian living that many Indians at first found unacceptable. Thus, five Franciscans were martyred in Georgia in 1597 for trying to introduce monogamy among local Indians. At Mission Santa Elena in South Carolina, the Jesuit Fr. Juan Rogel found that eight months of religious instruction led to nothing when a council of Indian chiefs objected to renouncing the devil before Baptism. (Many Indians worshipped the spirit of evil. It was to him they offered human sacrifice.)

In all, from Juan de Padilla in Kansas in 1542 to Antonio Diaz de Leon in 1834 in Texas, 80 Spanish missionary priests and brothers were martyred in America. Most of them were Franciscans, Jesuits and Dominicans. Twenty-one Franciscans died at one time in New Mexico in 1680. Eight Jesuits were killed at one time in Virginia in 1570 at a site near the Rappahannock River which would be within commuting distance of today's Washington, D.C.

The French arrived in what is now the United States later than the Spanish, but they, too, helped make most of the country what it first was: Catholic. Numberless existing place names testify to it, and none more gloriously than the "Gateway to the West," St. Louis, named for France's great King Louis IX, crusader, friend and patron of St. Thomas Aquinas, and a saint canonized in 1297 by Pope Boniface VIII after the Church examined 65 miracles attesting to his sanctity. "A Christian should argue with a blasphemer only by running his sword through his bowels as far as it will go," King St. Louis once declared. As for Boniface VIII, the pontiff who canonized him, he declared in his Bull *Unam Sanctam* in 1302: "We declare, say, define and pronounce that it is absolutely necessary for the salvation of every human creature to be subject to the Roman Pontiff."

(The " Feeneyites" have compiled more than 3,100 quotations from Scripture, the decrees of popes and councils, and the writings of Fathers and Doctors of the Church and hundreds of saints, blesseds and venerabili in support of their position on *extra ecclesiam nulla salus* [see *The Apostolic Digest*; ed. Michael Malone.] However, the quote from *Unam Sanctam* is one of the three they cite most often on account of their solemnity. The other two:

"There is but one universal Church of the faithful, outside of which no one at all can be saved." [Pope Innocent III, Fourth Lateran Council, 1215]

"The most Holy Roman Catholic Church firmly believes, professes, and preaches that none of those existing outside the Catholic Church, not only pagans, but also Jews and heretics and schismatics, can have a share in life eternal; but that they will go into the eternal fire which was prepared for the devil and his angels, unless before death they are joined with Her; and that so important is the unity of this ecclesiastical body that only those remaining within this unity can profit by the sacraments of the Church unto salvation, and they alone can receive an eternal recompense for their fasts, their almsgivings, their other works of Christian piety and the duties of a Christian soldier. No one, let his almsgiving be as great as it may, no one, even if he pour out his blood for the Name of Christ, can be saved, unless he remain within the bosom and the unity of the Catholic Church." [Pope Eugene IV, the Bull *Cantate Domino*, 1441])

The city named for St. Louis was founded fairly late, but before there was a United States. It was in 1764. By then, French explorers and missionaries had been active in and around today's U.S. for more than two centuries, the first being the Italian-born mariner Giovanni Verrazano. In the service of France's King Francois I, he became in 1524 the first European to enter New York Harbor. During that voyage he explored most of the East Coast from the Carolinas to Newfoundland.

The list of French who brought the Faith and European Catholic civilization to these shores is long. It includes Marquette, Cartier, Champlain, LaSalle (who opened Illinois to French settlement), the brothers Lemoyne (one of whom founded New Orleans in 1718), and others. None matter more than the eight canonized by the Church in 1930 as the Martyrs of North America. They are Sts. René Goupil, Jean Lalande, Isaac Jogues, Antony Daniel, Jean de Brébeuf, Gabriel Lalemant, Charles Garnier and Noel Chabanel, listed here according to the chronology of their martyrdom from 1642 to 1649.

We need to understand what it was that motivated these men and their Spanish brothers in the Faith. Why were these men willing to die as they did? ( In all cases it was horribly.) The answer is very relevant to our inquiry into the Boston Heresy Case. That is, if Fr. Feeney was never called upon to give his life (thanks, perhaps, to the mounted police who surrounded him on Boston Common), why was he ready to sacrifice his brilliant career and reputation as "an American Chesterton"?

In reference to the canonized North American Martyrs, Coulson's biographical dictionary, *The Saints,* tells us that Fr. Charles Garnier, born to considerable wealth in Paris, "would walk thirty or forty miles in the summer heat over enemy country just to baptize a dying Indian."

"Just" to baptize him? Did Fr. Garnier not believe that "baptism of desire" would be sufficient for the Indian? Sufficient to what?

The answer is suggested by Fr. Garnier's Jesuit superior, Fr. Paul LeJeune (all of the canonized Martyrs of North America are Jesuits). Coulson tells us that in his missionary travels, Fr. LeJeune "tasted the four worst aspects of Indian life: cold, heat, smoke and dogs. Of these he found smoke by far the worst. It filled the hut in which men, women and dogs slept together around the fire, and prolonged exposure to it usually brought blindness in the end, a fact which caused LeJeune to remark: 'Unhappy infidels who spend their lives in smoke, and their eternity in flames.'"

Taking Fr. LeJeune's words on their face, the canonized North

American Martyrs (like their uncanonized but heroic Spanish brethren) were ready to undergo all they did in order to save as many Indians as they could from eternal fire. They paid dearly for their charity. How dearly? Here is some of the account we have of the martydom of Fr. Jean de Brébeuf. (It is provided by another Jesuit missionary, Fr. Christophe Regnant. We shall begin by summarizing him, and then go to direct quotation.)

Taken captive by Iroquois, Fr. de Brébeuf was stripped naked and tied to a post. He was beaten with clubs. His fingernails were then torn out. In a mockery of Baptism, a cauldron of boiling water was poured over him. There followed a string of hatchets heated by fire to red-hot and which was strung around his neck. Next, a belt of pitch was tied around his waist and set afire. The Indians then cut out his tongue. After that they began to flay him, which is to say cut and strip the skin off his body.

They still were not done. Says Fr. Regnant: "Those butchers, seeing that the good father began to grow weak, made him sit down on the ground, and one of them, taking a knife, cut off the skin covering his skull. Another one, seeing that the good father would soon die, made an opening in the upper part of his chest, and tore out his heart, which he roasted and ate. Others came to drink his blood, still warm, which they drank with both hands."

Centuries later, in 1991, a feature film entitled *Blackrobe* would be made about the early encounters of French missionaries with American Indians. Not nearly as politically correct as another film of the day, *Dances With Wolves*—besides the savagery shown the missionaries, it realistically depicted Indian cruelty to other Indians—the movie did poorly at the box office. Besides its political incorrectness, the chief reason for the picture's poor acceptance was doubtless accurately fingered by the *New York Times'* senior religion writer, Peter Steinfels, in a review of the film. A contemporary audience, Steinfels said, simply could not understand the missionaries' willingness to sacrifice themselves. The missionaries looked misguided or positively idiotic to such an audience. It was not necessary for Steinfels to say this was because the audience would consist mainly of unbelievers, or at least of persons who do not believe as did the North American Martyrs—and all other Catholics once upon a time, it should be added.

Here is a piece of writing from the pen of another Jesuit missionary and canonized saint, Francis Xavier, the great Jesuit Apostle to the Indies who lived ( 1506-1552) a century before the North American Martyrs:

"Before their Baptism, certain Japanese were greatly troubled by a hateful and annoying scruple: that God did not appear merciful and good because He had never made Himself known to the Japanese people before, especially if it was true that those who had not worshipped God were doomed to everlasting punishment in Hell. One of the things which torments them most is that we teach that the prison of Hell is irrevocably shut, so that there is no escape from it. For they grieve over the fate of their departed children, their parents, and relatives, and they often show their grief by tears. So they ask us if there is any way to free them by prayer from the eternal misery. And I am obliged to answer that there is absolutely none."

So wrote St. Francis Xavier in the 16th century. But in the 20th, another Jesuit, James Brodrick, author of a biography of the saint published in 1952, could say of the Apostle to the Indies that "it is impossible not to feel a little sorry for the Brahmans whom Francis trounced so mercilessly [in a letter to Rome]. For one thing, it was their country, not his, and the religion which they professed and served had a title to some respect from a foreigner, if only by reason of its venerable antiquity, so much more impressive even than that of the Holy Catholic Church. Besides, it has a metaphysic, a philosophy of being, as profound in its own way as any of which the Western world can boast, but of that St. Francis was completely ignorant. He does not seem even to have heard of such deep-rooted and cherished doctrines as those of *karma, maya, bhakti* and *yoga*....Of course, St. Francis was not alone or singular in the hastiness and superficiality of his views. They were shared by all Western men of his time, and we too would have shared them had we been alive then, so there is no particular reason why we should imagine ourselves to be superior."

No, there certainly is not, one is inclined to respond. In fact, how many "Western men" today can be regarded as even equal to Francis Xavier and the countless other missionaries who took seriously Christ's last commandment to His followers, to make disciples of all the nations? The missionaries would include, first of all, the very Apostles who heard the commandment directly and set out to convert the lands of the Roman Empire, but also those who sought to make America Catholic beginning virtually as soon as Catholics discovered her. If these missionaries are today incomprehensible to "Western men," as *Blackrobe* was to its audiences, the incomprehension is rooted in unbelief. "Western men," which is to speak of men who used to be Christian, do not believe in the same things as did Francis Xavier and the North American Martyrs, or they do not believe in anything at all. Remaining Catholics among the "Western men" are apt to be of the "cafeteria"-type. They pick and choose which of the Church's teachings they will believe, including *extra ecclesiam nulla salus*, and then feel "free" to decide whether or not they will live according to them. They may do so, they contend, because every man enjoys "freedom of conscience." Every American knows that.

It was precisely such incomprehension and unbelief which Fr. Feeney foresaw if the leaders of the Church in the U.S. continued on the course they were following a half-century ago. He also understood it was a course to which the U.S. hierarchy had bound itself earlier. Did he additionally see that the heresy of Americanism with its view of liberal democracy as a model for the Church would spread far beyond the frontiers of the country to influence the life of the Church Universal? He was in decline during most of the years following Vatican II and until his death in 1978, and his sense of Americanism's triumph therefore may not have been very sharp. Besides, he might not have wanted to believe in the development, even if he foresaw it. After all, like Fr. de Brébeuf he had sacrificed himself in the conviction that the Church is *the* Church and outside her there is no salvation. To give them their due, most of the original Americanists probably shared his conviction. They simply held that in a Protestant nation the teaching *extra ecclesiam nulla salus* was not to be taught. Somehow they failed to understand that if it were not taught, one day it would not be believed.

Who were the Americanists? What were they about? To answer these questions now is to fast-forward our account of the devolution of Catholic America into the officially pluralistic and secular United States of the late 20th century, but without doing it at this juncture it will be impossible to understand how there arose the circumstances which eventually prevailed, were prevailing when the controversy surrounding Fr. Feeney was at it's height, and which prevail today.

Americanism was condemned as a heresy by Pope Leo XIII in 1899 in an Apostolic Letter, *Testem Benevolentiae*. The document was addressed to Baltimore's Archbishop James Cardinal Gibbons, Primate of the United States. Himself an Americanist, Gibbons tried to block the letter. At the last minute he even sent a cable to Rome, beseeching Pope Leo not to dispatch it. However, the cardinal's cable was received at the Apostolic Palace after *Testem Benevolentiae* was shipbound for transport to the U.S.

(Interestingly enough, no Archbishop of Baltimore has been canonically invested with the title of primate since Gibbons. The most recent one before today's incumbent was installed, William Borders, was not even made a cardinal.)

In his letter, Pope Leo says that Americanism can be identified by certain "doctrines" (his word) which it promotes. They may be summarized: Christian perfection can be attained without external spiritual guidance; natural virtues are superior to supernatural ones and should be extolled over them; even among natural virtues, the cultivation of "active" ones (doing good works), as compared to "passive" ones (praying or contemplating, for instance), is more suitable to modern times; religious vows are out of joint with these times because they limit human liberty; traditional methods of winning non-Catholics to the Church should be abandoned for new ones.

Of these "doctrines," the first and last interest us the most for purposes of tracing the historical background against which the drama of the so-called Boston Heresy Case would eventually play out. The first, that Christian perfection can be attained without external spiritual guidance, can lead to the view when developed far enough that the Church herself is not necessary for salvation. As for the last "doctrine," it had always been the way of the Church to proclaim her truths "from the housetops" (*Matthew,* 10:27). That was so from the days when St. Paul preached in the Athenian *agora.* It was still so with the North American Martyrs and St. Francis Xavier in India and Japan. The Americanists—Bishops John J. Keane and Denis J. O'Connell, Archbishop John Ireland and Cardinal Gibbons were among the leading ones—believed it should be otherwise. They saw that the evangelization of a Protestant nation suspicious of "undemocratic" Catholicism and "Popish plots" against separation of Church and state was a difficult problem. They proposed the "Americanization" of the Church as the solution. That would entail leaving untaught teachings which truly were undemocratic. Among them would be the teaching that membership in a particular religious body, theirs, was necessary for salvation. No democrat believing in the principle of equality—equality of beliefs as well as of men—would want to hear that.

Leo knew exactly what Americanism entailed. It is why he wrote that all of the "doctrines" summarized above were based on a single "First Principle": "That in order the more easily to bring over to Catholic doctrine those who dissent from it, the Church ought to adapt herself somewhat to [the Pope is being ironic] our advanced civilization, and, relaxing her ancient rigor, show some indulgence to modern popular theories and methods." The Pope then allowed himself to express the confidence that "the Bishops of America would be the first to repudiate and condemn" the First Principle. Otherwise, there would be raised "the suspicion that there are some among you who conceive and desire a Church in America different from that which is in the rest of the world."

Now, it needs to be known that the formal heresy of Americanism did not first arise in America. Its true home was France. However, it could not take root in that country in the late 19th century. It was only in America that it could possibly find the right soil for taking root at that time, and Leo knew very well what it could one day mean for the Church Universal if it did anywhere. Equally well, he understood that among the U.S. bishops were men who did desire "a Church in America different from that which is in the rest of the world," and who believed the one in the rest of the world should be as theirs.

One such has already been identified: Denis J. O'Connell. In 1898, the year the U.S. went to war against Spain ostensibly over Cuba, he was rector of the North American College in Rome. As such he was the man in charge of the formation of young clerics selected for training in the Eternal City in order for them to play leading future roles in the U.S. Church. Here he is writing from Rome to his good friend and fellow-Americanist,

Archbishop Ireland of St. Paul, in May of that year:

"For me this [the Spanish-American War] is not simply a question of Cuba. If it were, it were no question or a poor question. Then let the 'greasers' eat one another up and save the lives of our dear boys. But for me it is a question of much more moment:—it is the question of two civilizations. It is the question of all that is old & vile & mean & rotten & cruel & false in Europe against all this [sic] is free & noble & open & true & humane in America. When Spain is swept of [sic] the seas much of the meanness & narrowness of old Europe goes with it to be replaced by the freedom and openness of America. This is God's way of developing the world. And all continental Europe feels the war is against itself, and that is why they are all against us, and Rome more than all because when the prestige of Spain & Italy will have passed away, and when the pivot of the world's political action will no longer be confined within the limits of the continent; then the nonsense of trying to govern the universal church from a purely European standpoint—and according to exclusively Spanish and Italian methods, will be glaringly evident even to a child. 'Now the axe is laid to the root of the tree.'"

O'Connell continued: "Let the wealth of Convents & Communities in Cuba & the Philippines go; it did nothing for the advancement of religion."

There is still another, quite amazing passage of this letter which asks for citation: "Again it seems to me that above all nations, moving them on along the path of civilization to better, higher, happier modes of existence is the constant action of a tender divine Providence, and that the convergent action of all great powers is towards that common & destined end; to more brotherhood, to more kindness, to more mutual respect for every man, to more practical and living recognition of the rule of God. At one time one nation in the world now another, took the lead, but now it seems to me that the old governments of Europe will lead no more and that neither Italy, nor Spain will ever furnish the principles of the civilization of the future. Now God passes the banner to the hands of America, to bear it:—in the cause of humanity and it is your office to make its destiny known to America and become its grand chaplain. Over all America there is certainly a duty higher than the interest of the individual states—even of the national government. The duty to humanity is certainly a real duty, and America cannot certainly with honor, or fortune, evade its great share in it. Go to America and say, thus saith the Lord! Then you will live in history as God's Apostle in modern times to Church & to Society. Hence I am a partisan of the Anglo-American alliance, together they are invincible and they will *impose* a new civilization [emphasis added]."

Let us for a moment (but only a moment) abstract from the letter's obvious racism and voiced contempt for religious in convents and monasteries (they would be guilty of practicing "passive" virtues). O'Connell's letter is documentary proof that leading Americanists really did want "a Church in America different from that which is"—or then was—"in the rest of the world." Indeed, it shows they wanted a different Church Universal, one annealed to "the cause of humanity," not the cause of Jesus Christ (who is never mentioned).

It was said a few lines ago that we would soon return to the racism of Bishop O'Connell's letter, the note of Anglo-American superiority he struck, and we shall. Right now, there asks to be answered the question, why might the heresy of Americanism take root in America but not in France where it arose—and take root so deeply it would become known as Americanism? The answer is simple.

The heresy essentially represented an effort to accommodate the Revolution, the one that began with the Protestant Revolt commonly called the Reformation, which erupted politically in France in 1789, subverted most of Spain's empire in the Americas at the beginning of the 19th century, erupted again in 1848 in France and elsewhere in Europe, then in 1917 in Russia, and the spirit of which has held sway almost everywhere in ex-Christendom since 1945. This Revolution amounts to a revolt of man against God and it shows itself politically in the notion that society should be governed according to "the will of the people" instead of God's. But in France in the late 19th century there was an intense Catholic feeling, one so intense that monarchists for a time were the majority in the French parliament. It was this feeling that led to the construction on Montmartre, approved by the parliament as a public utility, of the spectacular Basilica of the Sacred Heart (the Sacré Coeur) in expiation for France's revolutionary sins.

In contrast to France, the U.S. was the nation where "the will of the people" governed as nowhere else in the world at that time, and given fallen human nature,"the people," if left uninstructed (and to speak in terms of the "doctrines" condemned by Pope Leo), will never readily concede the need for authoritative external direction for anything; will not even acknowledge supernatural virtues; will not imagine, if only due to sentimentalism, that anything could be more important than doing good; and will (at best) turn a deaf ear to truth. (At worst—we have already seen it—the bearer of truth may have to suffer martyrdom, if only a "dry" one.)

As for the racism of Bishop O'Connell's letter, it was doubtless more rooted in a cultural attitude than in actual belief in the superiority of one set of genes over another. ("Greasers" were seen as wont to "waste" time sitting in cafes—or praying in monasteries; things were run more "efficiently" in North America than in Latin America; Latins were not as democratic in their institutions; and so on.) Margaret Sanger worshipped Anglo genes, but the Church has never proposed the worship of anything or anyone except God, at least not until quite recent times when the spirit of the Revolution finally so infected her that most clerics began openly to suggest that serving creatures (like the "poor and oppressed") is more important than serving the Creator (exactly as if the Church really were dedicated to "the cause of humanity" instead of the cause of Jesus Christ).

In any event, it was the arrival on these shores of English-speakers, especially including Catholics among them, which began to undo the Catholic America founded by the Spanish and French. It was natural for Protestant Anglos to want to undo it, but more important to what transpired was the attitude of the Catholics among the new arrivals. They did not resist the Protestant enterprise. Search the history books as you will, you can find no instance of an early-arriving English-speaking Catholic ever saying more than that Catholics simply wanted their Church in this country to be equal to other religious bodies.

The Carroll family, the first Catholic family to enjoy real prominence in the United States, are emblamatic of all the Catholics in their day and ever since who were and have been American before anything else, and to such a degree that no one has ever spoken of Catholic Americans, but always of American Catholics.

Charles Carroll (of Carrollton), schooled by Jesuits in Maryland and Flanders, would be the wealthiest man in the colonies when he signed the Declaration of Independence in 1776. We are told by the old *Catholic Encyclopedia* (the edition of 1909): "As a democrat he opposed all distinctions and titles." He was also a champion of centralized government, that deadliest of enemies to true political freedom. On the personal level, he had seven children, four of whom died in their youth. Those who lived and married did so outside the Church.

John Carroll was the cousin of Charles and, like him, was Jesuit-trained. But John became a Jesuit, being ordained at Liege at the age of 34. That was in 1769, by which time the Society was no longer what it had been when it produced the North American Martyrs. Indeed, four years later Pope Clement XIV published his Bull dissolving the order. History best knows John Carroll, of course, as the first bishop named in the U.S., his see being that of Baltimore (which is what makes it the primatial one in the U.S.).

The old *Catholic Encyclopedia* tells us that although he accepted his office from Rome, he "hoped that some method of appointing Church authorities be adopted by Rome that would not make it appear as if they were receiving their appointment from a foreign power." That is a delicate way of saying John Carroll advocated the popular election of bishops.

It was not all he advocated. Again we turn to the old *Catholic Encyclopedia*. "Doubtless to him, in part," it says, "is due the provision in Article Sixth, Section 3, of the Constitution, which declares that 'no religious test shall ever be required as a qualification to any office or public trust under the United States,' and also the first amendment that 'Congress shall make no law respecting an establishment of religion, or prohibiting the free exercise thereof.'"

Helpful also in erecting the famous wall of separation between Church and state in the U.S. would have been John Carroll's brother Daniel, one of the two Catholics present in Philadelphia in 1789 as framers of the Constitution. Daniel also owned the land, which he gifted to the United States, on which the U.S. Capitol was erected. (The ceremonies for the laying of the Capitol's cornerstone, presided over by George Washington in the apron he wore as Grand Master of a lodge in Alexandria, Virginia, were Masonic.)

Such was America's first eminent Catholic family. In light of the lead they gave, there should be no surprise that when in a few decades the United States engaged in its first foreign war, the one it waged against Mexico in 1846, no important Catholic voice was raised against the aggression. That was even though the proximate cause of the U.S. invasion of Mexico was a law enacted by the Mexicans which required that U.S. citizens settling in Texas (then a state of Mexico) should be Catholic or convert to the Faith.

( If no important Catholic voice was raised against the war, simple Irish immigrants sent to Mexico in the U.S. Army quickly perceived the anti-Catholic nature of "the Crusade," as it was called in the U.S. They defected to Mexico and formed the *Brigada de San Patricio*, St. Patrick's Brigade. Also, Abraham Lincoln, a man who is not known to have joined any church and who was a member of the U.S. House of Representatives in 1846, was the only member of that body to speak out against the war. There is a statue of him in Mexico City on account of it.)

It is an aside but illustrative of how far America got away from her Catholic origins that from the seizure of half of Mexico's territory (Texas, California, Colorado, all of today's Southwest) in the war of 1846, to the "liberation" of Spain's last important colonies in 1898, to the dissolution of the Catholic Habsburg Empire demanded by Woodrow Wilson as a condition for peace in World War I, to the U.S.-approved overthrow and murder of President Diem in Vietnam, the Catholic interest has suffered in every foreign war fought by the U.S. That is with the arguable exception of the "police action" in Korea, but conducted as it was under the auspices of the United Nations, that fighting can be seen as a precursor to more recent undertakings in the Persian Gulf, Somalia and elsewhere in defense of the New World Order—which order is certainly inimical to the Christian one.

As for World War II, the atom-bombing of the principal center of Catholicism in Japan, Nagasaki, was celebrated by most Americans, but at St. Benedict Center in Cambridge, Massachusetts, the effect was traumatic, as we shall see. However, to speak already of the years of World War II really is to get us far ahead of ourselves.

The point has here been made that as late as 1800 all of today's U.S. which lay west of the Mississippi was still Catholic. That is because it was all Spanish. It should be added that east of the river, all of today's Florida and the coasts of today's states of Alabama and Mississippi also belonged to Spain. To give some sense of what Spain was doing to evangelize her lands, it is sufficient to know that in Florida alone there had been established 87 Spanish missions, with 17 Spanish forts to defend them.

A large section of Spain's North American lands, known as the Louisiana Territory and extending from the Mississippi River on the east to the Sabine River in the west and to the Missouri in the north, had been ceded to Spain by France in the Treaty of Paris of 1763. (The entire Mississippi Valley—most of today's Midwest—was claimed by France after La Salle explored the length of the "Father of Waters" in 1682.) The Louisiana Territory reverted to France after Napoleon's conquest of Spain soon after the turn of the 19th century. Subsequently, Napoleon literally sold everything claimed by France, from the Gulf of Mexico to the Canadian border, to the U.S. The latter still consisted of nothing but the former British colonies hugging the eastern seaboard, but already, merely 25 years after George Washington's installation as the first President, those states felt the westwards expansionist urge whose eventual fulfillment, our textbooks tell us, was the realization of "Manifest Destiny." Napoleon's sale of the territory is what we know as the Louisiana Purchase.

After it, much of the territory west of the Mississippi still belonged to Spain, and then to Mexico after that nation declared independence from Spain in 1821. We have already seen how this remaining Catholic territory came to be governed by the U.S. as a consequence of the war against Mexico begun in 1846. ( Florida was ceded by Spain to the U.S. in 1819, by which time there had grown up in addition to St. Augustine cities which are now known as Jacksonville, Miami, Gainesville, Tampa, Tallahassee and Pensacola. )

From a Catholic point of view, the importance of the takeover by the predominately Anglo, English-speaking Protestant U.S. of the lands west of the Mississippi cannot be exaggerated. As Bishop David Arias, Auxiliary Bishop and Vicar for Hispanic Concerns of the Archdiocese of Newark, explains in his 1992 book, *Spanish Roots of America* (he writes in the present tense): "The taking of this vast region by the United States is not like coming into an uncivilized land, but into a territory that is explored and unified. It is a territory with a culture deeply rooted in its people and cities. Also, this is a territory with mining, agriculture, cattle raising, and economy in progress. It is a territory with its Indian population, to a large extent, settled, civilized, and christianized from a slow but steady labor of Spain for over three hundred years." In a word, it was not wilderness. It was Catholic.

Bishop Arias, still writing in the present tense, also notes the terms of the 1848 Treaty of Guadalupe-Hidalgo by which Mexico lost all her territories north of the Rio Grande. "The Treaty includes three conditions for its validity: respect for the property of its present owners; keeping of the Spanish language, culture and customs of its people; and freedom to practice their Catholic faith. None of these conditions will be respected in the years to follow."

By way of illustrating the difficulties faced by Catholics in the former Spanish and Mexican lands after their takeover by the U.S., Bishop Arias points out that within a year of Guadalupe-Hidalgo, there were but 12 priests in the entire State of Texas to serve 20,000 Catholics.

The Indians of whom he speaks—"settled, civilized, and christianized to a large extent"—especially suffered as a consequence of the takeover. Great historians have acknowledged this, historians whose works, alas, were not the ones read at Harvard or the other exclusive eastern seaboard universities which for too long served as models for all so-called higher education in the U.S. In those schools, books like *The California and the Oregon Trail,* by Francis Parkman, were the preferred texts. What they provided—to generations of the sons of the nation's governing elite—was the notion of an unexplored Western wilderness finally being civilized thanks to its settlement by English-speaking Protestants.

One of the neglected historians was Herbert Eugene Bolton, author of numerous scholarly volumes on Spain's civilizing mission in the Western Hemisphere in general and North America in particular (*History of the Americas; Coronado, Knight of Pueblos and Plains,* etc.). It looked for a time during the 1960s that Bolton would finally enjoy the recognition he deserved, but the interest in him faded. It is even less likely that his work will be revived in these days of political correctness. "The conquistadores who threaded their way through the American wilderness," he wrote of the original explorers of the continent, "were armored knights upon armored horses; proud, stern, hardy, and courageous; men of punctilious honor, loyal to the king and to Mother Church, humble only before the symbols of their Faith." Of another time, the years after the U.S. began to expand into the formerly Catholic West, Bolton said: "We must admit that the accomplishments of Spain remained a force which made for the preservation of the Indians as opposed to their destruction so characteristic of the Anglo-American frontier."

Of course that was not about to be admitted, no more by Americanist bishops like Denis O'Connell than by Harvard professors.

Even before the Anglo-American frontier was pushed westward, the ideology driving the push found expression in the Monroe Doctrine, avowedly designed to exclude European influence from the Americas— and by European was meant Catholic. Theodore Roosevelt was explicit about that at the turn of this century after a visit to Argentina. "While these countries remain Catholic," he said, "we will not be able to dominate them." That European meant Catholic was again evident in 1982 when the U.S., in violation of the Monroe Doctrine, actually assisted England in its war against Argentina in the Malvinas Islands (called the Falklands by England).

At no time did the Catholic bishops in the U.S. or any Catholic laymen of note raise their voice in protest against the clear anti-Catholic policy of the U.S., much less try to stand athwart developments stemming from the policy. Either to protest or act, at least in a Catholic way, would necessarily have entailed the championship of undiluted Catholic truths. Of course a defense of the Church and her material interests within the settled U.S. was made, but it was made in an American way, on the basis of religious freedom, equality of beliefs, and so on. John Carroll, as we have seen, led in this way.

By mid-19th-century, so anxious were Catholics in the U.S. to show themselves as Americans before they were Catholic that even the greatest apologist the Faith has ever produced in this country, Orestes Brownson, felt obliged three years before his death to write: "I willingly admit that I made many mistakes, but I regard as the greatest of all the mistakes into which I fell...that of holding back the stronger points of the Catholic faith...of laboring to present Catholicity in a form as little repulsive to my non-Catholic countrymen as possible; and of insisting on only the minimum of Catholicity."

Having admitted his mistake to himself, Brownson ended his life (he died in 1876) as a vocal defender of the teaching *extra ecclesiam nulla salus*. Doubtless it helps explain why his name and work were let fall into obscurity after his death. (It took the archliberal Arthur M. Schlesinger, Jr., of all men, to revive the memory of Brownson. It was with his first book, published in 1939, *Orestes Brownson: A Pilgrim's Progress*.)

There can certainly be no doubt as regards the reason for the silencing of the Redemptorist priest Michael Mueller, another 19th-century figure. He was the Bishop Sheen of his day, but without television. His medium was books, and his principal theme was *extra ecclesiam nulla salus*. The books were always best sellers for that era. Fr. Mueller's publishers could not print them fast enough. Yet, he was silenced. Today his name is hardly known. The present writer did not know it until I started the research for this book.

If there could ever have been a time when U.S. Catholicism might develop in other than an Americanist direction, it was probably precluded from doing so by a single factor: From the days of the signing of the Declaration of Independence until very recently, the majority of the republic's Catholics have been Irish or of Irish extraction. Well before the end of the 19th century it was the same with the bishops. Even today, with the majority of the Church in the U.S. likely to become Hispanic in the near future, the Irish influence remains predominant. More bishops are still of Irish extraction than any other, for instance.

For a time in the 19th century and early in this one, German-speaking Catholics centered in the northern Midwest offered some challenge to the Irish influence, but the Germans generally fell into silence in the face of the widespread anti-German feeling that seized the U.S. during World War I.

Also in the 19th century there were numerous Spanish and French bishops in the U.S., but their mere arrival within these shores seemed to change them. An example would be the famous Archbishop Lamy of Santa Fe, New Mexico, a Frenchman and the model for Willa Cather's justly celebrated novel, *Death Comes for the Archbishop*. Archbishop Lamy, like the majority of the bishops from the U.S., was an inopportunist at Vatican I.

(The record of Vatican Council I shows that Ven. Pope Pius IX and the majority of the bishops at the council—they were continental Europeans—intended the dogmatic definition of papal infallibility precisely in order to strengthen the papacy's ability to defend Catholic truths against the spread of the democratic conception of liberty of ideas and freedom of conscience. Besides the Americans opposed to the definition, another inopportunist was the Englishman, Henry Cardinal Newman.)

In terms of the U.S. Church developing in an Americanist direction and thus becoming one virtually certain to condemn Fr. Michael Mueller in the 19th century and Fr. Leonard Feeney in the 20th, what is the significance of the Irish influence? To answer in as few words as possible, Irish Catholicism by the time it reached America was deeply imbued by the spirit of Jansenism. No one will dispute this. It is too widely recognized. Had a Catholic gone to confession as recently as 30 years ago in Dublin or Boston or New York, and then confessed the same sins in Naples or Marseilles or Buenos Aires, he would have had sharply different reactions from the priests. Your Irish-American priest in Boston would have been outraged, and rightly so, at the confession of a sexual transgression. The priest in Naples would also be disturbed by that, but it would probably draw his first attention if you additionally confessed, say, purposely harming another man's reputation.

There would have been no question of the priests practicing different religions. Had you asked the one in Boston and then the one in Naples to draw up a list of ten grave sins, they could well end by listing the same ones, but it would have been in a different order. Generally speaking, the Irishman would put sins of the flesh at the top.

That there was a Jansenist spirit in the Irish Church has significance in the story of the so-called Boston Heresy Case because most of the great Irish immigration into the U.S. that followed the Potato Famine and during subsequent years was via the Northeast, and for a long time stopped there. It made Boston, as it did New York City, a great Catholic center. Unfortunately, New England after Plymouth Rock had become the heartland in America of Protestant Puritanism. This native Puritanism simply reenforced the Jansenist tendencies of the Irish immigrants and their clergy. The tendencies reenforced, they made the Irish-American Church—that is essentially what the Church in the U.S. became—a very peculiar institution. No doubt the Church everywhere and in every age should be anxious for the sexual morals of her sons and daughters, but the concern of the Irish-American Church could be excessive. There are women living today who can remember being instructed by parochial-school sisters not to look at the toes of their patent leather shoes. At home they were made to wear a slip when they bathed.

Though it certainly did not shape his outlook as it would that of countless others, even Leonard Feeney was not untouched by the Jansenism of the Irish-American Church. Some of his poetry could be quite sensual. (One thinks, for example, of a poem he wrote about the martyrdom of St. Catherine of Alexandria.) On the other hand, during the years he spent in New York City as a critic for *America* magazine, he never went to the theater, not even to the most serious of plays, for fear of exposing himself to impurity.

But the effect of the Irish-American Church on her individual members is not our real concern here. Rather, the larger point that wants to be made is that a predominantly French or German or Italian immigrant Church would have been immunized against the native Puritanism of New England. The predominantly Irish one was not. However, the native Puritanism did not simply make her even more Jansenist than she was at home. It made her, from the beginning, American—i.e. different from what then was the Church in the rest of the world and especially in *her* heartland, continental Europe. The real question is, how could a Church which was American from the beginning ever have been disposed to convert America? The answer is that she never was.

The tragedy is that non-Catholics did not believe the Church in the U.S. was not disposed to convert the nation. They looked at the Church in Europe and Latin America and supposed the one at home was the same. Seeing that this is what they believed, Catholics in America, and especially the Catholic clergy, became all the more determined to prove they were as American as everybody else. They proved it by *becoming* exactly that, even though it meant ignoring Our Lord's last commandment to his followers, the one we have already recalled: to make disciples of all the nations. In time, they would feel driven to go beyond ignoring Christ's injunction. They would positively deny that the Church had a mission to convert the nation, and to deny also the reason for converting anyone: that outside the Church there is no salvation. In other words, they began by asserting that the Church sought no special position for herself in the U.S., she simply wished to be equal with other "denominations," and hence Bishop Carroll's instigation of the First Amendment. They ended by teaching that there is nothing special about the Church, period. You could get to Heaven without her. If pressed, some might allow that it was "better" to be Catholic, as it is "better" to ride first-class on an airplane. But you'll still arrive at the destination if you're seated in coach.

With that teaching is how they ended, it was said a moment ago. However, it was not quite the end. In fact, the U.S. bishops took the teaching with them to Rome in 1962, and the result was Vatican II's promulgation of the Declaration on Religious Liberty. That particular Americanist triumph is another story, however, one already told by Michael Davies as here earlier noted.

We have said that the Church in the U.S. went from ignoring Christ's commandment to make all nations Catholic to denying positively that the Church had such a mission, and that she was driven to do so in order to prove the sincerity of her Americanism. It remained that many persisted in not believing in her sincerity.

One such was writer Paul Blanshard. Wrong as he proved to be, his name is not much remembered today, but in 1949 it was a household one. Blanshard was a lawyer by training who became a very successful professional anti-Catholic. In 1949, Beacon Press, a Boston publishing firm run by Unitarians and with national reach and respectability, brought out one of his books, *American Freedom and Catholic Power*. To describe the book as merely a best-seller would be seriously to misrepresent it. The thing in fact went through no fewer than 26 printings in its first edition. In a word, its sales were phenomenal.

We want briefly to look at Blanshard's book, bearing in mind that the year it came out, 1949, was also when the controversy surrounding Fr. Feeney and St. Benedict Center was at its height.

Blanshard posited a "struggle between American democracy and the Catholic hierarchy." That there was no such struggle is right now beyond the point. Catholics, Blanshard said, were "outbreeding non-Catholic elements in our population," and once they became the majority in three-fourths of the states, there would be "Catholic control of the United States." Once this "control" existed, went the line, there would be passed "three comprehensive amendments to the United States Constitution."

The first Blanshard styled as the "Christian Commonwealth Amendment." It's first provision, as imagined by the best-selling writer: "The United States is a Catholic Republic, and the Catholic Apostolic and Roman religion is the sole religion of the nation." Another provision: "The First Amendment to the Constitution of the United States is hereby repealed." That, of course, was the amendment in part contrived by Bishop Carroll in the first place.

Blanshard's second imagined amendment was the "Christian Education Amendment." Two of its projected provisions, which the writer said "could be expected with confidence": "1. American religious education belongs pre-eminently to the Roman Catholic Church, by reason of a double title in the supernatural order, conferred exclusively upon her by God Himself. 2. The governments of the United States and the states shall encourage and assist the Roman Catholic Church by appropriate measures in the exercise of the Church's supreme mission as educator."

Finally, Blanshard said there would be a "Christian Family Amendment". Some of its provisions, as envisioned by the writer: "1. All marriages are indissoluble, and the divorce of all persons is prohibited throughout the territory of the United States, providing that nothing herein shall effect the right of annulment and remarriage in accordance with the Canon Law of the Roman Catholic Church. 2. Direct abortion is murder of the innocent even when performed through motives of misguided pity when the life of a mother is gravely imperiled. 3. Birth control, or any act that deliberately frustrates the natural power to generate life, is a crime."

Now, cradle Catholics who grew up in the U.S. during the forties and fifties know that Blanshard's notion of a Catholic threat to American democracy was preposterous. They know that the Catholic hierarchy did not seek a "Catholic Republic". However, the present writer can testify that non-Catholic Americans often did believe the kind of things Blanshard claimed. It is exactly the kind of stuff I used to hear around the house, growing up in the forties as a Protestant.

To the non-Catholics, Blanshard's predictions seemed plausible for two reasons. First, Catholics at that time *were* "outbreeding" the rest of the population. Indeed, had the practice of contraception and then abortion not become as widespread among them as the rest of the population, they would be the majority today. However, more important to Blanshard's credibility was the fact that he could point to the predominantly Catholic nations of Western Europe and Latin America where at that time divorce, abortion and the sale of birth-control devices were all still illegal. (Of course in 1949 abortion was still illegal in all the states of the [non-Catholic] United States except in cases where the mother's life was supposedly gravely endangered.) As far as that goes, in two heavily Catholic states, Connecticut and Massachusetts, the sale of contraceptive devices over the counter was illegal. What Blanshard chose to ignore was that by 1949, Catholic politicians in the U.S., *with no censure from their bishops*, were already ignoring Rome's teachings. For instance, the young John F. Kennedy, then a member of the U.S. House of Representatives, was telling his constituents that he was opposed to the continued prohibition against the over-the-counter sale of contraceptive devices in Massachusetts. Kennedy always enjoyed the support of his family's close friend, Richard Cardinal Cushing.

Yet, in 1949 there was still one nationally-known cleric, a priest standing in the same line as his heroic Spanish and French predecessors to these shores, who publicly preached that there was no salvation outside the

Church and that accordingly, for the sake of her citizens' souls, America should be Catholic. She would become that by converting non-Catholic Americans as well as by "outbreeding" them. Preaching this is exactly what now made the cleric nationally known since he was no longer writing much poetry, but he did not merely preach it. Working out of a storefront operation in Cambridge, Massachusetts, he was successfully converting hundreds of young men and women, students of Harvard and Radcliffe, including members of some of the country's wealthiest and most powerful Protestant families.

The assimilation of Catholics in the U.S. as complete social equals is what was wanted by the leaders of the Church in the U.S. Assimilation would not be as easy, it could be made impossible, if families belonging to the nation's governing elite were antagonized.

The cleric in Cambridge was Rev. Leonard Feeney, S.J. Unless he and his associates were silenced now, in 1949, and a cloak of obscurity cast over the teachings they upheld, it would be impossible to prove once and for all that Blanshard and his ilk were wrong, that the Catholic hierarchy was not at odds with American democracy. Of course, too, if the teachings continued to be proclaimed in America and accepted by very many on account of their proclamation, it would be impossible (at least it would be much more difficult) for the Church elsewhere in the world to be persuaded and to accept that it really was desirable for her to "adapt herself"—we are quoting Leo XIII in *Testem Benevolentiae*—to liberal, democratic, pluralistic "advanced civilization."

Chapter Three

St. Benedict Center began as a storefront operation. Catherine Clarke is believed to have been the one to spot the location, a vacated furniture store on the ground floor of an apartment building which stood where two streets with the unlikely names of Bow and Arrow intersected. This was in Cambridge, Massachusetts, across the Charles River from Boston proper. The building still stands at Bow and Arrow.

No sharp corner is formed by the intersection of the streets. The facade of the building which housed St. Benedict Center is curved. In front of the building is an urban space like a small European piazza or square. Across the way, as a half century ago, sits a Catholic church, St. Paul's. When I visited the neighborhood on a Sunday afternoon in September, 1992, the doors of St. Paul's were locked. (No doubt the neighborhood has changed a great deal during the past five decades, especially the last couple, and not for the better. It is so nearly everywhere.)

When St. Benedict Center was at Bow and Arrow, someone coming out its front door and turning right had only to walk a block and then to the other side of Massachusetts Avenue to reach the campus of Harvard University. That Catherine Clarke chose well the location for a student center is attested by the fact that today, the Archdiocese of Boston's Harvard/Radcliffe Student Outreach Center is just a bit further down the block and across the street.

In September, 1992, I stood before the glass doors of the Archdiocesan operation, wondering how much money was spent on it. Looking past a polished lobby, I could spy a room with four or five persons gathered around a conference table. Seeing me peer in, the woman at the head of the table got up and came to the door. She was middle-aged, burly, and wore a black turtleneck sweater. She could have been taken for a women's wrestling coach except there was a large silver cross without a corpus hanging from her neck.

She wanted to know if I wished to come inside for some reason, or wished anything else, and she wanted to know it *now*.

"No, thank you," I said. "I'm researching a book on Fr. Leonard Feeney and St. Benedict Center, and I'm just looking around the neighborhood."

"Oh," Sister Whomever said, closing the door and turning away. Clearly, St. Benedict Center and Leonard Feeney were names not unknown to her. Equally clearly, the center and the priest were unpalatable subjects for conversation.

Involuntarily, a picture of Catherine Clarke, always described as charming, came to mind. Then, as I made the short walk from the Harvard campus to the former site of St. Benedict Center, it was easy to imagine a cold autumn or winter afternoon in 1946 or '47 and someone, perhaps a young veteran of the recent fighting in Europe or the Pacific with the collar of his coat turned up and hands gloved, walking briskly along in these same steps, leaving behind the hubbub of Massachusetts Avenue, fleeing a classroom lecture on Hegel—that philosopher-precursor of Hitler as well as Stalin—and looking forward to Mrs. Clarke putting into his hands in a few moments a cup of coffee or steaming hot chocolate. Afterwards would follow some good conversation with like-minded friends.

What would make them like-minded? They would be other young men and women who did not imagine history in the fashion of Hegel's thesis-antithesis giving way to synthesis. They would be Catholics who knew history to be a continuing unfolding of the will of God.

St. Benedict Center did not come into being out of nothing. Earlier, in 1936, the St. Thomas More Lending Library and Book Shop was opened on Church Street in Cambridge by three young women, Evangeline Mercier, Mary Stanton and Martha Doherty. The three friends were from locally prominent Catholic families and they intended more than a simple bookstore. To help them achieve it, they hired as their store manager the vivacious, red-haired wife of a postal worker, Henry (Hank) Clarke. This was Catherine Goddard Clarke. (Hank and Catherine had two young children whom they had adopted.)

In a way that is hard to feature today, there was a real intellectual ferment going on in Catholicism in the U.S. during the 1930s. Having begun earlier in the century and paralleling a similar development in England, it followed on the efforts of numerous continental European figures to apply the teachings of the Faith to the social and political domain. So it was that when the three young women and their new manager opened their bookstore in Cambridge, they had the idea, beyond the selling of books, of providing a place where Catholics could gather to attend lectures, discuss the work of such as Jacques Maritain, Christopher Dawson and Dorothy Day, and thereby help perhaps to develop a Catholic perspective on issues of the day which might even—Who could say?—exercise some national influence.

A distinctive national Catholic influence seemed possible in those days for two reasons. The first: Catholics were still distinguishable from the rest of the population. The second: Catholics were becoming increasingly accepted socially, distinctive as they still were. (A sign of the growing acceptance was the bestowal in 1937 by Harvard University of an honorary doctorate on Boston's Archbishop William Henry Cardinal O'Connell.)

Members of two groups, St. Andrew's Club and St. Clement's Society, both of which met in private homes, made up most of the regular attendance at the sessions on Church Street. But on occasion, the audience swelled in size, the premises became too small.

At about the time their enterprise was obviously outgrowing its base, Martha Doherty became engaged and her two friends decided to enter Carmelite communities. Thus it was that Catherine Clarke had an eye out for a location where a new Catholic center could be set up. She and others did not want to see such a fruitful beginning come simply to an end.

Exactly who all signed the lease in March, 1940, for the former furniture store at 23 Arrow St. is not clear today. It may have been Mrs. Clarke by herself, but two other persons were also important in the creation of the new center. One was Christopher Huntington, a Harvard assistant dean who also taught government. The other was Avery Dulles. One day he would be one of the most famous members in the world of the Society of Jesus, but in March, 1940, he was a student at Harvard Law School. He was also the scion of one of the nation's leading Presbyterian families (his father, John Foster Dulles, became Dwight Eisenhower's secretary of state during the 1950s). Young Avery was very close to Catherine Clarke. This is by all accounts. It was she who stood as his godmother when he was received into the Church with a conditional baptism in November, 1940.

Another who knew Mrs. Clarke has already been quoted in these pages as saying, "You couldn't talk with her without coming away burning with zeal." The zeal she imparted to young Avery Dulles is evident in an article he wrote for the first issue of *From the Housetops* when St. Benedict Center launched that publication. "We must resolutely refuse to expose ourselves unnecessarily to the contagion of false doctrines and false values," he said. "We must cease to regard 'broadmindedness' as a virtue....We should on the contrary...concentrate primarily on the difficult process of saving souls."

As with the question of who signed its lease, no one today is sure of who named the new center. There apparently was a thought to name it after St. Robert Bellarmine. George B. Pepper says Avery Dulles remembers John Julian Ryan, a professor of literature at Holy Cross College and another who was present at the center's creation, as being the one to suggest the name of St. Benedict.

(George B. Pepper is the author of a sociological work, *The Boston Heresy Case in View of the Secularization of Religion; A Case Study in the Sociology of Religion*, published in 1988. Besides the recollections of persons interviewed for the present book and articles published over the years in various newspapers and other periodicals, Pepper's volume is a source for what is here related regarding the history of St. Benedict Center. Even more so is Catherine Clarke's own book, *The Loyolas and the Cabots*, recently reprinted by the branch of St. Benedict Center in Richmond, N.H. Sr. Catherine's book is indispensable to anyone interested in the so-called Boston Heresy Case. Pepper's account of the history of St. Benedict Center is quite complete for its brevity—61 pages in a volume of 196—but he is a sociologist and suffers from the deficiencies of one, including little grasp of history, as manifested when he refers to the "medieval works" of St. Augustine. Another book about Fr. Feeney—and also Orestes Brownson—is important for the documentation it provides. This is *They Fought The Good Fight* by Bro. Thomas Mary Sennott, M.I.C.M.)

The three, Clarke, Dulles and Huntington, together with the nine or ten others who were its original nucleus, now had premises for their center, and a name. It remained to decide, if not yet a complete program for St. Benedict Center, what form it would take, as well as some purpose for it on which they could all agree.

All agreed that St. Benedict Center had to include a lending library of Catholic books. Further, they decided the center was to be a place where non-Catholics, as Sr. Catherine describes it in her book, "could find out from Catholics what the Church was teaching without getting in touch with any of its professionals."

Christopher Huntington felt especially strongly on the last point, for it was at such a center—one with a library but where no clergy intruded—that he discovered the Faith and eventually converted from Episcopalianism while a student at the University of Wisconsin in Madison.

With some form and a limited purpose for St. Benedict Center agreed upon, a couple of organizational details remained before the door at 23 Arrow St. could be opened to the interested public. For one thing, there were numerous Catholic students at Harvard by 1940, though each was supposed to have the permission of his pastor, and they had a group, the Harvard Catholic Club, with a priest from St. Paul's as its spiritual director. In his capacity as an assistant dean, Christopher Huntington spoke to the Dean of Harvard College about the proposed new center, pointing out that the existing campus organization offered no library and the new body would have no clerical involvement. The dean responded with the advice that the center be set up as an entity independent of both Harvard and the Church. Accordingly, St. Benedict Center was legally established as a corporation in the city of Cambridge.

If the center was envisioned, at least for the time being, as a place free of "Church professionals," it was still desirable to have the good will of the pastor of the local parish, St. Paul's. The pastor was Msgr. Augustine F. Hickey. Informed by Catherine Clarke of the center's plans, and indeed of the fact that the center was to be located just across the way in the former furniture store, Msgr. Hickey reacted in a positive way, even offering to help pay the rent. He also smoothed the feathers of the priest attached to the Harvard Catholic Club who had not been told about the center.

The center was independent of Harvard as well as the Church, but

Harvard's was the dominant intellectual presence in Cambridge; the center existed in the university's shadow; and as long as it was in Cambridge, the majority of those active in its apostolate or whose lives were touched by it were either students or faculty from Harvard, as was foreseen and meant to be the case. At the center, they were always very conscious of the presence up the street.

What was the nature of that presence? Harvard, as it never ceases to remind the nation, was the first college founded in what is now the U.S. That was in 1636 (83 years after a university was opened in Mexico City). Though it was called a college, and that signifies to us today an institution of "higher learning," Harvard's curriculum for a long time corresponded approximately to the program of a European secondary school nowadays, except that there was a religious stamp on education at Harvard that no longer exists in most state schools in Western Europe. At Harvard, the stamp was of course Puritan.

That was the case until 1817 when Unitarians took control of the School of Divinity. They retained control until 1878, at which time the school became non-denominational, as it remains to this day.

Being "non-denominational" is uniquely American. Anywhere in Catholic Europe or even in Protestant England in 1878, it would have been recognized as being nothing, religiously speaking.

Over the years, as Harvard moved from Puritanism to non-denominationalism and ever since, its prestige as the nation's premier institution of "higher learning" was never seriously challenged, not even by other eastern seaboard schools—Yale, Princeton, and so on—attended by sons of the governing elite. When Stanford University in distant California took on some academic luster, it became known as "the Harvard of the West," such was Harvard's prestige.

There were numerous Catholic students in attendance at the university by 1940, but it was still as it had always been, and as it would remain through the fifties: a bastion of WASPism, male WASPism (the institution did not go co-ed until the 1970s).

We still have some WASPs around, although whether another will reach the pinnacle of political power as did George Bush must be an open question. The interesting thing about them is that their history in this country as men exactly parallels that of their religion. They began as Puritans and now stand for nothing, except as symbols of what once was. What was that? Catholics as recently as 40 years ago might have been on the verge of "outbreeding" everybody else, as Paul Blanshard contended, but the nation was WASP. The WASPs ran it, and the WASPs therefore are the ones who bear the responsibility for its becoming as it has—even less civilized than it was when it was run according to their lights.

There is a temptation to believe WASP standards were better than having no standards at all, and in a sense that is true. But today, it is as much the WASP as anyone else who lacks standards. How did this happen to him, and to the society he once led? How did society in the U.S. lapse into moral anarchy?

It happened because the WASP was always a liberal, even when he was a Puritan. After all, to decide for yourself what you believe, instead of believing as God intends, is to put yourself in His place. This is what has made every Protestant in America from Plymouth Rock to Rev. Jerry Falwell a liberal by definition.

To be sure, the development of historical Protestantism's essential liberalism was not yet complete 50 years ago when Catherine Clarke and her friends first opened the doors of St. Benedict Center. To the undiscerning, the thing still gave the appearance of having some Christian substance. However, the complete development could be seen by July, 1993, at a joint assembly in St. Louis of the Christian Church (Disciples of Christ) and the United Church of Christ (UCC), a body in direct lineal descent from the New England Puritans of old. The assembly criticized President Bill Clinton for failing to sign an executive order opening the ranks of the military to practicing sodomites, and heard a speech from South Africa's Anglican Archbishop Desmond Tutu urging an end to all discrimination "on the basis of race, culture, gender or sexual orientation." The Disciples then passed several resolutions, including one that called for the legalization in the U.S. of the French RU-486 abortion pill. The UCC voiced its support for animal rights and Indian rights, and wrung its collective hands over the plight of battered women in prison, that burning issue. It also endorsed the notion of a "multicultural church."

At St. Benedict Center 50 years ago, the essentially liberal character of Protestantism in all its forms, including the Puritan, and in all the institutions it spawned, including Harvard, was sufficiently understood to be assumed. The fear was that liberalism, already infecting the Catholic Church in the U.S. through the virus of Americanism, could one day produce in her a full-blown illness, even a fatal one such as is now killing the Disciples of Christ and United Church of Christ (both have lost more than half their membership in the past three decades).

The fear felt at the center was not unreasonable, no more than the hope to prevent further infection which was born there. The hope was not unreasonable because the Church is given a mandate for eternity. As for the fear, there is no promise the Church will endure in a particular land.

St. Benedict Center at last opened, Catherine Clarke next asked herself how additional persons could be drawn to it, especially passersby. Her thought was to have a bookstore in addition to the lending library as one of the center's activities. (No doubt she was thinking of her experience at the Thomas More Bookstore.) Msgr. Hickey, the pastor at St. Paul's, was initially hospitable to the idea of there being a Catholic bookstore in his parish. However, he subsequently changed his mind, offering no explanation as to why he did. Yet, he continued to lend his support to the center, where a series of lectures on philosophy had begun. Soon, a course in Church Latin was also being offered. By then, the student group of a dozen with which the center started its work had grown to about 50.

One of the first on the scene after the center opened was Fred Farrell, young son of a Boston attorney and then a student at Harvard. Now Bro. Leonard Mary and in his seventies, superior of a California branch of St. Benedict Center, no one alive today has been associated with the apostolic enterprise for a longer time.

Neither he nor anyone else thought in the early days of the center to keep a list of the persons who spoke there. Nor is there available now a detailed record of all the courses offered at the center in its first years. It is for sure that Catherine de Hueck, director of the famous Friendship House in Harlem, was a featured speaker. Dorothy Day of the *Catholic Worker* spoke more than once. Some Europeans who found refuge in the U.S. at the start of World War II gave talks at the center. One such was the celebrated Parisian composer and music teacher, Nadia Boulanger. She spoke in the autumn of 1942, by which time the center, though not yet a school as such, had a full-fledged program of lectures and courses, a number of them taught by Harvard instructors. Besides philosophy and theology, which were overseen by Fr. Feeney, there were courses in classics, literature, French, Italian, creative writing and drama.

One of the center's principal philosophy lecturers was a young Lebanese named Fakhri Maluf. He first visited the place in 1942 while on a Harvard fellowship after earning a Ph.D. at the University of Michigan. It was in the winter of 1943 that he began to lecture at the center on every Tuesday evening. Fifty years later and as Bro. Francis, M.I.C.M., he was still lecturing at the New Hampshire branch of St. Benedict Center, which he served as superior, and one evening a week in the church hall of a traditional Catholic parish in the outskirts of Boston. Eighty years old in the summer of 1992 and apparently full of vigor, Bro. Francis was interviewed for this book and we shall see more of him.

When the center's lease was up for renewal in 1942, it was not clear to Catherine Clarke whether she and her associates were still in Msgr. Hickey's favor. He had lately seemed somewhat remote. Accordingly, she hesitated to approach him. In the event, there was no reason to fear that St. Paul's pastor no longer supported the center. His praise for its work was generous. "We were relieved and overjoyed," Sr. Catherine writes.

The center came to enjoy the approval fairly early of another churchman, one who would eventually rise well beyond the rank of monsignor. This was John Wright. He became a visitor after Fr. Feeney was a fixture. Exactly how the two clerics became acquainted is not known, but Bro. Leonard Mary believes that Fr. Feeney was Wright's confessor. "At least the two of them would go to the back when Wright came to the center, and I supposed that was what was happening," Brother says. It would be through Wright that the center became known to Archbishop Richard Cushing. For a time, it had his support.

Fr. Feeney was first seen at the center in 1942. A friend of Catherine Clarke named Mary Perkins took him there. Perkins had come to know the Jesuit priest while he was an editor at *America* in New York City and she was working at the Catholic publishing firm, Sheed and Ward. Fr. Feeney was teaching at the Weston School of Theology when Perkins took him to meet Catherine Clarke. We already know something of that meeting (see Introduction ). More substantively, Fr. Feeney offered the view that the center's aims, once Catherine Clarke explained them, constituted "a wonderful idea."

The center had of course been planned as a lay entity. The participation of clergy was not envisioned by Catherine Clarke, Christopher Huntington, Avery Dulles and the others who formed the center's founding nucleus. However, as the months passed and the student body grew, an increasing number of students were asking for a priest to sit in on their discussions. Their desire can probably be seen as a reflection of the clericalism that has marked the Irish-American Church for as long as it has existed and which persists among some to this day: "Tell me what to think as well as believe, Father."

That has been the way of Catholics in the U.S. But the selection of Fr. Feeney as the center's priest was fortuitous. It initially seemed unlikely that he could be a part of the program. After all, by the time a female student, Betty Reichart, suggested Fr. Feeney as spiritual director for the center, he was nationally celebrated as "an American Chesterton". Even if he were inclined to become active at the center, how could he find the time? And why should he be inclined?

Providence had its reasons. Catherine Clarke wrote to Fr. Feeney, inviting him to become active at the center. The text of her letter is lost to us today, but it was obviously persuasive because the priest agreed immediately to become a member of the center team.

Thursday evening became Fr. Feeney's time to lecture at the center. To describe his presentations as popular would be to minimize their impact. World War II was raging, some of the young men who were original members of the center were off in the armed forces (they included Fred Farrell, Christopher Huntington and Avery Dulles), but the crowds on Thursday evening grew and grew. As many as 200 young persons had to be turned away on some occasions. It was no time at all before some of the young men and women were seeking instruction in the Faith. Others sought preparation for marriage. Others wrestled with personal problems and needed direction. Soon, Fr. Feeney was being driven in from Weston to keep appointments at the center nearly every day of the week. This was apart from his Thursday evening lectures.

The students were not all from Harvard. Radcliffe, M.I.T., Cambridge Junior College—those and other educational institutions had their representatives at Fr. Feeney's lectures.

Reference was made to World War II a few lines ago. The life of St. Benedict Center was not much affected by the conflict until the very end. It might have been otherwise had the center been located elsewhere, but the point has already here been made that Boston is insular. The hard realities of the fighting in Europe, and the fighting in the Pacific even more, were very far away from the city, and especially very far from the Harvard campus and its environs. Harvard men were engaged in the war, of course, but not too often in the actual fighting. They tended to gravitate into staff work and such specialities as intelligence or, like Christopher Huntington, commuications.

In Rome soon after its "liberation," Huntington was one of a small group received in audience by Pope Pius XII. Prior to the audience, a report he prepared on St. Benedict Center was presented to the Supreme Pontiff. As a result, Huntington obtained from His Holiness a papal blessing on the center and its work, a blessing which eventually found expression as a very large, richly calligriphied and illuminated parchment. Sr. Catherine describes it in *The Loyolas and the Cabots*, and the thing itself may be seen today, along with many other mementos of St. Benedict Center, in a hallway of the main house of St. Benedict Abbey in Still River.

We here recall Pius' blessing because when Catherine Clarke went across the street to tell Msgr. Hickey about it, she took the occasion to ask a favor. This was in early 1945. Given the amount of time Fr. Feeney was now spending at the center, would Monsignor consider writing to Archbishop Cushing, asking him to ask the Very Reverend John J. McEleney, newly appointed Provincial for New England of the Society of Jesus, to appoint Father full-time to the center?

Msgr. Hickey thought the appointment unlikely in light of the importance to the Society of Father's teaching at Weston, but he agreed to write the letter. In due course, Fr. Feeney was in fact appointed to the center by Fr. McEleney. The latter's action was not entirely disinterested. As he would ackowledge two years later during a visit to the center, "I am grateful to St. Benedict Center for the unusually fine boys it has sent, through Fr. Feeney, to the Jesuit Order." He surely knew that could be expected as one result of Fr. Feeney's work at the center.

Conversions were another. We have already related that more than 200 young persons were received into the Faith by Fr. Feeney during the time he and the center were in Cambridge. We shall want to look at a couple of the conversions in particular.

Before then, the one event of World War II which did affect the life of the center wants to be considered. It took place in the closing days of the war. To say that it so traumatized the center as to make it henceforth a gravely serious enterprise in purpose and direction should not be construed as suggesting that Catherine Clarke and Leonard Feeney were ever frivolous either in their persons or their aims. However, Catherine Clarke herself writes:

"We were never quite the same, at St. Benedict Center, after the dropping of the atom bomb. It seemed to have shocked us awake. It was almost as if we saw the life around us for the first time. The scales fell from our eyes, and we beheld clearly as actualities many things which we had dreaded might one day be the outcome of our exclusively humanitarian society." In a word: "The atom-bombing of Japan, to our thinking, was unChristian." Further: "We could not find it in our hearts to rejoice over the wholesale slaughter of innocent people."

That last sentence leaps off the page to this writer's eyes, as it must to the eyes of anyone who was living in the U.S. in August, 1945. I was a child, but well remember the rejoicing of the adults around me. "Just imagine," the mother of a playmate down the street said to me and her son, "we destroyed an entire city with a bomb the size of a baby tomato!"

That was not quite true (the bomb was much bigger), but it is hardly the point. Why did they not rejoice at St. Benedict Center over America's deadly technological puissance? Why did they see the atom-bombing of Hiroshima and Nagasaki as unChristian when an entire supposedly Christian nation was celebrating it? Why did the bishops of the U.S. not condemn the atom-bombing if it was unChristian? Was it possible that the nation was not truly Christian, that the bishops were more American than Catholic?

Such are the questions we can ask today. They were asking them at St. Benedict Center a half century ago, and coming up with the answers. As they did, there was another transformation besides that wrought in the center itself. Cathcrine Clarke explains:

"Father Feeney had despaired of doing anything about Catholic Liberalism until he was at the Center for several years. When so much came clear to us about the state of a world which would permit the dropping of the atom bomb on Japan; when the boys came back to study and found in every class, practically, the same philosophy which had brought on the war; when we came to the realization that we must speak out no matter who was hurt or whose sense of expediency was outraged,— Father knew we at last saw the problem. And when Father had, finally, strong and holy men and girls (become so under his direction) who were as eager as he was to work for the Truth, then he knew that something could be done about it.

"He changed, then, from the 'poet priest' his admirers had known. (Father used to say that this title gave one the impression of a poet who did a little priesting on the side.) He changed from the priest who had been lionized in literary circles in many cities, who had been in demand as a dinner speaker, a lecturer, a famous humorist, who had delighted all and challenged none. He became instead the thundering, fighting missionary who, warring in the name of the Wonderful Mediatrix of all Graces, God's Mother, filled students with a love for God which sent them into all the churches around for daily Mass, which led them to spend their spare time studying the Scriptures and the Doctors, which fired them to make sacrifices so heroic that they left homes, parents, prestige,—to face disgrace, ignominy and persecution."

Chapter Four

"Father Feeney had despaired of doing anything about Catholic Liberalism until he was at the Center for several years," Catherine Clarke wrote.

We have already had some discussion of libealism in these pages, but what is it exactly when it presents itself under specifically Catholic coloration? Here is a passage of her book wherein Catherine Clarke undertakes to answer the question:

"We have been asked many times what we mean by a 'Liberal'. It is evident we do not mean a Liberal in the political sense, but in the religious sense, and as pertaining to the Catholic religion, inasmuch as religion in the abstract has no meaning to a Catholic. A Catholic Liberal is one who, having taken all his cultural standards from a non-Catholic society, tries to make his Catholic dogmas square with these standards. Liberal Catholicism can occur in any country because it is a relative thing. Our battle with it is particularly as it has occurred in the United States, where non-Catholicism anteceded the advent, in large numbers, of Catholics. This situation induced Catholics to attempt to reconcile beliefs they had brought over from Europe with the humanitarian, utilitarian, pragmatic and political ideals of the new world into which they now moved. As a result, Catholics stopped being interested in Christ, and started being interested in Christianity. This term Christianity quickly became hyphenated with the various secular group movements, and it ended up by leaving Catholics with a set of relative standards as regards religion, and caused them to abandon, little by little, their dogmatic certitudes.

"The Liberal Catholic, it may be said, is one who always knows how God *should* behave. God's behaviour is invariably made to conform with the Liberal's own fine feelings in any situation. Father Feeney once said, 'A Catholic Liberal tries to make the Jesus described in Holy Scripture square with his own preconceived notion of how an incarnate God should talk and behave. He wants to seek first the mercy of God, and expects that His justice will be added to it.'

"A Liberal Catholic does not like the statement 'No Salvation Outside the Church,' because 'it isn't nice.' One of his favorite expressions is, 'My dear grandfather was not a Catholic, but he was a good man in every way.'"

Catherine Clark went on to explain that Fr. Feeney had come to know Catholic Liberalism in England and the U.S., in his work at Oxford and in New York City. "He had come to be aware of it with that sixth sense which is the poet's, that keenness of perception which is denied those who are not poets, and which is the cause of much suffering for the possessor of it because he must wait until his more unseeing brothers catch up with him."

It has seemed useful to quote Catherine Clarke at a little length on the subject of the liberal Catholic. We could have given our own understanding of what he is, but it is better to have from the founder of St. Benedict Center in her own words an explanation exactly of what it was she and Fr. Feeney saw themselves up against. At the same time it is desirable to underscore Catherine Clarke's point about Fr. Feeney's transformation beginning in about 1945—his "change from the priest who had been lionized in literary circles," etc. Besides simply relating that he was several years with the center before he felt its members ready to join him in a fight against the liberal Catholic, Catherine Clarke highlights the truth that the apparent transformation was merely outward, that he had been onto the evil of liberalism in Catholicism for a long time. She does this by quoting one of his poems, *The Hound of Hell*, written in 1935 when all he was writing—supposedly—was "light" verse. It is now quoted here, the only poem by Leonard Feeney quoted in its entirety in this book, for the same reason Catherine Clarke quoted it. It shows the "whimsical Leonard Feeney" as author of a poem "as stark and challenging as any poet of modem times has uttered."

Pray for the fragile daughter,
And the frail, infant son,
Whom, at the font, the baptismal water
I pour upon.

The cycle has swung to sorrow,
Our ranks have begun to fail;
We know not what gate of Hell tomorrow
Will not prevail.

The foam-at-the-mouth is frothing
In the Beast with the flashing tooth;
The Hound that was sent on the scent of Nothing,
Has found the Truth.

The guns will be hard to handle
In the forts we will soon forsake.
Pray for the light of the single candle
On the birthday cake.

The vision which that poem lays before us is appalling even in the 1990s after so much has happened. The poet who had it in 1935 necessarily was a prophet as well as a poet. No wonder *The Hound of Hell* and other similar work by Leonard Feeney was ignored when published amid the poet's "whimsical" stuff. Who would want to see the vision it imparted? How many could?

Doubtless Fr. Feeney's vision as prophet as well as poet helps account for the tone and content of *From the Housetops*, the quarterly whose first issue was published by St. Benedict Center in September, 1946. Officially, Avery Dulles was the editor of the review's first issue, but still as one with the center and its purposes as he then remained, it was more than his personal point of view which infused the publication.

Once again, we shall turn to Catherine Clarke and let her explain the thinking behind the review. It began with the realization that Catholic truth was no longer being conveyed to Catholic students at Catholic schools. (That they would have to do without it at Harvard, Radcliffe, M.I.T. and other such places was always a given at the center, and was why the center in part was founded: to help supply the truth to the students at those institutions.) How to help the Catholic students of Catholic schools?

"The sum of our duty was clear," Catherine Clarke writes, and listen to the excitement—the *zeal*—with which she talks of the decision four years after it was made. "*Someone* had to tell the truth before it was too late. The full, unequivocal, uncompromised message of Jesus Christ had to be thundered in the world again. It could not merely be told. It had to be shouted, bellowed, because the world was deaf, asleep, already half-dead. Polite talking would not wake it, nor would vague reference, large gesture, platitudinous utterance. 'Never give offense' seemed to be the Catholic policy of the day. We knew that it was impossible to tell the truth, and not give offense. Christ had given offense to the Pharisees of His day, and to the Sadducees (the free-thinkers of His time), who robbed Jewish children of their full birthright of revealed doctrine...

"We would give the full Catholic message by every means God had given us in the Center. Father Feeney would tell it on Thursday night. We would study it in our courses; we would write it.

"We would *write it*—we would bring out a magazine, and we would call it, this magazine which would have to borrow from the saints and doctors their thunder, this magazine which we hoped would go roaring into the highways and the byways, which would shout the truth, we would call it *From the Housetops*."

When it came out, Msgr. Hickey, the pastor at St. Paul's who was still supportive of St. Benedict Center, walked across the street to say he liked the first issue of *Housetops* very much. More significantly, John Wright, still a monsignor, let the center know that Archbishop Cushing would be pleased to contribute an article to the new publication. Accordingly, a piece over the prelate's signature appeared in the quarterly's second issue (December, 1946), and still another was published in the third number (March, 1947). No one supposed for a minute that Cushing actually wrote these articles, but it did not matter. The publication became bolder with each issue. Articles signed by the archbishop provided protection from anyone offended by the boldness. Meantime, subscriptions were coming in from most of the states of the U.S., and from Canada, Latin America, Europe, the Near East, the Far East, India and the Philippines.

Little wonder. It is to digress, but like anyone who was associated with *Triumph* magazine, the present writer has spent the past two decades listening to persons lament that publication's demise in 1975. In fact, at this writing, one publisher is talking about getting out a volume, *Best of Triumph*. Certainly I am proud to have been part of the team which produced a Catholic publication regarded by so many as "irreplaceable."

Well, men who are now 50 and were reading *Triumph* during their twenties would have been children when St. Benedict Center launched *Housetops*. They did not read it. They do not know what "irreplaceable" is.

There appear to be but two complete sets of the review extant. I had access to both while preparing this book and spent time reading some of every issue. I think it is the publication we were trying to be at *Triumph*, at least in the early days, only we did not know it. Philosphy, theology, history, music, literature—such were the subjects of the review's articles. There were also apologetics, short stories, wonderful poems (not all of them by Leonard Feeney). There can never have been in the U.S. another Catholic publication offering such a variety and depth of material. Most of it was written by center members, and out of that fact arises the second striking thing about the periodical after the high quality of its thought and excellence of its writing:

Apart from Avery Dulles, who abandoned his commitment to the center and its mission to combat liberalism in Catholicism, the names of all the men and women who wrote so wonderfully for *Housetops*—persons who ought to have enjoyed brilliant careers as thinkers and writers—have been consigned to so deep an obscurity as to be unknown today. Even Catherine Clarke and Leonard Feeney himself are not known today as they should be, at least not as writers.

Of course, with the exception of *Triumph*, neither has any intellectually serious effort to fight liberalism in Catholicism been mounted in the U.S. since *Housetops*, not by means of a publication. Two branches of St. Benedict Center, one in Still River and the one headed by Bro. Francis (Fakhri Maluf) in New Hampshire, do continue to put out publications called *From the Housetops*. Both the publications are well worth reading for their piety, but they are not deep and original in the way of the original *Housetops*. Nothing on today's scene is.

Before we continue looking at *Housetops* and see what happened following publication of its issue of September, 1947, we want to return to a point made a little time ago: that Catholic education was already failing Catholic students in the 1940s.

This was not at first understood at St. Benedict Center. In fact, center students who had resigned from Harvard and Radcliffe often went to Boston College and other Catholic schools for advanced work on the recommendation of Fr. Feeney—a recommendation he made in good faith. As the students quit the Catholic institutions and returned to the center,

Catherine Clarke and Leonard Feeney began to understand what was going on.

Catherine Clarke explains what it was: "The Catholic colleges did not say outright that man is in the world for the achieving of his own ends, that he is the alpha and omega of all things. They did not say, as the teachers in secular colleges, that man's eternal destiny is only an idea that some theologians and philosophers like to play with; that it is the notion which made for the backwardness of the Dark Ages and the superstition of the Middle Ages; that it is, in fact, the reason why Catholic countries today are without modern improvements, such as bathtubs and showers! But the courses in the Catholic colleges were, nevertheless, completely secularized. The religion course was in a compartment all by itself, and its presentation was dull and mediocre, without fire, and it communicated its message not at all to the other courses in the curriculum. These courses seemed to be set up only with an eye to making the student, later on, a rich man or a power in some field where his scientific prestige or political aggrandizement would redound to the glory of the college. Even a mediocre student could, for the most part, be assured of a good job upon graduation. And every student could be sure that he would look like and be like every other college graduate of every other college in America, whether Catholic or non-Catholic. That he was totally unaware that his Faith was the most exciting thing in the world, and that the full living of it would change the world, seemed not to matter to anyone."

Elsewhere in her book, and referring to the young veterans attending classes at the educational institutions surrounding St. Benedict Center, Catherine Clarke says, "they were being taught, by professor after professor, the very doctrines which had brought on the war they had just been fighting...the philosophy of Hegel, the psychology of Freud, the sociology of Marx."

If the young men and women who gravitated to St. Benedict Center risked losing the Faith (or at least would not be buttressed in it) at any of the surrounding educational institutions, secular *or* Catholic, could the center itself do the necessary job? That is, could it provide the education which was wanted? This was the question Fr. Feeney, Catherine Clarke, Fakhri Maluf and other center leaders raised among themselves. The question raised, the effective answer was that it was their duty to try. They would become a faculty.

That they could do the job was obviously recognized by even the secular educational authorities since St. Benedict Center School, once it was set up, was given accreditation. Accreditation of itself really proves nothing about a school and the worth of its curriculum, except that the institution and curriculum are at least deemed on a par with other accredited schools, but it was necessary for St. Benedict Center School to have it so that a number of veterans in the student body could qualify for government-provided tuition under the G.I.Bill.

Here are some lines from the *Statement of Aims* of St. Benedict Center School as they appeared in the school catalogue:

"St. Benedict Center at the present time is deliberately a small school. Its faculty, however, is an eminent one, and its library excellent. Its aim is to give a thorough education in Liberal Arts, modelled on the classic traditions of the best universities in Europe, at which its faculty, with the exception of three or four, have studied.

"St. Benedict Center is interested in close cooperation between faculty and students, and for that purpose the teachers mutually attend each other's classes, and are at the call of the students for special instruction or query at almost any time of the school day. The teachers thereby see exactly what instruction is being given the student in every subject, and this contributes enormously to that most difficult of all educational problems, personal guidance....St. Benedict Center is qualified to offer academic work leading to B.A., M.A., and Ph.D. degrees. It's work is mainly in the field of special research in the classics."

Especially troubling to some of the young men and women of St. Benedict Center who were Harvard and Radcliffe students was the presence of religious in their classrooms. The Jesuits alone had 24 priests attending Harvard when St. Benedict Center School was set up. "Our students often saw the priests sit, apparently unmoved, in the classes of atheists and Marxist sympathizers," Catherine Clarke writes. "The priests listened while these professors frequently denied Christ, questioned His claims, belitted Him, or cast reflections on devotions to the Blessed Virgin Mary, the Mother of God. Through it all, the priests remained, if not smiling and serene, at least without open protest and complaint, the kind that any true priest is required to give under circumstances like these."

Fr. Feeney forbade the Harvard Jesuits to visit St. Benedict Center. This was three years before he would be expelled from the Society of Jesus for "disobedience."

We have heard from Catherine Clarke as regards the importance to the center of its quarterly, *From the Housetops*. We know what the publication was meant to do. We want now to take a look at the review itself.

The very first issue had as its lead article an essay by Fr. Feeney in which he defined religious faith. The article is perhaps most remarkable when read today on account of what it does not say, rather than what it does.

Religious faith "is an act," Fr. Feeney wrote, "by which a human being worships and adores through his highest faculty, his intellect, the intelligence and truthfulness of God. This surrender constitutes the generic notion of faith. It is the subordination of a creature in his noblest attribute to a Creator in His noblest attribute." A little later, the priest adds to his thought: "Faith is an act of worship addressed by a human intelligence towards a Divine intelligence, which consists not in mere acknowledgment of a Deity who *has* a superior intelligence, but in an adoration of the *truth He possesses* by reason of being a superior intelligence, which truth He has condescended to reveal *to me*." In other words, an act of faith is the offering of one's intelligence to God, which offering is made possible by Him because He has revealed Himself to one.

What is missing from Fr. Feeney's definition is any of today's liberal cant about "love." Fr. Feeney talks about truth.

Besides his essay and the remarks by Avery Dulles which were quoted here in Chapter Three, the offerings of the first issue of *Housetops* included some poems and an article condemning the absence of Christian truth (that word again) in the U.S. education system on account of the system's secularism.

The second issue of the center's quarterly was most notable for an article by Fahri Maluf on the limits of scientific knowledge, a subject even more pressing today than a half century ago. The young philosopher was perhaps the most telling when he wrote of the imbecility of consulting physicists on the morality of something as momentous as dropping the atomic bomb.

An article by Fr. Feeney in the third issue of *Housetops* was especially striking to the present writer. In "Catholicism is Also a Manner," the priest makes it clear that the Faith is something to be lived, not merely held; and when it is lived, a culture results. The culture is what was called at the center an "integral Catholic culture." The term simply signifies living in a Catholic way. At the center it meant that even the games—often a sort of Catholic Trivia—were spun out of the Faith. I experienced something of what it was like to play one during a car-trip with Bro. Francis (Fakhri Maluf).

We were returning to St. Benedict Center in Richmond, New Hampshire, following a lecture Bro. Francis had given at a traditional parish in the outskirts of Boston. Besides the lecture, he had given a little lesson in Latin, enabling a couple of children present to translate a sentence in just a few moments. I spoke of how impressed I was by that. Brother then made a remark about games that teach. I asked for a demonstration.

"Can you name all the ecumenical councils in chronological order?" he asked.

"No way."

"I can teach you to remember them in less than ten minutes, and you'll have fun."

He did, and I had. It is not his fault if I could not now repeat the list. I am a convert who does not live in an "integral Catholic culture."

"Father Feeney used to say," Catherine Clarke writes, "that the tragedy of conversions to the Faith was that after the catechumen had finished instruction and had received the sacraments, he had no Catholic culture into which to return with his Faith. He was obliged to go back into our secularized society, where it was impossible to tell a Catholic from a non-Catholic. There used to be a time when this was not so, when becoming a Catholic meant a conversion in a total sense. This is no longer true in the United States, due, in no small part, to the secularization of our ecclesiastics, themselves."

One rather doubts that Sr. Catherine truly believed a genuinely Catholic culture had ever existed in the U.S. She herself writes in another passage of *The Loyolas and the Cabots*:

"The American Catholic is a sort of diluted Catholic, made so by force of circumstance, and the Boston Catholic is a sort of Catholic all by himself."

She goes on, in a vein similar to one we followed earlier in these pages: "Some very brilliant and bright Irish were brought over to America, because persecution made it impossible for them to make a living in their own country. The auspices, however, under which their priests began to function in Boston was more of a church-building, housing problem than it was of ardent plans for the spreading of the Faith. The regime was holy and God-fearing. The Italian Apostolic Delegate who said, 'The Irish do not love God; they fear Him,' was being, as anyone can see, more racial than religious. But those of us who have Irish blood in our veins might well wonder if he was not hitting a little too close to the truth for our comfort.

"The Irish, and may I say particularly in Boston, were a warm, generous and loving people. The formality and restraint of their religion came from having merely good men and not saints as priests. Their settling among the Puritans of Boston did not help either, for Puritanism and Jansenism have too much in common. There was a wide streak of Jansenism in the Irish priest. Irish theology and Plymouth Rock manners are one of the weirdest and most difficult-to-live-under regimes this world has ever experienced."

As we continue to look at *Housetops*, the reference that has been made to center games which taught is a reminder that the center's faculty and students were not deadly serious, not single-mindedly dedicated to nothing but high purpose, every waking moment of every day of their lives. No one can be. Even cloistered monks, who are often quite a jolly lot, have periods of recreation. It is inhuman never to let the interior spring come unwound, and at the center they had their fun.

Fr. Feeney was in the middle of it often as not. It has been mentioned that he had a gift for mimicry. He used to keep everyone in stitches by doing things like an imitation of Eleanor Roosevelt giving the ringside commentary of a boxing match. (Anyone with a memory of Mrs.

Roosevelt's New York upper-class speech can imagine the hilarity.)

Father's mimicry could sometimes have a sharp edge, and there are "Feeneyites" who say, tongue not entirely in cheek, that the center's troubles with the Boston chancery really began when the priest started "doing" Bishop Wright.

The future cardinal was not the only center visitor at whose expense fun was had. There was an occasion famous among "Feeneyites" when the English Catholic novelist Evelyn Waugh stopped by the center. *Life* magazine was paying the way for his trip to the United States and Clare Luce had urged him to make the acquaintance of the "brilliant" priest. Fr. Feeney was about to deliver a lecture when Waugh arrived, and knowing full well that the novelist was close friends with Msgr. Ronald Knox, he launched into a talk on Knox's shortcomings as a Catholic scholar and writer. Fr. Feeney was parading his Irishness: picking a fight, being contrary for the sake of being contrary, and loving every minute of it. The students understood. Waugh did not. He stormed out of the center before the lecture was done, and contended forever after that Fr. Feeney had to be quite mad.

Not every fellow luminary who encountered Fr. Feeney felt like that, because Fr. Feeney was not like that with every luminary. Jacques Maritain, who spent the years of World War II in North America, asked Fr. Feeney to be his spiritual director. Fr. Feeney declined, on what stated grounds we do not know. The true reason can be surmised, however. Fr. Feeney would have understood that a direct line could be drawn from the 19th century's Félicité-Robert de Lamennais to the 20th's Jacques Maritain. The difference between the two was that Lamennais died in open apostasy after his exaltation of democratic ideas was condemned in two encyclicals by Pope Gregory XVI, *Mirari Vos* and *Singulari Nos*, whereas Paul VI wanted to make Maritain, another champion of the same ideas, a cardinal. The passage of a century had made that much difference in the life of the Church, at least in its uppermost reaches. It did not with Fr. Feeney. He probably recognized, if Maritian did not, that there was a gulf between them across which could not be thrown the kind of lines which must exist between a spiritual father and son if their relationship is to bear good fruit.

Socially, the two men got on very well. On one of several evenings they spent together with mutual friends, the philosopher felt much entertained when the priest, accompanying himself on the piano (musicality was a Feeney family trait), sang French peasant songs he had learned when the Jesuits sent him to Europe.

An article by Fr. Feeney in the fourth issue of *Housetops*, "Sentiment and Emotion," may be seen as prefretory to an essay by Fakhri Maluf which appeared in the issue of September, 1947 (Vol. II, No. 1). The latter's title was "Sentimental Theology."

One of 17 articles and poems in this issue, it was the first piece by anyone writing for *Housetops* to refer to the dogma outside the Church there is no salvation. To see the reference in context, a surrounding passage of Maluf's essay will here be quoted, but it wants to be read against the background of some lines from Catherine Clarke on the period which followed the article's appearance. First she observes that with publication of Vol. II, No. 1, "the shouting *From the Housetops* really pierced the ears of the Liberals. One article, principally, caught their attention." That, of course, was the article by Fakhri Maluf.

Catherine Clarke continues: "After the publication of that article, we were able to discern, far out, signs of a gathering storm. However, we were too busy trying to get to the bottom of Liberalism to regard these signs as ominous. We had come to know that our work of the moment, namely, the charting of clear values to replace the shattered certitudes of the students, was work on the periphery only. There was, somewhere, a serious disarrangement of truth, and we knew that if we prayed hard enough, groped long enough, worked steadily enough we would find the doctrine, the displacement of which had made Catholic Liberalism possible."

With Catherine Clarke's remarks about a missing doctrine, a "serious disarrangement of truth" and a "displacement" which made possible liberalism in Catholicism, we turn to Fakhri Maluf's article:

"...Sentimental thinking about religious matters is very much with us today. A great deal of what is being said by Catholics today sounds in very sharp contrast with the accent of the authentic voice of the Church, teaching, warning, defining. The sharp weapons of Christ are being blunted, and the strong, virile doctrines of the Church are being put aside in a conspiracy of silence.

"While talking to a Catholic group recently, I was shocked to a realization of what is happening to the faith under the rising wave of liberalism. I happened to mention casually the Catholic dogma, 'There is no salvation outside the Church.' Some acted as if I were uttering an innovation they had never heard before, and others had the doctrine so completely covered with reservations and vicious distinctions as to ruin its meaning and destroy the effect of its challenge. In a few minutes, the room was swarming with the slogans of liberalism and sentimentalism, utterances which are beginning to have the force of defined dogma. Taken in their totality and in the manner in which they were used and understood by their utterers, these slogans constituted an outlook incompatible with the Catholic faith and with the traditions of the Church. 'Salvation by sincerity,' 'Membership in the soul of the Church,' 'Don't judge,' 'Don't disturb the good faith of unbelievers,' 'It is not charitable to talk about hell or to suggest that anybody may go there,' and 'Isn't faith a gift?' and 'How about bapitism of desire?' and so on. I am not concerned with these phrases as they might occur in a theological treatise with sufficient explanations and with only proportionate emphasis; I am, rather, concerned with a practical attitude of mind which seeks and selects precisely these phrases and builds them into a closed system of thought, ready to justify every act of cowardice and disloyalty to the Church....

"The Catholic Church does not proclaim the exclusive salvation of one race or one class of people, but invites every man to the great joy of being united with Christ in the communion of saints. The Catholic truth is not a sad story for which we need apologize; it is a proclamation of the greatest good news that could ever be told. No matter how sternly its message is phrased, it is still the one and only hope in the world. Only love and security can afford to be severe. When we say that outside the Church there is no salvation, we are also and at the same time announcing that inside the Church there is salvation. The world already knows the sad part of our story, because the world finds no salvation in the world. The Church does not have to tell unbelievers that they are in sin and in despair; they know that in the depths of their hearts. What is new to the world in the Christian story is that, through Mary, the gates of heaven are opened and that we are invited to become brothers of Jesus in the Eternal Kingdom of God. This is not a story which can be told with the subdued and hesitant voice of sentimental theology."

Again, "Sentimental Theology" appeared in September, 1947, and Catherine Clarke would later write that after its publication "signs of a gathering storm" could be "discerned." She does not say exactly when that was. Whenever, the very next month, October, Archbishop Richard Cushing paid a very public call on St. Benedict Center.

As boys, Richard Cushing and Leonard Feeney were actually schoolmates for a time. Like Leonard, Richard also sought admission to the Society of Jesus, but the Jesuits did not accept him. Thus, when he was eventually ordained it was as a secular priest. Besides the early connection between the two clerics, Catherine Clarke had spent a period doing secretarial work in Cushing's office. We have already seen that Cushing's auxiliary bishop, John Wright, was a frequent visitor to St. Benedict Center. In other words, the principals in the so-called Boston Heresy Case were not strangers to one another.

When Archbishop Cushing called on the center in October, 1947, he could not have been more lavish in his praise of its work and of Fr. Feeney. His visit had been publicized in advance. Standing before a crowd which overflowed the center and filled the little square outside to the point that police had to be called to take care of the jam, he five times declared in different ways that the center enjoyed the approval and gratitude of the archdiocese. "As regards Fr. Feeney," he said, "we feel about him the way the little boy felt when he knelt down one night and said his prayers, this way: 'Dear God, please bless my mother and daddy, and all my aunts and uncles; and please, dear God, *please* take care of Yourself. If anything happens to *You*, the whole show's over!"'

Seven months after Archbishop Cushing's visit, the prelate still seemed supportive of the center and Fr. Feeney. That was at the beginning of May, 1948. In February a statue of the Infant of Prague, one blessed by the Archbishop of Prague, the heroic Josef Beran, had been received by the center. The gift was arranged by Count Edmund Czernin, a native of Prague who was a member of the center. On May 2, 1,200 students and friends of St. Benedict Center processed through the grounds of Archbishop Cushing's residence with the statue, carrying it to an altar in a garden in back of the mansion. Besides hearing remarks from Archduke Rudolph von Habsburg, Count Czernin and others, the crowd was greeted by the archbishop, who also stood by and listened to the promises made to the Infant Jesus by the students of St. Benedict Center School.

If the Archbishop of Boston still seemed as supportive of the center as he pronounced himself to be the previous October, in fact the storm whose gathering signs could be discerned after publication of "Sentimental Theology" was now nearer to breaking. Other articles published after that of Fakhri Maluf assured it.

Notable among such articles was one by Catherine Clarke, "Common Objectives," which appeared in the issue of March, 1948. This was at a time when ecumenism, then commonly called the "interfaith movement," was first being seriously promoted in the same spirit and by many of the same agencies as had given rise to the United Nations a few years before. As ever since, "brotherhood" (including its interfaith variety) was a notion so widespread, and the thing itself regarded as so desirable, that challenging it was bound to provoke a reaction. It is what *Housetops* did in publishing Catherine Clarke's condemnation of the interfaith movement and its fundamental tenet, expressed by her as that "the things on which we agree are vastly more important than the things on which we differ."

In the same issue of *Housetops* was an article entitled "Schism," by Raymond Karam, another early member of the center who would become a priest. It was in this article that the doctrine, outside the Church there is no salvation, figured in the center's quarterly for the second time.

Finally, there was a piece by Clare Booth Luce in Vol. II, No. 3. Entitled "Sincerity," it did not amount to very much, but the appearance of the celebrated Mrs. Luce's work in this issue, as also the next, doubtless helped serve to defer any official archdiocesan action against the center and its publication—beyond Bishop Wright asking Fr. Feeney to censor *Housetops'* contents. (That had already happened. We shall presently see when and under what circumstances it was done.)

It was with publication of the issue of *Housetops* which came out at the end of 1948 that open confrontation between St. Benedict Center and the Archdiocese of Boston became inevitable, especially with this issue's appearance capping other developments we shall begin to trace in a few moments.

What drew attention to this issue of *Housetops* was another article by Raymond Karam. This one was entitled "Liberal Theology and Salvation," and it said:

"Our age is witnessing a terrible defection of Christ's word in the minds of innumerable Catholics. Infected with liberalism, surrendering their minds to teachers of error and heresy, they minimize the importance of dogma and of Catholic unity, and they distort the meaning of Charity, changing that sublime supernatural virtue into a sentimental shadow which, at best, can be termed mere charitableness....The eternal salvation of man is achieved by adhering to the word of Christ, by abiding in the vine. Those alone bear good fruit who have been faithful to the word of Christ....It is part, therefore, of the doctrine of Jesus Christ that no man can be saved outside the Catholic Church."

The importance of Karam's article in the history of the so-called Boston Heresy Case is considerable, but before we deal with the aftermath of its publication we want to look at other factors which contributed to the eventual interdiction of St. Benedict Center by Archbishop Cushing. The chief of these factors: the conversion by Fr. Feeney of numerous young persons, some of them children of rich and powerful families; the resignation of some students from Harvard and Radcliffe; Fr. Feeney's increasingly strained relationship with the Society of Jesus.

Chapter Five

More than 200 young men and women were received into the Church by Fr. Feeney during the years St. Benedict Center was in Cambridge and he was its leading figure. However, there were also young persons expelled from the center. One such was Robert Kennedy. *The* Robert Kennedy.

John Kennedy is supposed to have said that when the controversy over St. Benedict Center broke out, it made for more than one lively conversation around his father's dinner table. Since the Kennedy brothers, John, Robert and Edward, have all been notable for their liberalism, it might be assumed that the head of the family, old Joe Kennedy, would have been among those who urged Archbishop Cushing to move against the center when upholding the doctrine *extra ecclesiam nulla salus* became the heart of its mission.

That was not the case, according to M.I.C.M. religious who were on the scene in those days. In fact, they conjecture that the pro-Feeney side of any Kennedy dinner-time argument would have been led by Joe. One M.I.C.M. religious says there was a daughter of the family who thought seriously of joining the Slaves of the Immaculate Heart of Mary. Pressed as to which Kennedy girl it was, the religious confesses not remembering.

In any event, a cocky young Bobby Kennedy came into the center one day, swaggered up to Fr. Feeney and said, "I understand you're sending my Protestant friends to Hell."

Fr. Feeney gave the young man a look and said, "I'm not sending your Protestant friends to Hell. I'm just telling them that if they want to be saved, where they've got to find it."

"I know more Protestants who are going to Heaven than Catholics."

"That's not a way to talk to a Catholic priest. If that's the way you're going to talk, you can get right on out of here."

Momentarily taken aback, Bobby quickly gathered himself together and demanded, "Do you know who I am?"

Fr. Feeney answered, "I don't care who you are. That's not the way a Catholic young man talks to a Catholic priest. There's the door."

The future U.S. Attorney General and U.S. Senator, son of the rich and powerful Joe Kennedy, was so flumoxed by the order that he obeyed it without another word.

Not a regular at the center but frequently in attendance at Fr. Feeney's Thursday evening lectures was another young man who also one day would have an important public role to play in Boston, in Massachusetts and even nationally. This was Humberto Medeiros, a seminarian at the time. We have already heard that when he was Cardinal-Archbishop of Boston, he did not refrain from asking for the blessing of the "excommunicated" Leonard Feeney.

Other young persons in the orbit of St. Benedict Center might not in future play as large public roles as Robert Kennedy and Humberto Medeiros, but they came from families more exalted in U.S. society at that time than the Kennedys. That is because the families were Protestant. As already here recorded a Dulles—Avery, son of the future Secretary of State John Foster—helped found the center and had Catherine Clarke for his godmother when he came into the Church.

Unlike Christopher Huntington, another member of the center's original nucleus who became estranged after the war and moved on to become a priest, Dulles at least continued to lend his material support to the apostolate. That is, before taking his vows as a Jesuit, he set up a bank account to provide funds on a periodic basis to the center. (In a truly Jesuitical maneuver, after the Society of Jesus expelled Fr. Feeney, Dulles' superiors released him from his vow of poverty long enough for him to close the account.)

Morgan—as in J.P.—is a family name which has not yet here been mentioned. When Temple Morgan, a member of the family, was baptized on Holy Saturday, April 5, 1947, with Catherine Clarke as his godmother, he was the 18th person Fr. Feeney had baptized at St. Paul's across the way from the center since February, 1944.

Not only was Temple a Morgan, his maternal grandmother was an heiress to the fortune of John Jacob Astor. Morgan served as an officer in the Army Air Force during World War II, and when he came to Harvard after his discharge, he was following in the traces of generations of the men in his family. Thus, when he resigned from Harvard on the Thursday following his baptism and enrolled at St. Benedict Center School—he was one of three men to leave Harvard for the center that spring alone—it produced consternation in the family. They immediately sent a representative, a family lawyer, by chartered plane from New York to Boston to speak to Temple. Also, Archbishop Cushing and Fr. Feeney's Jesuit superior began receiving phone calls from members of the Morgan family and their representatives. Also:

"The Boston hierarchy, as well as the sons of St. Ignatius of Loyola," Catherine Clarke writes, "came in for unusual attention at this time, in the form of dinner invitations from people who had heretofore held them at arm's length. This was a strange alliance. We were reminded of the famous quatrain:

And this is good old Boston,
The home of the bean and the cod,
Where the Lowells speak only to Cabots,
And the Cabots speak only to God.

We have succumbed to the temptation, as doubtless the reader has noted, of substituting 'Loyolas' for 'Lowells' in the above stanza, with more than unsatisfactory results. "

Temple's conversion, his resignation from Harvard and his family's reaction all followed by days a conversation in which the young man indicated to a senior Harvard dean that he had become interested in the Church after listening several times to Fr. Feeney lecture at the center. "Don't you know the Church is dead?" the dean asked.

Whatever the impact of the phone calls and invitations on Archbishop Cushing may have been, the results were not immediately visible. This all happened in the spring of 1947, after all, and in October of that year the prelate was still ready to visit the center and heap praise on it and Fr. Feeney, as we have seen.

As for Fr. Feeney's Jesuit superior, Rev. John J. McEleney, Temple, Fred Farrell and another young man called on the Provincial for New England a little time after Temple's conversion. The young men were interested in applying for admission to the Jesuits. Temple was told, reasonably enough, that he had not been Catholic a sufficient time for consideration. Farrell needed to work on his Latin before he could be considered. The third man was accepted. But the real significance of this visit is that it was the occasion when Fr. McEleney allowed that "Fr. Feeney is the greatest theologian we have in the United States, by far."

None of the pressure from Temple's family accomplished anything with him. He remained at the center, became a Slave of the Immaculate Heart of Mary when Sr. Catherine and Fr. Feeney founded the order, then lived as a Benedictine at St. Benedict Priory in Still River, and at this writing is a Trappist monk at a monastery on an island off the coast of Wales.

Although for some time no action was taken against St. Benedict Center and Fr. Leonard Feeney as a consequence of conversions like that of Temple Morgan, something was bound to happen eventually if such conversions continued to be made, and if there were more resignations from elite educational institutions. The Irish-Catholic hierarchy's hallowed policy of Americanization dictated it. That policy existing as long as the hierarchy, which came into being the same year as the liberal republic, it was not going to change in the late 1940's, especially with Paul Blanshard selling his books in incredible numbers.

Students of the history of the Church in the U.S. will be familiar with a famous article written by John Gilmary Shea which was published in the *American Catholic Quarterly Review* in the summer of 1883 when ethnic Germans in the Midwest were resisting Irish domination. They did so by emphasizing and promoting their own ethnicity—seeking German-speaking parishes separate from the Irish English-speaking ones, and so on. Shea's article was entitled "Converts—Their Influence and Work in This Country," and a passage of it is here quoted because it shows the psychology of the Americanists—their fear that Catholics be seen as a foreign presence in the liberal U.S. and their determination that they not be so seen—decades before the so-called Boston Heresy Case hit the headlines.

Shea contended that Americans who converted to the Church became isolated among their foreign-born fellow Catholics. At the same time they were cut off from the larger native-born, non-Catholic population to which they formerly belonged. The isolation was especially intense if the convert lived among German Catholics insisting on their ethnicity and whose newspapers, according to Shea, made "the most contemptuous allusions to American and Irish Catholics." The whole question of nationality, he said, was a "canker eating away the life of the Church in the United States." Shea went on:

"Those who labor mainly among Catholics of foreign birth, as well as such Catholics themselves, rarely form a conception of the extent to which we Catholics, as a body, are regarded by the people of this country only as a sort of foreign camp in their midst, who will in time scatter and be lost in the mass of the Protestant, or at least non-Catholic population. Though the census will show that the Catholic far exceeds the foreign population, only part of which is Catholic, it is not easy to convince or disabuse them. Many things which they see and know keep up the delusion. A Protestant will point to the map and say: 'Where are your American Catholics? The whole country is laid off in dioceses, as though you owned it, but how is it that your Popes have never found an American Catholic fit to occupy a see west of the Mississippi and Lake St. Clair? There are thousands of miles where no American-born bishop has ever been seen.'"

By the end of the 1940s nearly all the bishops in the U.S. were American-born, but their anxiety that the nation might perceive the Church as other than thoroughly American remained as acute as the fear reflected by Shea. The problem with conversions, especially when there were so many in one place as to draw attention (the more so when the converts included members of prominent families) was that they could make the sincerity of the bishops' Americanism questionable in the minds of non-Catholic Americans. This was the problem presented by St. Benedict Center and Fr. Feeney. Naturally it only became worse when Fr. Feeney began to preach in a very loud way that outside the Church there is no salvation.

Before that happened, Evelyn Uberti, a young Catholic woman and an honor student at Radcliffe, resigned from that college and joined the center school. This was at the beginning of the fall term, 1947.

Miss Uberti's parents were extremely upset at what their daughter had done and they went to John Wright, now Archbishop Cushing's auxiliary bishop, and made their distress known. As with Temple Morgan, the reaction of her parents did not deter Evelyn Uberti at the time or afterwards. (She is today a sister at St. Ann's House in Still River.) However, Bishop Wright did send for Fr. Feeney after the visit of Mr. and

Mrs. Uberti.

It was on this occasion of the two clerics meeting that Fr. Feeney was asked to censor all articles written for *Housetops*. Further, he was requested to submit to his Jesuit superiors articles written by himself. The requests followed a complaint voiced by Bishop Wright that the contents of the center's quarterly were published without the approval of Church authorities.

When Fr. Feeney acceded to the first request, he became, in effect, *Housetops'* editor. The second request filled his colleagues with wonderment when they heard of it. It amounted to requiring that contents of their journal have an imprimatur. What other Catholic magazine, they asked themselves, was required to have an imprimatur?

As the two clerics discussed the question of censorship, Bishop Wright allowed that Fakhi Maluf's article, "Sentimental Theology," stirred so much interest at the diocesan seminary, St. John's, that a group of faculty theologians met to discuss it.

"Did they find anything doctrinally wrong with it?" Fr. Feeney asked.

"No, they didn't," came the bishop's reply, "but they said there were some controversial statements in it."

Was this the reason, they wondered at the center, that *Housetops* had to be censored? Was it because the presentation of a defined dogma of the Church was "controversial"?

Bishop Wright had a second complaint at the meeting. Students, he said, should not be allowed to resign from schools like Harvard and Radcliffe without the permission of their parents and home pastor.

"What if a student is clearly losing his Faith because of attendance at these colleges; he says he is; and his parents and his pastor will do nothing about it?" Fr. Feeney asked.

"Oh, that is an entirely different matter," Bishop Wright replied.

It would not be a "different matter" when students, as soon happened, began leaving Catholic schools, including very notably ones run by the Jesuits, in order to enroll at the center. There were a number of such resignations, mostly of veterans on the G.I. Bill, from Holy Cross College and Boston College in late 1947 and early '48. These resignations caused additional strain between Fr. Feeney and the Society—additional to the strain which first arose when Fr. Feeney told the Harvard Jesuits that he did not want any of them volunteering their "help" at St. Benedict Center.

Given the pressure generated by the combination of Protestant and Catholic parents with Harvard officials and the Jesuits, Boston Church officials might have moved against St. Benedict Center even without its upholding the doctrine *extra ecclesiam nulla salus*. On the other hand, it is unlikely there would have been defections to the center, or as many, if undiluted Catholic truth was not being upheld by Fr. Feeney and other center figures—Catholic truth in opposition to Americanism because it was undiluted.

At first, the moves made against the center were somewhat oblique. For instance, in May, 1948, Bishop Wright accepted an invitation to speak at the Liberal Union on the Harvard campus. It is reasonable to surmise that the invitation had been sought. A Catholic bishop being invited to address Harvard's Liberal Union would not have happened out of the blue—no more than that Archbishop Cushing at about the same time was invited to dine at Lowell House, a Harvard students' residence.

Thw two prelates were not simply looking to improve relations with Harvard. They knew at St. Benedict Center that there was more than that to Cushing and Wright's Harvard visits. For one thing, a Harvard faculty member who was also the father of a center student had written his son: "The President and Fellows of Harvard College are taking the matter of Father Feeney under serious consideration." Additionally, Catherine Clarke explains that "the Catholic wife of a man who had been on the faculty at Harvard wrote her sister telling her that Catholics of prominence, who were outraged and ashamed that Father Feeney should be talking so plainly, had taken the matter into their own hands; and a scheme had been worked out which would take care of the removal of Father Feeney and St. Benedict Center. Part of the scheme was read to us over the telephone."

Archbishop Cushing's attendance at the Lowell House dinner was part of the plan to close down the center, "not because St. Benedcit Center was not telling the truth, but because it was not telling the truth in quiet and measured words, in general phrases intelligible only to the few and which would move no one to do anything about it. The Center was shouting from the housetops, and that was offending people."

At the Lowell House dinner, a student asked Archbishop Cushing point-blank, "Do you approve of St. Benedict Center?" Now, the archbishop had visited the center, praised it and Fr. Feeney, and he had written, or at least signed, two articles for publication in the center's quarterly. Further, at the beginning of this very month he had hosted the Infant of Praque dedication ceremony at his residence. However, he answered the student: "I don't know anything about them. I was invited over there to speak once, and I spoke there. But I speak anywhere. I am not sure I approve of their method. I will have to look into that."

When news of the archbishop's remarks reached the center, as it did immediately, some alarm naturally was felt. A group of the center's students (on their own initiative, Catherine Clarke says) sought to speak with the archbishop. They went to his residence, and he saw them. A report of the meeting was subsequently entered into the *Center Log*, a record of center doings that was finally being kept (the happenings of the center's earlier days having gone unrecorded).

"When we arrived, the Archbishop came in to see us immediately. He asked jokingly if we were a contingent protesting military conscription [the subject of Bishop Wright's speech at the Liberal Union].

"We said, 'We have come here, Your Excellency, because we have heard that St. Benedict Center is going to be closed down.'

"The Archbishop answered that we were old enough not to believe in rumors, and that if St. Benedict Center was to be closed down there would be a thorough hearing...

"We told him that we needed his support for our work at Harvard. He replied, 'If we didn't support you, you would be shut down.'

"We answered, 'We don't think your going to Lowell House, and the Bishop's going to speak at the Harvard Liberal Union, is support.'

"'Well, it wasn't my idea to go over there,' the Archbishop told us. 'I didn't even know where the Lowell House was. The Chancery Office told me that it would be a good thing to go over there. I would eat anywhere. I would eat with Stalin if he invited me. The subject of St. Benedict Center only came up once. Some boy asked me what I thought of St. Benedict Center.'"

The archbishop then confirmed that he answered as he did by repeating the exact words already quoted here. The students were astounded by the confirmation.

"We then spoke about Bishop Wright's talk at the Liberal Union and the effect which that talk and the supper at Lowell House had upon our work. We said that everybody at Harvard knows that the Center stands in opposition to the teachings at Harvard, and that these two visits from the hierarchy seemed a repudiation by the hierarchy of the work of the Center.

"The Archbishop repeated several times during this part of the interview, 'This is all a revelation to me!' He said that he knew nothing about anyone leaving Harvard, nor about the vocations from the Center, nor the school, nor the *Housetops*, nor any of the work of the Center, nor Father Feeney's many conversions!

"We then told him about Harvard. Several of us who had done work in the various fields discussed the situation in those fields. He said that he knew nothing about Harvard, or that many Catholic boys lost their Faith there. We told him how few Catholics went regularly to Mass. He replied, 'If all the Catholics in Boston went to church, there wouldn't be enough room for them all in the churches!'....

"Before leaving, we brought up again the question of the closing of St. Benedict Center. The Archbishop assured us that there would be no steps to close the Center. If the question ever came up 'there would be a thorough investigation.' We would have a complete hearing, and a chance to present our case. He said that he wouldn't think of closing down an organization that had such zeal, and that it would be very much against his interests to suppress such a group of boys.

"We asked for and received his blessing."

Before the students left the archbishop, he told them to go and see

Bishop Wright. "He takes care of all these things," he said.

Faithful to the archbishop's injunction, the day after their meeting with him the group of young men called on Bishop Wright. He said he would not meet with the entire group, but two representatives of it. The entire *Center Log* entry on this meeting is here being quoted because it is so revelatory of the episcopal attitude confronting St. Benedict Center:

"Bishop Wright was very angry with us because we had gone over his head to the Archbishop. [The students had in fact tried to see Bishop Wright, but he was out of his office.] We explained that he had not been in, and that we had then gone to see the Archbishop, but only after first trying to see him. Why hadn't we waited until he returned? We told him that the Center had been threatened with being closed, and we considered it such an urgent matter that we could not wait. He told us that we were grown men and should be more mature, and should not listen to every rumor we heard.

"We explained that we had several sources of evidence that the Center was going to be closed, but he said he knew nothing about any of them. We made some criticism of the Archbishop's presence at the Lowell House dinner, at which the activities of the Center were under discussion. The Bishop said, 'There will be no discussion of where, when and why the Archbishop eats dinner. He will go where he wants and when he wants. Is that quite clear?'

"We mentioned again that the existence of the Center and the teachings of the Center were under question at this dinner, and that the Archbishop by his remarks to those present (Harvard professors and students) had undermined the work of the Center. Also, what the Archbishop had said would lead us to believe that he not only questioned whether the Center were teaching true Catholic doctrine, but that he planned to investigate the Center and close it. We reminded the Bishop that the men to whom the Archbishop was speaking were not our friends, and that he had discussed our very existence with them. Whereupon, in a very firm and decisive manner, the Bishop said, 'We have no enemies!' We said we were speaking about the enemies of the Church. He insisted that the Church had no enemies. We were appalled at this statement, and asked him, 'What about the Communists, in Russia, in the countries of eastern Europe?' He answered that they weren't our enemies. They were merely misguided!

"We made an appointment with Bishop Wright for an interview with the whole group on the next Thursday morning."

The meeting a week later of the center delegation with the auxiliary bishop was significant enough that the *Center Log* account of it wants quoting, like the report of the first meeting, but not due simply to what it reveals of the episcopal temperament. Besides the procedural difficulties stipulated by Bishop Wright, the reader will want to note His Excellency's criticism of Fr. Feeney's methods and the reason for it; his theory of *Civitas Dei vs. Civitas Satanae*; his remarks on this occasion regarding the Uberti family as compared to what he had earlier said to Fr. Feeney ("Oh, that is an entirely different matter"); and his striking remarks on the Natural Law. Finally, and almost as if it were despite everything else he had been saying, there is his parting reassurance. That certainly asks to be underlined.

"After we had waited exactly one half hour, Bishop Wright entered the room. He spent twenty-five minutes outlining procedure 'in order to save time, for he was very busy.' He spent twenty-five minutes laying out such rules of speech as limiting us to one adjective to a noun. He set forth three topics for the discussion: 1) Harvard, 2) the Center and Harvard, 3) the Center and the Church. Almost every point we brought up for discussion was deferred by him as belonging to one of the other two topics not then under discussion.

"We began the talk by saying that we were come as children to our Bishop. Bishop Wright answered, 'I take for granted that you come as children to your bishop.' However, he then outlined the rules of grammar for our talk. We repeated several times, 'But we are as your children!' until finally he said, 'I am not your bishop! The Archbishop is!' (The Archbishop had told us that we were to go to see the Bishop.) Bishop Wright added: 'We are all meeting here as Catholic men met to discuss the problems of the Church.' And so he continued to discuss procedure.

"We discussed Harvard as much as possible under the rules of procedure. Bishop Wright said, 'There are two methods of dealing with non-Catholics. *The method of infiltration, which I prefer; and the direct method, which is the method Father Feeney uses.* Both methods have a tradition in the Church.' He gave us several names which he considered to be on one side or the other.

"One of us said, 'The important thing is that the truth should be told, rather than a concentration on what manner of method is to be used. Our Lord said, "Do not be solicitous about what you say, for it will be given to you." So the important thing is that Father Feeney is telling the truth to the students of Harvard. That's more important than the method. But if you want to speak of method, Our Lord Himself tells us how to tell His Truth: "The Kingdom of Heaven is taken by violence" and "shake the dust" and "whosoever does not heed the admonition of the Church, let him be to you like the publican and the heathen." And St. Paul said, "A man that is a heretic, after the first and second admonition, avoid."'

"Then the Bishop said: 'Christ also said, "If your enemy forces you to walk with him one mile, walk with him two."'

"Raymond Karam answered, 'What if you have walked the second mile with him?'

"The Bishop had nothing to answer.

"Bishop Wright said, 'The Church has no enemies. The war is between the *Civitas Dei* and the *Civitas Satanae*, not between the Church and the institutions of unbelievers.'

"The way Bishop Wright developed this theory of his shocked all of us, because it was clear that he conceived of the war as being between two purely spiritual kingdoms, and that we men had nothing to do with this war, but were helplessly used by one side or the other. It sounded Manichean. And what about the Visible Church, the Church Militant, we asked ourselves? This was a queer way for a bishop of the Roman Catholic Church to talk.

"Again he criticized Father Feeney's method of dealing with Catholic students who were studying in secular colleges. He gave us the example of an unnamed girl (who, we knew, was Evelyn Uberti) who had left Radcliffe College against her parents' will. When we said, 'She certainly felt she could not stay there in conscience without seriously endangering her Faith,' he said, 'Even then, leaving a school against her parents' will is against the Natural Law.' We answered, 'In matters like this, where a person's Faith is seriously endangered, one is allowed to act against one's parents' will.' Bishop Wright replied, 'It is against the Natural Law to disobey one's parents in anything. I believe in the Natural Law just as firmly as I believe in God!'

"This completely astounded us!

"Apart from the method used by Father (the direct method), he said that he had nothing against the Center. Except, however, he did add that an article which appeared in the *Housetops* was questioned and examined by a board of theologians. The article was found to be very controversial. (This was Dr. Maluf's article, 'Sentimental Theology,' which contained the doctrine of No Salvation Outside the Catholic Church.) Bishop Wright said, 'As a result, I had to ask Father Feeney to have the *Housetops* censored. Father Feeney said that he was competent to censor the articles which were submitted to him. Then I told him it would be wiser if at least he submitted his own contributions to be censored by some theologian of his own choice, and Father Feeney chose Father Gallagher.'

"Aside from this, Bishop Wright said he had no criticism of Father Feeney or the Center. He said that he had always thought that the Center was all right, but now he was starting to suspect it because of the jitteryness of us all.

"We answered that we were not jittery, but that we had heard reliable reports that the Archbishop and the Chancery did not approve of the Center and of Father's teachings. Bishop Wright said, 'If anyone would question my orthodoxy I would not worry, unless it were the Pope.'

"He ended by reassuring us that there was no danger for the Center."

In her book, *The Loyolas and the Cabots*, Catherine Clarke says of the meeting and its concluding reassurance: "Despite this promise, the Center men came away from the interview with Bishop Wright disturbed, and vaguely apprehensive."

There was good reason for their apprehension, and on that point one is aware that a reader without personal experience of episcopal mendacity may be dubious of its existence. I recall my own shock as a young Catholic writer when I realized that a cardinal, looking me straight in the eye, had told me a lie. The worst part of it was that he certainly understood I would not expose the lie because it would have been his word against mine. As for Archbishop Cushing and Bishop Wright, the insincerity of their assurances regarding St. Benedict Center would be exposed by their own actions.

Chapter Six

Before we come to the events which cumulatively came to be known as the Boston Heresy Case, let us recapitulate the story of Fr. Feeney, Catherine Goddard Clarke and St. Benedict Center as it has been related up to this point. This is desirable so that all the background will be in mind as a compact whole when we come to the events which produced the crisis, and then the crisis itself.

The center was founded in 1940 by Catherine Clarke, a married woman with two adopted children who had earlier managed a Catholic bookstore. The center was located in Cambridge, Massachusetts, a few steps from the campus of Harvard University. Nowadays its purpose would be described as providing Catholic "outreach" to students at Harvard and other schools in the Boston area. It was a lay operation. No clergy were involved initially. However, during its early existence it enjoyed the friendship and support of Msgr. Hickey, pastor of the neighboring Church of St. Paul. This is not to speak of the support eventually manifested, for a time, by Boston's Archbishop Richard Cushing and his auxiliary bishop, John Wright.

A mutual acquaintance of Catherine Clarke and Fr. Leonard Feeney brought the priest to the center and introduced the two in 1942. Fr. Feeney was in his forties and teaching theology at that time, but he was no ordinary teacher, nor an ordinary priest. Probably the most famous Jesuit in the U.S. and perhaps the world, his verse and "light" essays had earned him the reputation of being "an American Chesterton." And writing was not the only art at which he excelled. A small man, slightly built and dark complected thanks to having a Spanish grandfather, when he spoke or lectured it was usually with such an intense concentration of mind and energy as to make him by all accounts spellbinding. On the other hand, when he was not speaking, when he was not "on," his personality did not simply flatten out. The poet's side of his temperament getting the best of him, he could fall into a quite subdued mood. Bro. Leonard Mary, eventually the superior of a branch of St. Benedict Center in California, was for many years Fr. Feeney's driver. He says that he and Fr. Feeney could sometimes be in the car for hours without the priest saying a word to him.

St. Benedict Center began with Catherine Clarke, a nucleus of a dozen or so young men and a small lending library, its volumes provided by the center's founding members. Soon there were 50 students who were regulars at the center, and lectures and even courses (in Church Latin, for instance) were being given. Some of the students began to express a desire for having a spiritual director. Someone mentioned the name of Leonard Feeney. Catherine Clarke wrote him, asking if he would consider helping the center. She was not optimistic when she made her request. Here was a priest, after all, who wrote best-selling books, spoke on the radio, was in demand all over the country, had hobnobbed in New York with the rich and famous, and was now preparing young men for the priesthood as a professor of sacred theology. He had been to the center only once. What interest could he have in her students? To her surprise and delight, Fr. Feeney answered that he would be happy to help. He even undertook to offer a lecture every Thursday evening.

Before then the United States had entered World War II. Military service took away a number of the young men who were founding members of St. Benedict Center, but life at 23 Arrow Street was not much touched by the war for most of its duration. Indeed, after Fr. Feeney became involved, the center really began to have its impact. On some Thursday evenings, as many as 200 young persons would have to be turned away from the priest's lecture. There was no room for them. Another popular lecturer was Dr. Fakhri Maluf. He came on board in the winter of 1943 and his field was philosophy. Today, as Bro. Francis, he is the superior of the branch of St. Benedict Center in Richmond, New Hampshire.

If the center was generally unaffected by World War II as the conflict unfolded, it was traumatized by the atomic bombing of Japan in the last days of the fighting. Up until then the center was simply providing "outreach"—making known the Faith to interested persons. With the bombing of Hiroshima and Nagasaki, "the scales fell from our eyes," Catherine Clarke later wrote in her book, *The Loyolas and the Cabots*. They wondered at the center why all the U.S. celebrated something so unChristian and therefore uncivilized as the purposeful killing of hundreds of thousands of women, children and old men. They wondered why the bishops did not speak out against the outrage. Why did not the hierarchy act to arrest America's decline into barbarism? "In the end, of course, we were forced to ask ourselves what we were doing about it all."

In the 1990s every Catholic might ask himself what he is doing to help lift U.S. society out of the barbarism into which it is sunk so much more deeply than it was even by 1945.

At St. Benedict Center, the main thing they did was set out to discover what was preventing the Church from fulfilling her mission—the one defined by Christ: to make disciples of all the nations. After all, if the U.S. were a "disciple," she would not kill the hundreds of thousands of non-combatants in Japan (nor the 4,000 pre-born babies now murdered every day through "legal" abortion). So, the intent was to "find the doctrine, the displacement of which had made Catholic Liberalism possible." Study and prayer were their means for seeking what they were after.

In retrospect, and if you read their own many lucid defenses of the missing doctrine written after they identified it, you wonder why their search took two years. They make the necessity of upholding it so clear.

Non-Catholics, and even some members of the Church (given the sorry state of catechesis today), may wonder as to the point of seeking a "displaced" or lost doctrine. They may suppose that if a Church teaching is "displaced," the Church has changed her mind about it; that must be the reason the doctrine is no longer taught.

A doctrine or teaching (the words mean the same) expresses a truth. The truth expressed by a teaching does not cease to be the truth if or because the teaching is no longer taught. Usury used to be loudly condemned by the Church. It remains an evil even though the Church no longer teaches in a loud way that it is so. Bad as it has been for the social order that the teaching on usury stopped being taught as it should, it has been disastrous for the Church that she has not taught as she should that outside herself there is no salvatioin. Not simply did membership in her thereby become less than imperative even to most who claimed membership. To most, she eventually became irrelevant to the living of their lives.

Of course men still feel the religious impulse. Thus there occurs a phenomenon like the one reported on the front page of the *New York Times* in October, 1993: Mass attendance and vocation rates continue to decline in western Europe, at least for the conciliar Church, but more Catholics are making their way to pilgrimage sites, especially Marian ones like Lourdes and Fatima, than have done in years. In other words, the Church has made herself irrelevant, or at least no more relevant than any other religious body, by not upholding the teaching *extra ecclesiam nulla salus*, but men still long for God, and they are seeking Him now at places where His mother has been. She provides a link to Him which the Church, absent the Mother of God, no longer seems to do—largely because the Church no longer proclaims she does.

That the Church risked becoming irrelevant in the lives of men was perfectly understood at St. Benedict Center, once they identified the doctrine whose "displacement" made possible liberalism in Catholicism. Though it took two years for the point of identification to be reached, the life of the center was not slowed. It accelerated. Fr. Feeney was having to spend so much time in Cambridge instructing, counseling and lecturing, that exactly when he was needed most—in order to direct the search for the cause of liberalism in Catholicism—permission was sought and granted from his Jesuit superiors for him to work full-time at the center. This was in 1945.

Considering that when Fr. Feeney was assigned to the center, his main job was to teach sacred theology to Jesuit seminarians and that the Jesuit Provincial for New England was prepared to acknowledge him to be "the greatest theologian we have in the United States," releasing him from his seminary teaching to serve full-time in Cambridge has to be regarded as a commentary on the Jesuits' view of the center at that time. Clearly, they saw it as such a worthy and important enterprise that they would back it to the extent of assigning their best man to its work.

Their view would only begin to change when the man denied other Jesuits—those enrolled at Harvard—the opportunity to "help" at the center. The changed view sharpened in the summer of 1947. It was that summer when Fr. Feeney, constantly discussing the matter with other center faculty and members, determined which was the "displaced" doctrine.

Physically, St. Benedict Center was set up so that when you entered from the front door the space formerly occupied by a furniture store, you came into an area with sofas and chairs, like a living room. Beyond that area was set up the center's library with long tables for study and writing as well as the book shelves.

At one point in the summer of 1947 Fr. Feeney spent considerable time, silent and withdrawn, in an armchair of the living-room part of the center. He looked as if he could be in one of his moods. He was not. Five decades of life experience as a Catholic and his years in the priesthood, in addition to the two years he had just spent as the center's spiritual director and leading light, had brought him to this moment. Though he led them, he had spent the past 24 months studying and praying with the other center members. Now he was mentally bringing to bear that work and all that had gone before. Now everything was to bear fruit.

No one says Fr. Feeney jumped out of his armchair one day in 1947 and cried "Eureka!" However, he did get up from it one day in July and let it be known that he understood what was missing from the current presentation of Church teaching, what was of such importance doctrinally that its absence could allow Catholicism to be infected by liberalism.

Although strain was beginning to build between Fr. Feeney and the Society of Jesus, and although local Church authorities were obviously vexed that the center was making converts—notably Temple Morgan in April, 1947—it can be said that the so-called Boston Heresy Case flowed more-or-less directly from Fr. Feeney's July announcement to the center that surely *extra ecclesiam nulla salus* was the "displaced" linch-pin doctrine they sought and which the Church needed to reaffirm.

Perhaps more precisely, it can be said that the case flowed from center actions which followed the announcement. For one thing center members began to write about the doctrine in their publication, *From the Housetops*. A reference to it in one article produced "controversy," according to Bishop Wright in a meeting with Fr. Feeney, making it clear that such a thing was unwanted at the chancery. Even as they began to write about it, Fr. Feeney and other center faculty also started to speak about the doctrine—and speak about the necessity of its being upheld. News of what they were saying got around. If it got to Bobby Kennedy, as we have seen it did, we can be sure it reached Bishop Wright and Archbishop Cushing quite soon.

On the face of it, preaching *extra ecclesiam nulla salus* constituted veritable defiance of the U.S. bishops' historical policy of Americanism, and that was serious enough. It was worse that converts were being made at the center in a greater number than ever, as was the case, now that its faculty were openly championing the doctrine.

Another factor in the picture: When St. Benedict Center transformed its lecture program into St. Benedict Center School, neither the Society of Jesus nor the Archdiocese of Boston was consulted. Strictly speaking, there was no reason why a lay-run operation chartered in the city of Cambridge as an independent corporation had to consult them. However, the lack of consultation further alienated the Jesuits and was irksome to the chancery.

For some time there was not publicly manifest either the alienation or the disfavor which followed upon being irked. Fr. McEleney, the Jesuit Provincial for New England, *was* ready to acknowledge Fr. Feeney as "the greatest theologian we have in the United States." Archbishop Cushing *was* prepared to visit St. Benedict Center and to praise it and Fr. Feeney before a crowd large enough that police were needed to keep traffic going through the overflow standing outside 23 Arrow Street. Archbishop Cushing *did* tell a delegation of center students that there would be no steps to close down the center. A week later, Bishop Wright *did* tell the same young men that the center was in no danger from the chancery.

Yet, even as the episcopal assurances were proffered, Bishop Wright had already spoken before the Harvard Liberal Union, Archbishop Cushing had accepted an invitation to dine at the university's Lowell House, and when asked if he approved of St. Benedict Center he had said to the Harvard professors and students with whom he dined that he did not know anything about the center and was going to have to "look into" it. At the center they heard immediately what the archbishop had said. They had also been informed that His Excellency's attendance at Lowell House was part of a plan for "the removal of Fr. Feeney and St. Benedict Center." Accordingly, they remained apprehensive of their future despite the episcopal assurances.

Such was the background of the events cumulatively known as the Boston Heresy Case. There were some other elements of the picture which lay in the background, but we have traced the most important. The next thing to be known is that when the storm finally broke, the one Catherine Clarke said the center could sense to be gathering as soon as "Sentimental Theology" was published in *Housetops*, it was an action of center members which unleashed it.

What they did was give witness to Catholic truth. They stood up for it. They acted as did St. Jean de Brébeuf and other heroes of the Faith who were commemorated in our Chapter Two, that great army of missionary priests and brothers who came to America from Spain and France in order to bring salvation to the inhabitants and thereby make the land Catholic and civilized. The work of those heroes had been undone. Now Fr. Feeney, Catherine Clarke and the young men and women they had filled with zeal would seek to renew the earlier mission.

Unlike the missionaries of that earlier time, no one from St. Benedict Center lost his physical life for giving witness, but in terms of family ties broken, prestige lost, reputations slandered, persecution and much else undergone, Fr. Feeney, Catherine Clarke and the others would pay dearly for what they did. No doubt the most unjust punishment and greatest irony is that they are now remembered, when they are remembered at all, as "heretics."

Chapter Seven

We have said that at St. Benedict Center conversions to the Faith began to be made in a greater number than ever after Fr. Feeney and his colleagues started preaching and writing about the doctrine *extra ecclesiam nulla salus*.

It was not merely the number of conversions which increased. During the winter of 1947-48 three more men resigned from Harvard. Two of them came straight to the center school. The other, Robert Colopy, transferred to Holy Cross College in order to continue premedical studies. However, he found at Holy Cross the same essentially secularistic materialism which had marked Harvard's curriculum. In disgust, he resigned from the Jesuit college and enrolled at the center school.

Then, in May, 1948, three more men resigned from Harvard and came to the center school. Another young woman, Lenore Miller, left Radcliffe. About the same time that she did, still one more man quit Harvard for the center. His resignation was followed by those of three men from Jesuit-run Boston College. With one exception, all the men who resigned from Harvard, Boston College and Holy Cross were war veterans.

However, it was not the continued—nay, increasing—conversions and academic defections which unleashed over St. Benedict Center the storm whose coming could be felt as soon as Fakhri Maluf's article, "Sentimental Theology," was published in *Housetops*.

The climate for the storm settled in during a conversation between Dr. Maluf and Fr. John Ryan, S.J., director of Boston College's Adult Education Institute. The conversation took place subsequent to the publication of "Sentimental Theology."

It needs to be understood at this juncture that while still a Ph.D. candidate at the University of Michigan, Fakhri Maluf met a young American woman. They married. They remain married today, but have been as brother and sister for very many years. Only insofar as they are both members of the religious community he serves as superior, the branch of St. Benedict Center in New Hampshire, can they be said to be "together."

There were children by the Maluf marriage. A daughter is now a member of the branch of St. Benedict Center in Vienna, Ohio. There are two sons.

In the late fall of 1947 the young Malufs were still early in their life as a family. The family had to be supported. So it was that Dr. Maluf, on the recommendation of Fr. Feeney, had found work as an assistant professor of philosophy in the Adult Education Institute of Boston College. (A second man from St. Benedict Center, James Walsh, was at the college as an instructor in mathematics. A third man, Charles Ewaskio—he was another of Fr. Feeney's converts—joined Boston College in the fall of 1948 as an assistant professor of physics. One more center man, David Supple, taught German at Boston College High School.)

Fakhri Maluf and Fr. Ryan met late in 1947 to discuss what courses the young philosophy scholar might next teach. Dr. Maluf volunteered that he would like to teach a course in Apologetics. Thereupon occured the following exchange, according to Bro. Francis and as first recounted by Catherine Clarke in *The Loyolas and the Cabots*.

"No, you had better stick to something like Logic or Cosmology," Dr. Ryan told Dr. Maluf.

"May I know why, Father?" Dr. Maluf asked.

"I do not agree with Fr. Feeney's doctrine on salvation outside the Church," came the answer.

Dr. Maluf was taken aback. "What is your doctrine, Father, on this subject. I know that Fr. Feeney's doctrine is the doctrine of the Church, and if you teach a different doctrine I would be very much concerned to determine definitely which of us is in error, because I am completely with Fr. Feeney."

The priest looked at his watch. "I have an appointment now," he said. "We will have to discuss it some other time."

If the atmosphere for the storm settled in with that conversation, it thickened the following May. That month, James Walsh, already an instructor in mathematics and slated for the next academic year to become an instructor in philosophy, was summoned to the office of Rev. Stephen A. Mulcahy, S.J., Dean of the College of Arts and Sciences of Boston College.

Fr. Mulcahy did not beat around the bush. He flat-out told Walsh that if he wished to be a philosophy instructor he was not to teach "Fr. Feeney's doctrine that there is no salvation outside the Church."

Walsh bridled at the doctrine being described as "Fr. Feeney's." He said, "This is a defined dogma of the Catholic Faith."

"We have the Department of Religion to take care of these matters," the priest answered, "and I am not having a religious controversy with you. Boston College has gone on very well for over seventy years without bringing this question up, and you're not to teach it now. You are to teach philosophy, of which theology is only the negative norm, so there is no reason for you to talk outside your field. We don't want men here going home and telling a non-Catholic father or mother that they have heard this doctrine at Boston College, thus causing their parents to have erroneous consciences."

"But this might be the cause of their salvation, Father," suggested James Walsh.

"And it might not," came back the clerical answer. "But I don't intend to discuss the matter with you. I'm just telling you not to teach it."

During this same term of 1947-48, Boston College launched a fundraising drive for a new building. One day Fr. Francis McManus, S.J., walked into a class conducted by Dr. Maluf and asked if he could speak to the students on behalf of the drive.

"I am appealing to you to get behind the drive for the Business School Building," he said. "You know that Boston College is for all denominations. We do not proselytize here. Students come to Boston College from all religions, and nobody bothers them about their beliefs."

On February 16, 1948, even as money for the new building was being raised at Boston College, the *Boston Daily Globe* published an article under the headline, "Archbishop Asks End to Feuding Among Religions." In the article, Archbishop Cushing was quoted as "calling for an end of feuding over religious dogmas and a resurgence of tolerance and magnanimity."

In the archbishop's own words: "We cannot any longer afford the luxury of fighting one another over doctrines concerning the next world, though we must not compromise these. We are faced with a situation in which all men of good will must unite their forces to save what is worth saving in this world."

Scripture, of course, has something to say about "this world" not being worth a man's soul. To anyone who remembers that, the archbishop's words are striking even at the remove of nearly half a century. It is easy to imagine their impact at St. Benedict Center at the time of their delivery.

Something the archbishop said at Milton, Massachusetts, on August 8, 1948, was felt still more sharply at Cambridge. This was in remarks to benefactors of St. Columban's Seminary. He said: "I cannot understand any Catholic who has any prejudice whatsoever against a Jew or other non-Catholic. If there is any Catholic organization harboring such prejudices, I will assume the responsibility of remedying it. A Catholic cannot harbor animosity against men, women and children of another creed, nationality or color." According to the *Boston Globe* of August 9, His Excellency added: "Some of the finest benefactors to the Boston Catholic Archdiocese are non-Catholics."

Commenting on the remarks delivered in Milton, Catherine Clarke writes in her book:" Does St. Benedict Center come under the category described by Archbishop Cushing? Of course it does not, but we knew when we read the newspaper account of this speech of the Archbishop that he undoubtedly had no one else in mind, because the accusations contained in it were often made of St. Benedict Center since our avowal of the doctrine of No Salvation Outside the Church. The President of Boston College, Father Keleher, said the same thing of us later on, and it was headlined in the newspapers."

Catherine Clarke goes on to reflect that center students included young men and women not merely from Great Britain and most of the countries of Europe. They also came from China, Japan, India, South

America, Mexico, the Philippines, Costa Rica, Puerto Rico and Trinidad. In other words, they were of many nationalities and colors.

She continues: "Now, Father Feeney is well known for the number of his Jewish converts and friends. There is much in the Jewish people which Father admires—a life, vivacity, warmth, capacity for deep spirituality. He never finds it difficult to get down to fundamental truths with a Jew. He invariably says to him, 'What is the matter with you? The Queen of Heaven is a little Jewish girl!' Some of the Center members are Jews who have come into the Faith. And so, race as such is not inimical to St. Benedict Center.

"What is it, then, which makes St. Benedict Center at cross purposes with Archbishop Cushing and Bishop Wright?"

Having posed the question, Catherine Clarke answers it: "St. Benedict Center does not hold that it is truth or that it is charity, either to ourselves or to anyone else, to tell men, in order to create social good feeling, to meet a political expediency, or to receive donations of money, that we do not care what their creed is, and that the things we hold in common are more important than the things on which we differ, when the things on which we differ are God and our salvation. We believe it is charity to say to our neighbor not so much 'You are going to hell!' as 'Are you going to heaven?'"

How much did the center people's position put them at cross purposes with Archbishop Cushing? Two weeks after His Excellency spoke at Milton, Fr. Feeney was ordered by his Jesuit Provincial to leave St. Benedict Center and report to Holy Cross College in Worcester, which was outside the Archdiocese of Boston. This was on August 25, 1948. It was the long-expected storm's first unmistakable crash of thunder.

When Fr. McEleney, the Jesuit Provincial for New England, wrote to Fr. Feeney ordering him to Holy Cross, no reason for the transfer was given. The letter was brusque.

"Dear Father Feeney: You are to go from St. Benedict Center to Holy Cross College. You are to report there on September 8. This will give you time to report at Holy Cross and get things cleared up at St. Benedict Center...." English is what Fr. Feeney was going to teach at the college.

At the center, they understood the risk if Fr. Feeney did not report to Holy Cross. It would provide "an opportunity to obscure the doctrinal challenge by making the whole thing [i.e. any action taken against Fr. Feeney on account of not reporting to Holy Cross] appear to be disciplinary." That is how Catherine Clarke put it.

She also relates that upon receipt of Fr. McEleney's order, Fr. Feeney asked to see him. In the *Center Log* was recorded an account of the meeting. Obviously it would be Fr. Feeney's account. (The Jesuits' files on Fr. Feeney and the so-called Boston Heresy Case remain closed.)

Some of the account from the *Center Log*:

Feeney: "What is the point of my being changed, Father?"

Provincial: "Higher authorities."

Feeney: "What higher authorities?"

Provincial: "We can't go into that."

Feeney: "You mean by higher authorities the archbishop or the bishop?"

Provincial: "I'm not saying it was anyone. You are being changed, dear Father, for the good of the Province."

A bit later in the conversation, Fr. Feeney asks: "Can't you revoke the decision?"

Provincial: "No, Father, I am not in a position to do that."

Feeney: "Well, would you, if you could?"

Provincial: "No, I don't think I would."

Feeney: "....What is being objected to in what I am doing?"

Provincial: "Your doctrine."

Feeney: "My doctrine on what?"

Provincial: "I'm sorry, we can't go into that."

Now, as with the matter of episcopal mendacity, readers unfamiliar with how things are done in the Church, and unfamiliar especially with how dirty work is done, may be shocked as to the timing of the provincial's order. It came while the "higher authorities" were out of town and thus apparently uninvolved. That is, Archbishop Cushing and Bishop Wright were on an ocean liner on the way to Italy.

A cable signed by "Your Loving and Devoted Children of St. Benedict Center" was sent to Bishop Wright on board ship: "Beseech you for the love of Christ to cable at once to Monsignor Hickey and Father McEleney, Jesuit Provincial, to stop all action as regards Father Feeney and St. Benedict Center until you or the archbishop returns."

(Besides being pastor of St. Paul's, Msgr. Hickey was vicar general of the archdiocese, the official in charge of it while Archbishop Cushing and his auxiliary were away.)

The cable went unanswered, as did one from Fr. Feeney to Archbishop Cushing (emphasis added): "I beseech you to cable Monsignor Hickey and my provincial to hold up my removal from St. Benedict Center until you return and make the investigation *you promised.*"

By getting away from Boston, not simply could the "higher authorities" give the appearance of being uninvolved in Fr. Feeney's removal from St. Benedict Center, they could ignore the most urgent of messages.

Catherine Clarke sums up in a single paragraph why they wanted the priest out of St. Benedict Center and out of Boston: "Father Feeney was asked to leave the diocese because the truth he was teaching was embarrassing to too many people. The feeling of College Officials about the resignations of students from Harvard, the discomfiture of priests studying at Harvard, and social Catholics with Harvard connections—on the one hand—and, on the other, the hierarchical policy of expediency, had conspired to bring about Father's removal from St. Benedict Center. The Church in Boston was saying, not in words so much as in action, 'Hush, hush! Father Feeney. This isn't the time to preach the doctrine of No Salvation Outside the Church. There is a time for that, but this is not the time."'

The founder of St. Benedict Center also writes about how "Father's two shabby bags were packed and waiting by the door, not to take him on a lecture tour this time, but for the trip to Worcester, and away from us, for good."

That is all Catherine Clarke writes about the packed and waiting bags. She lies about nothing, but insofar as the Society of Jesus would expel Fr. Feeney on grounds of disobedience for not reporting to Holy Cross, the impression is left that the bags went nowhere. As a consequence, every writer using *The Loyolas and the Cabots* as a source since its publication has written as if the bags stayed put. They did not. No more than Catherine Clarke told it, the information is not today volunteered at any of the existing branches of St. Benedict Center, but Fr. Feeney in fact did leave Cambridge and go to Holy Cross in Worcester. Thereupon, two of the center's young men, Temple Morgan and Hugh MacIsaac, drove out to Worcester, found Fr. Feeney and begged him to return to Cambridge at least to hear the students make their case for his remaining with them.

Actually it was not so much a case they made as a plea they laid at the feet of their spiritual director. The plea was not to abandon them, especially not now that he had brought them to the point where the center was beginning to advance the neglected dogma *extra ecclesiam nulla salus*. They also spoke of the "contract" he had with them. It was not a signed one. It was what lawyers call an "implied contract," purely moral in character. He himself had spoken of this "contract" in his conversation with his provincial. He had also invoked his place in the "status," the name the Jesuits gave to the publication in early summer of assignments for the following year. It was rarely changed and Feeney was down in the current status as being assigned to St. Benedict Center.

As far as Fr. McEleney was concerned—or, more properly, Fr. McEleney and the "higher authorities"—neither the status nor the "contract" with the students in Cambridge, many of whom had come from out of state expressly to study at the center, could influence the irrevocability of the decision to remove Fr. Feeney. Fr. McEleney was not influenced even when Fr. Feeney said to him, "The hundreds of boys and girls who have trusted me, and all the children I had in religion, will be scandalized if you throw me out like this without warning, without a hearing. They will be confused if you tell them my doctrine is wrong without a hearing on that doctrine."

Said the provincial in response to that appeal: "We have considered all that."

Clearly, then, if nothing else turned on Fr. Feeney's decision now that he had heard the students' plea, his own life did. He had to know that if he did not leave Cambridge as ordered (leave for good, that is) he would risk expulsion from the Society of Jesus, his "home" for all his adult life. Yet, much more than the direction of Fr. Feeney's life would be determined by his decision. For when he decided, as he did, to remain in Cambridge, the stand he thereby took not merely assured that the storm over St. Benedict Center would not soon abate. Famed sociologist John Murray Cuddihy would later call the stand "a kind of 'Last Hurrah.'" This was in his 1978 book, *No Offense: Civil Religion and Protestant Taste*. "Father Feeney and the Boston Heresy Case" he wrote, "was a kind of 'Last Hurrah' of unreconstructed, ultramontane, Tridentine Catholicism in the United States."

Although with that remark Cuddihy captured the momentousness of what Fr. Feeney and his Cambridge associates were about, and thus captured what the priest was deciding back then in 1948, he was not quite correct. After all, the Catholicism described by Cuddihy—i.e. *undiluted* Catholicism—continues to have its "Last Hurrah," it continues to be upheld by the existing "Feeneyites," kept in obscurity as they have been. On the other hand, if the Body of Christ in the United States is confused with the episcopacy and its governance of the Body, then the Catholicism described by Cuddihy never had a "Last Hurrah" in this country. It never existed, for the bishops of the country have never in their history corporately upheld a Faith that could be described as ultramontane, undiluted, or anything like it.

Once the decision was taken to remain with the center, its members and students collectively signed a letter to Fr. McEleney. Some of its language (drafted by Catherine Clarke) is revelatory and will here be emphasized.

"Inasmuch as you have consistently and rudely refused us a hearing, we, the members and students of St. Benedict Center, wish to inform you that Father Leonard Feeney of the Society of Jesus has commitments towards us to be our director and instructor throughout this academic year. On the basis of Father Feeney's promise, we have made all our plans and undertaken very serious commitments. *We have placed before Father Feeney's conscience the seriousness of his commitment to us, and the fact that he has no right under God's law to break his contract with us at this time.*

"We are hereby informing you that by our unanimous request Father Feeney will continue to lead our work until we get a fair hearing from higher authorities."

Fr. McEleney did not deign to answer the letter from St. Benedict Center, but he wrote Fr. Feeney the next day. His letter began: "For your sake and for the Society's, I plead with you to end all connection with St. Benedict's Center at once and to report to Holy Cross next Monday."

Not very much would here be gained by quoting the remainder of Fr. McEleney's letter nor any of the rest of the subsequent correspondence between the Provincial for New England and Fr. Feeney. What is wanted now is understanding on two points. 1) How may a Catholic, belonging as he does to a Church hierarchically ordered by Providence, justify disobedience to a superior? 2) What was the nature of the "commitment" made by Fr. Feeney to the center and why or how could it supersede his commitment to the Jesuits and 34 years spent with them?

On the first point, at St. Benedict Center they located the answer in St. Thomas Aquinas' *Summa Theologica, Secunda Secundae*, Question 104, Article 5, wherein the Angelic Doctor finds different kinds of obedience to exist:

"Accordingly we may distinguish a threefold obedience; one, sufficient for salvation, and consisting in obeying when one is bound to obey; secondly, perfect obedience, which obeys in all things lawful; thirdly, indiscreet obedience, which obeys even in matters unlawful.... [Moreover], it is written (*Acts* V, 29): 'We ought to obey God rather than men.' Now sometimes the things commanded by a superior are against God. Therefore superiors are not to be obeyed in all things."

The key to the thinking at the center on that passage of Thomas was the fact that Fr. Feeney was being denied a hearing—as he always would be. As Catherine Clarke expresses things, "St. Ignatius himself had come up before the Inquisition, on a matter of doctrine. Yes, it will be said, but St. Ignatius was correct in his doctrine. Granted, we answer, but he was before the Inquisition precisely because he was accused of error in doctrine. The Inquisition gave Ignatius a hearing on his doctrine—which is all that Father Feeney asked for. In this age of ours, which considers itself superior to an Inquisition, Father was denied what would have been his right in the sixteenth century—a hearing."

As regards Fr. Feeney's commitment to the center—i.e. the reason for his decision not to leave Cambridge—George Pepper's insight is keen, sociological though it be. In his study of the so-called Boston Heresy Case, he writes of the decision to remain at the center:

"It is necessary to probe this decision as far as we can because it constitutes the critical turning point for subsequent happenings. The first observation to be made is that Fr. Feeney did not write the letter announcing his refusal to leave the Center; it was done by the members and students of the Center. Therefore, it was a collective decision, but one that Fr. Feeney must have participated in and subscribed to...

"Father Feeney had apparently reached a point in his relationship with the Center people where he could not decide the issue solely in terms of his prior priestly commitment. His interests and the Center's had then merged sufficiently to determine the future course of his priesthood. Something transacted between Fr. Feeney and the Center people whereby his priestly life could not proceed without ceding to the Center people an essential role in his decisions regarding it. Although they always looked to Fr. Feeney as a leader, sought his judgment in deciding important questions, and went to him as confessor, they had also reached a point where they felt that he could not reject their conscience claims upon him. 'We have placed before Father Feeney's consience...the fact that he has no right under God's law to break his contract with us at this time,' wrote Clarke.

"Since the contract is not a written one, we have to envision what the agreement included. It could not just have been Fr. Feeney's teaching assignments at the Center for the coming year, since such an agreement can be cancelled by supervening reasons. The Center members, rather, had accepted Fr. Feeney's view of what a Catholic life meant, and had committed their careers and future to that ideal. In turn, Fr. Feeney must have found in the St. Benedict community the fulfillment of all his own Catholic and priestly commitments and ideals. That vision of Catholicism that animated the Center's life had been termed 'an integral Catholic culture'.... Fr. Feeney found, in the reception given to his vision of Catholicism by the Center, a fulfillment of self and communal identity as a priest."

We have already said that when Father Feeney and center members spoke of an "integral Catholic culture," they referred simply to Catholics in a society living a Catholic way of life, in contrast, say, to a materialistic way of life, or a hedonistic one, or entirely pointless one. The society in which they live can be the smallest, the family, or the large one we call the nation. It could also be—for them it was—the society of St. Benedict Center and, later, the Slaves of the Immaculate Heart of Mary. In any event, there is nothing very mysterious as to why an "integral Catholic culture" appealed to Fr. Feeney in his moment of decision. Any man, if he is to live in full integrity, will want to live according to his ideas and beliefs.

As for the "transaction" between Fr. Feeney and center members, that is sociologese for what Christians know as love. That men are largely ignorant of it nowadays, though the word be constantly on their lips (along with "compassion"), is too bad for them. That Fr. Feeney loved the center's students, and they him, and that they would be faithful to one another as a consequence, arose naturally from their "integral Catholic culture." That is because wanting nothing but the best for your brother is the essence of loving, and to the Christian it means, above all, wanting the brother's salvation—the highest good there is for any man.

Once Fr. Feeney decided to remain at St. Benedict Center instead of taking the teaching position at Holy Cross as ordered, a certain inevitability marks events. So it seems today, at least. Whether at the time the players on either side, at St. Benedict Center or in Archbishop Cushing's chancery and the Boston headquarters of the Jesuits' New England Province, foresaw the events in detail is doubtful, however. The inevitable is not necessarily foreseeable. We usually only say of a thing afterwards that it was inevitable. Besides their seeming inevitability, the events unfolded at a faster pace once Fr. Feeney decided he could not obey his provincial.

As we begin here to watch the events unfold, it may be conjectured that if Fr. Feeney did not talk about it—he probably would not have done so at length with anybody except Catherine Clarke—in his own mind he must have seen himself as having broken with the Jesuits, if not yet irreparably separated from them. However, and as will be seen, his sense of having broken with the Society of Jesus, if indeed he felt it, did not weigh on him, or did not to the extent of keeping him from the coming fray. In fact, from now on is when he becomes truly combative.

One more item to keep in mind as we proceed with the story of St. Benedict Center after Fr. Feeney's decision to remain in Cambridge: The letter of September 9, 1948, from the center to Fr. McEleney was signed by all the members present at the center at the time the document was written. Among them were Fakhri Maluf, David Supple, James Walsh and Charles Ewaskio, the center members who were teaching at Boston College and Boston College High School. Catherine Clarke writes that it flashed across her mind that their signing the letter to Fr. McEleney could conceivably cost them their jobs, "but I dismissed the thought as petty and improbable. The Jesuits were an old teaching Order, and the men would be protected by their right of academic liberty."

Not for long.

As early as October there were signs the letter could cause trouble for the four men. Then, in November, Fakhri Maluf was asked to see his new department head at Boston College, Fr. Duncan. At the meeting, inconsequential matters were discussed until the end, when Fr. Duncan let drop, "Oh, by the way, the question about the letter of St. Benedict Center to Fr. McEleney has come up officially, and I think Father Rector would like to discuss it with you. He might send you a notice to come to his office, but I would advise you to go to see him first on your own."

The president of Boston College, Rev. William L. Keleher, S.J., was called by the title "Father Rector" by the staff and students of the college.

Fakhri Maluf decided to wait for a notice, and when it reached him a week later, he reported for the meeting. A record of it was entered into the center's *Log*.

Fr. Keleher did not delay getting down to business. As soon as he told

Dr. Maluf that he had been looking forward to meeting with him, he said, "The occasion for my calling you today is the question of St. Benedict Center, which is getting to be a matter of great concern to the authorities here. This measure, you see, did not proceed from Fr. McEleney, but from the Bishop, and we are very anxious to keep in harmony with the diocesan authorities."

Dr. Maluf asked, "Do you mean Bishop Wright?"

"I mean even the Archbishop," answered Fr. Keleher.

To that, Dr. Maluf responded, "But the ultimate origin of this order [i.e. the order to Fr. Feeney to leave the center] did not proceed from the Bishop or the Archbishop."

" From whom, then?"

"It is fairly common knowledge at Harvard that certain people connected with Harvard were dissatisfied with the Center."

"Do you think that the Bishop and the Archbishop are likely to be influenced by people coming to them with such a demand?"

"They do not have to come to the Bishop and the Archbishop. Archbishop Cushing had dinner at Lowell House in the spring, and Bishop Wright had dinner there just two or three nights ago."

"Then you think that there are politics behind this measure?"

"I have no doubt whatsoever about it."

No doubt the atmosphere between the two men was becoming charged by this point. With nothing gained for the center, it would become a bit less so. That was after Fr. Keleher asked, "Do you think that Fr. Feeney's stand is serving the interests of the Church?"

Fakhri Maluf did not hesitate in his answer: "Yes. And the fruits of St. Benedict Center's work are the proof." By way of justifying his statement, Dr. Maluf quickly offered a summary report of the center's activities and the results of them—above all, the conversions which resulted.

Fr. Keleher thereupon allowed that "I have the highest respect for Fr. Feeney, and I have always been edified by his exemplary life and that of his brother, Fr. Tom. [Rev. Thomas Feeney, S.J., had followed his older brother into the Society of Jesus. He would remain a Jesuit until the end of his life.] And I believe that the work of St. Benedict Center is the work of God. It has given to our Order not merely in quantity a large number of vocations, but some vocations of whom the whole Jesuit Order is extremely proud."

With those last remarks of Fr. Keleher's, Dr. Maluf thought he saw an opening. "Fr. Keleher, I believe that it is a very great grace to you as a priest that you should know the holiness of Fr. Feeney, and the nature of our work at St. Benedict Center. And I think that this grace imposes on you the duty to defend and support what you know to be God's work. I assure you that the Center is capable of doing for the glory of God far more when it receives official support in place of the present persecution."

Fr. Keleher then alluded to a conversation he had earlier had with Fr. Feeney. He said he had told Fr. Feeney that he would have liked to do something about "this situation," except "I could not agree with his doctrine on salvation. When he was here talking with me I tried to get his answer to this question, but he went on talking without giving me a satisfactory answer. He kept repeating such phrases as 'There is no salvation outside the Catholic Church.'"

Fakhri Maluf commented, "The doctrine that there is no salvation outside the Church is a defined dogma."

At this juncture, Fr. Keleher admitted of himself, "I have never gone into the theology of it." He continued: "But I know that not merely our Department of Religion here at Boston College, but also the theologians of St. John's Seminary and Weston College disagree with Fr. Feeney's doctrine on the salvation of non-Catholics."

"We know that," replied Dr. Maluf, "and we are very anxious to fight the doctrinal issue with those who disagree with what we consider to be the defined doctrine of the Church. We have challenged them to fight the doctrinal issue with us, but they refuse to meet us on the matter of doctrine, and instead they maneuver to destroy our work by reducing the issue to one of discipline."

"But nobody is trying to destroy the work of St. Benedict Center. And the stay of Fr. Feeney there is becoming a scandalous matter."

"The removal of Fr. Feeney is, to everybody's understanding who is in any way concerned, a disavowal of his doctrine. Should Fr. Feeney give up the doctrine, *that* would be the scandal."

From talk of scandal, the conversation between the two men turned to the subject of loyalty—the center members' loyalty to Fr. Feeney and his to them—and then it moved into a discussion of obedience.

Fr. Keleher: "I don't think you realize sufficiently the traditions both of the Jesuit Order and of this diocese. The Jesuit Order is based on the vow of obedience, and this diocese—even before the present regime—has had a tradition of extremely rigorous discipline. For example, under Cardinal O'Connell [William O'Connell, Archbishop of Boston from 1907 to 1944 and Archbishop Cushing's immediate predecessor], one of the greatest men we ever had here at Boston College, Fr. Thomas I. Gasson, to whom we owe everything here at the Heights, by falling into disfavor with the Cardinal, was ordered out of the Province. He spent his last days teaching grammar, somewhere in Canada."

Fakhri Maluf: "But, Father, did that—or did all these things—redound to the greater honor and glory of God? Do you think it was Fr. McEleney's kind of legalistic obedience which sent St. Francis Xavier to the Indies? And is it not right for those who love God, and have zeal for His honor, to withstand injustice and tyranny? Do you think that God could leave His servants so fatalistically helpless? Father, I cannot understand how a priest can know all that you know and not feel called upon to do something about it. It is very clear that a new policy, new methods, fresh realization of the Faith, and a return to the order of the virtues, as understood and interpreted by the likes of St. Ignatius and the great saints of the Jesuit Order, is needed if we are to protect our children from what is coming."

Fr. Keleher: "Let us both pray that this situation will come to a conclusion in accordance with the will of God."

With that, Fakhri Maluf asked for and received Fr. Keleher's blessing, and left.

Besides Dr. Maluf, Fr. Keleher also called in James Walsh for a conversation, one that centered on the "scandal" supposedly caused by Fr. Feeney's "disobedience"—i.e. his decision to remain at St. Benedict Center—but as far as concerns events in the month of December, 1948, we want to turn our attention in another direction—actually in two directions.

First of all, before the end of the month (it was on the 29th), Fr. McEleney once again wrote to Fr. Feeney, once again appealed to him to leave St. Benedict Center, announced that a replacement for him at the center had been chosen, and said: "With the end of the calendar year your diocesan faculties will cease. I have not judged it expedient to present your name to the Chancery for a renewal of your faculties."

The threat to Fr. Feeney's faculties produced some consternation among center members, as can be imagined, and troubled Fr. Feeney himself, but he consulted a canon lawyer and was told how to protect his faculty to hear confessions until such time as he was finally granted the hearing he began seeking as soon as the order to leave Cambridge was first received. (Again, a real hearing never was granted.)

Something else also happened that December. Raymond Karam, like Fakhri Maluf a native of Lebanon (he was eventually ordained a priest of the Maronite Rite, taking the name in religion of Cyril, and founded a branch of St. Benedict Center in Petersham, Massachusetts), was just then taking a course in Modern Science and Philosophy in the Graduate School of Philosophy at Boston College. The course was given by Rev. Joseph P. Kelly, S.J. That December Karam recorded into the center *Log* some of the statements he had heard Fr. Kelly make. Among them:

"It is possible for any man to be saved outside the Catholic Church."

"Any man who would say that there is no salvation outside the Church is a heretic."

"If you say that there is no salvation outside the Catholic Church, you are a heretic and cannot save your soul."

"The Catholic Church never defined or even suggested that there is no salvation outside it. No pope, no council, no Doctor of the Church ever taught that no one can be saved outside the Catholic Church."

"Not only is it possible to be saved outside the Catholic Church, it is even possible to be saved while being an enemy of the Church and actively fighting against it."

"St. Paul was not sinning while persecuting Christ and His Church."

"The dogma that there is no salvation outside the Church [this was said after Karam pointed out to Fr. Kelly that it was a defined dogma] applies exclusively to Catholics who have personally left the Church."

"When a pope or council, or when a Doctor of the Church says that there is no salvation outside the Catholic Church, the meaning of this statement depends on what is meant by the Catholic Church."

"Baptism is not necessary for salvation."

"Many people who are totally ignorant of Christ and His Church can be saved because their ignorance excuses them and confers on them baptism of desire."

"A person can have baptism of desire, even if he is ignorant of the baptism of water, even if he refuses to be baptized by water."

The upshot of Fr. Kelly's teaching was not simply that Raymond Karam withdrew from the priest's course and subsequently resigned from Boston College. Karam also wrote an article, "Liberal Theology and Salvation." It appeared in the issue of *Housetops* published that December, 1948.

Less than a month after his article's apperance there began to be circulated on the campuses of Harvard and Boston College a paper, "Some Observations on the Question of Salvation Outside the Church." By Rev. Philip Donnelly, S.J., the head of the Department of Theology at Weston College, it was clearly a response to Karam's article. More precisely, it was clearly meant to refute the article.

Fr. Donnelly's intended refutation was met by a further rejoinder, another article by Karam, but one which he prepared in close consultation with Fr. Feeney. Entitled "Reply to a Liberal," it appeared in the Spring, 1949, issue of *Housetops* and is a key document in the history of St. Benedict Center, as well as a kind of summary of the position center members took in their defense of the dogma, *extra ecclesiam nulla salus.* Thus, it merits some examination, along with Fr. Donnelly's paper. The examination must wait, however. To look at the documents at this juncture would be a distraction from the events and developments that followed Fr. Feeney's decision to remain at the center.

In terms of those developments, the next significant date is January 17, 1949. Two things happened on that date, the first during the day, the other that evening. First, Msgr. Hickey, the pastor of St. Paul's, walked over to St. Benedict Center with one of his curates and orally served notice on Fr. Feeney that publication of *Housetops* was to be suspended by order "from the Chancery Office, and therefore from the archbishop." Msgr. Hickey left the center and returned to his rectory immediately after delivering the message.

At the center they mulled over the message a little time, and then

Fakhri Maluf was sent over to St. Paul's to speak to Msgr. Hickey. The two men had this exchange:

"Monsignor, I have come to ask you to send us the order with respect to the *Housetops* in writing."

"I will see about that," the monsignor answered. As Dr. Maluf then stood up to leave, the cleric added, "So you don't trust my word?"

"We would like to receive this order officially, and in documentary form, because we intend to appeal it to the Holy Office."

"If I were you, I wouldn't try that."

"I don't think we will take your advice here, Monsignor. We know we are fighting a battle for the preservation of the Faith, and we know that the final judgment of our Holy Church cannot let us down."

A written order to suspend publication of *Housetops* was never received.

The other event to take place on January 17 was much more momentous than Msgr. Hickey's visitation. It is the date that the religious community, Slaves of the Immaculate Heart of Mary, was founded by Fr. Feeney and Catherine Clarke. The community's title was conceived by Catherine Clarke, inspired by St. Louis Marie de Montfort's *True Devotion to Mary* and William Thomas Walsh's *Our Lady of Fatima*. Some twenty center members took simple, private vows on the evening of the 17th: "I promise to make the first interest of my life the doctrinal crusade of St. Benedict Center and I promise obedience to Father, and to whomever he may delegate."

We see from the simple vow that from its inception M.I.C.M. brothers and sisters have had slavery to the Immaculate Heart of Mary *and* defense of the dogma *extra ecclesiam nulla salus*—their defense of it was their "doctrinal crusade"—as duo charisms of their religious community.

The Slaves of the Immaculate Heart of Mary still exist. Except at the Abbey of St. Benedict in Still River, Massachusetts, and a branch of St. Benedict Center in nearby Petersham, all of the brothers and sisters of the various existing branches are M.I.C.M., and even at the abbey, some of the brothers remain M.I.C.M. as well as members of the Benedictine community. The reader really already knows this. The fact is here recalled only to underscore that what was begun in January, 1949, was something lasting, and grows. The proof is that apart from Bro. Francis and his wife at Richmond, New Hampshire, Bro. Leonard Mary in California, the three or four brothers at the abbey and some of the sisters at St. Ann's House in Still River (one of them is the former Radcliffe student, Evelyn Uberti), none of today's M.I.C.M. brothers and sisters were present at the creation in 1949. They are all younger than that.

So, from this point in our narrative, we shall be telling the story of the Slaves of the Immaculate Heart of Mary as well as that of St. Benedict Center and the so-called Boston Heresy Case, and we shall be doing it now even as we recount the events and developments that followed soonest after Fr. Feeney's decision to remain at the center—even as, amid the events, the members of the center transformed themselves into a religious order. Why did they do that?

Sr. Catherine—sister is what she now was—explains in one paragraph towards the end of her book, *Gate of Heaven:* "We were beginning to realize the character of the battle before us, not only for the preservation of the sacred dogmas of the Church, but actually for their restoration. It was to prepare ourselves by prayer and discipline, and to secure graces enough to enable us to face such a battle, that we became a religious order."

Sister goes on: "It will be asked of us, 'Who are you that you should take responsibility for the Church's doctrine?' The answer is that the sacred doctrine of our Holy Church is the responsibility of each Catholic, be he powerful or lowly, learned or unlettered, clergy or laity, rich or poor. Each of us is the Catholic Church. God's Truth belongs to each of us, and we are each responsible for it."

It may also be asked, "Who were they to set themselves up as a religious order?" The question could be asked by a non-Catholic ignorant of the Church's ways, or by an equally ignorant Catholic, of which nowadays there are more than a few, too little having been done for too long even in Catholic schools to instruct the Church's members in her ways. The fact of the matter is that Rome does not launch religious orders. They are not set up by bishops, either. What happens is that some man or woman, perhaps a holy one, or perhaps a merely pious one, will gather unto himself or herself a group of friends or disciples, the group will take vows and then they will live according to a rule or constitution, often (but far from always) the famous Rule of St. Benedict or an adaptation of it. That is how a former gunnery officer and likely father of two illegitimate children, Ignatius of Loyola, began the order to which Leonard Feeney originally belonged, the Society of Jesus. After a time, and provided it endures, the order will present itself to Rome for Rome's approval.

"We are waiting for the time when we can present our Order to the Holy See, as all Orders must eventually be presented," Sr. Catherine writes in *Gate of Heaven.* "We know that many of the Orders in the Church whose work was most lasting and fruitful began under circumstances similar to ours. We know that many men and women who were later placed upon the rolls of the saints were at some time in their lives under the ban of interdict, and even excommunication. St. Joan of Arc died excommunicated; St. Ignatius of Constantinople died under threat of excommunication. We are not saints—though we pray we may be—and we are not excommunicated. We have offered our lives to God, and have consented to die, if need be, for our Holy Faith, in the saddest way (to our minds) that is possible to die—under the ban even of excommunication."

The vows taken by members of an order always include a vow of obedience. They must. In practice, some orders operate more democratically than others, but none is a democracy. An order, like a family, has to have an undisputed head, and the head must be obeyed. If he is not, the order will eventually dissolve, as have too many families in the decades since the authority of every family's natural head, the father, came to be disputed.

Someone may now ask, "Is it not strange that Fr. Feeney would ask obedience to himself when he refused it to his Jesuit superiors?" Indeed, Fr. Feeney would be disobedient again. It would be the proximate cause of his "excommunication" in 1953. When his only disobedience was his decision to remain at the center, Sr. Catherine wrote about it in *The Loyolas and the Cabots* (the Fr. McCormick of whom she speaks was the Rev. Vincent McCormick, S.J., Fr. Feeney's onetime teacher at Woodstock College and in 1949 the American Assistant to the General of the Jesuits, Rev. John Baptist Janssens, S.J.):

"We were startled and disturbed to find that the concern of Father McEleney, Father McCormick, and—we came sadly to find out—Father Janssens, was not for the honor and glory of God and the preservation of the Faith, but always for the prestige and well-being of an organization, the Society of Jesus. We have letter after letter, reported interview after interview, in which this policy is clearly brought out. This was the sorry condition to which Liberalism had reduced the great Order founded by St. Ignatius.

"It was, evidently, for the *political* good of the New England Province of the Society of Jesus that Father Leonard Feeney be transferred. His brand of honest orthodoxy, direct and unequivocal, was embarrassing to too many people, whom the truth would hurt. Now, ironically, St. Ignatius, the founder of the Society of Jesus, would have recognized in the protests surrounding Father Feeney the very signs he had always looked for in his priests, signs that they were doing the work of God. It is told of St. Ignatius that when he noticed his priests getting along exceedingly well and no noise was heard from their quarter, he would write the priests, asking, 'What is the matter? You can't be telling the truth of Jesus Christ and be getting along so well! You must be compromising. "As they persecuted Me, so will they persecute you!"'

"Compromise is the language of the weak. Legalism is the weapon of the tyrant. St. Ignatius of Loyola never called the virtue for which he wanted his sons to be famous 'obedience.' He called it 'holy obedience,' to keep his sons secure in their allegiance to the Pope and to the dogmas of the Faith. Father Feeney was disobedient legally, technically. But his disobedience was by way of being loyal to something higher than the political intrigues with which even Jesuits can become involved in a city like Boston. St. Ignatius knows that Father Feeney was a loyal Jesuit in the substance of his vow, even though he was banned in Boston."

Banned in Boston? He was not quite yet. Nor was the center itself. But on January 24, 1949, an action was taken that can be seen now as advancing the day when a ban would fall. On that day Charles Ewaskio, Fakhri Maluf and James Walsh, the three center members who taught at Boston College, addressed a letter to Fr. Keleher, the college's president:

"It is a matter of conscience with us to inform you, as the Rector of Boston College, that we are scandalized and grievously concerned about some of the doctrines being taught in this college, and we are especially concerned about the salvation of souls entrusted to the care of the faculty of Boston College. We have intimated to you before, in personal discussions, our worry, and it is clear you have done absolutely nothing about it.

"We are placing before your conscience the duty of thoroughly investigating whether, among other things, implicitly or explicitly, the following heresies are being taught at Boston College: 1) that there is salvation outside the Church; 2) that any man can be saved without submission to the authority of our Holy Father the Pope."

Clearly, it had been decided at the center that if they faced a battle for the preservation and even the restoration of Church teaching—and that was the reason given by Sr. Catherine for their becoming an order—the best defense of it would be to mount an offense. They would not wait to see what local archdiocesan and Jesuit authorities might do about them. They would take the initiative. This is why the letter to Fr. Keleher was followed by one to Archbishop Cushing on February 11.

It also wants noting that in the letter to Fr. Keleher, someone has put in writing for the first time an accusation of heresy, but it is center members who do it, and the accused are Jesuits teaching at Boston College. It is not the other way around, and the heresy of which the Jesuits are charged is the teaching that there is salvation outside the Church.

The letters to Fr. Keleher and Archbishop Cushing (there was never any reply from His Excellency) were not the only ones composed by center members early in 1949. In fact, the same day they wrote to Archbishop Cushing, February 11, they sent a letter to Pope Pius XII. They did this knowing that every Catholic has the right, when it comes to a matter of doctrine, to appeal directly to the supreme pontiff. The letter was signed by Sr. Catherine in her capacity as president of St. Benedict Center, as well as Ewaskio, Maluf, Walsh, and David Supple, who was teaching at Boston College High School. It said, in part:

"We are convinced that in this our country there is at this moment a very real and grievous threat to the integrity of our Holy Faith. The wave of error is not beyond control yet, but it will be very soon if not checked, for the poison of false doctrine is spreading by means of educational institutions, magazines, newspapers, books, even receiving official Catholic approval, and the people to whom the Faith is still the pearl of great price can only appeal to you, the successor of St. Peter, for protection.

"The insidious heresy that there may be salvation outside the Catholic Church and that submission to the Supreme Pontiff is not necessary for salvation has been taught by implication in many ways but is now getting to be more and more of an explicit teaching.

"In more than one way people are made to believe that a man may be saved in any religion provided he is sincere, that a man may have baptism of desire even while explicitly refusing baptism of water, that a man may belong to the soul of the Church while persisting in his enmity to the true Catholic Church, indeed even while actively persecuting the Church.

"These dangerous doctrines are beginning to manifest themselves even in the practical order in such popular demonstrations as interfaith meetings where a common denominator is sought, giving people to believe that something less than the entirety and integrity of the Catholic Faith may be sufficient for salvation, to the detriment of every dogma that is peculiar to the Catholic Church. Such slogans as 'one religion is as good as another'; 'we are saved by personal sincerity'; the 'things on which we agree are vastly more important than the things on which we differ'—such slogans are being accepted even by Catholics as substitutes for the Creed.

"We assure Your Holiness, as your most loyal children, that if this avalanche is allowed to continue, it will lead to a veritable catastrophe to the Kingdom of Christ and for the scandal and perdition of souls."

A fortnight after writing to the pope, on February 24, another letter was sent by Ewaskio, Maluf, Supple and Walsh to Rome. This one was addressed to Fr. Janssens, General of the Society of Jesus. It said, in its entirety:

"We are appealing to you on a matter of great gravity, involving the protection of our Holy Faith and the salvation of many souls.

"We are professors at Boston College, which is under the direction of the Society of Jesus. We are convinced that at Boston College many doctrines are being taught by members of the Society of Jesus which are contrary to defined dogmas of the Faith. They are teaching implicitly and explicitly that there may be salvation outside the Catholic Church, that a man may be saved without admitting that the Roman Church is supreme among all the churches, and that a man may be saved without submission to the Pope. We assure you that we would not have appealed to your high office unless we had exhausted every legitimate means of alerting all the proximate authorities of the Society without avail. We further assure you that we have very ample evidence to support our charges, which evidence will be produced at your demand."

The letter was incendiary. It was also naive to such a degree that we are left wondering whether the four men who signed it really did not know what they were doing. Yet, even today there are Catholics who do not understand that when they write to competent authorities in Rome to complain about scandal, wrongdoing, bad teaching or other malfeasance on the part of clergy or even a bishop, the first result, and often the only one, is that a copy of their complaint is sent to its object. The Boston College teachers would learn about this hard truth on April 11 when they received a notice (the same one was sent to each of them) by Fr. Keleher.

"I have just received from Father Jannsens word of your letter to him under date of February 24th," the notice began. "In connection with this matter, I would like to see you in my office on Wednesday, April 13th, at 2:30 p.m. In the event that any teaching assignment here at Boston College may conflict with this hour, I have notified the various deans that I shall expect you here and they will take care of the classes."

According to the account in the center *Log*, Fakhri Maluf did most of the talking for the three men when they met with Fr. Keleher.

Fr. Keleher: "I have written to you in connection with the letter you sent to the General of the Jesuit Order. I have received instructions to the effect that the signatories of that letter be presented singly before a Board of one priest and two laymen and be asked certain questions by me."

Fakhri Maluf: "Your letter invited us to meet with you personally, Father, and if we are to be presented before a Board we should have been given the right to know that ahead of time."

Fr. Keleher: "This arrangement was indicated to me by the General and I was asked to send you only the information that was given you in the letter. And besides, the members of the Board are not going to ask any questions, because I am going to do all the talking."

Fakhri Maluf: "What directions you might have received from the General do not concern us. We are shocked at the way the General handled our appeal, because we made it clear to him that we had no confidence in you to be the judge in this matter. And whatever directions you have received from him, we still feel that it is our right to know what we were invited for and whom we were invited to meet. In your letter you explicitly invited us to meet you, personally."

Fr. Keleher: "You will merely be asked to retract your statements and, in case you refuse to do that, your connection with Boston College will be severed as of this moment."

The talk continued for a little time, but the men retracted nothing, appeared before no board, and left Fr. Keleher's office dismissed, for doctrine, from the faculty of Boston College. David Supple was also fired from his job at Boston College High School.

"Four B.C. Teachers Fired After Probe," headlined the *Boston Post* the next morning, April 14. That same day, the *Boston Evening Globe* headlined a front-page article: "B.C. Replies to Ousted Teachers." The Globe article included a statement issued by Fr. Keleher. A line of it will here be emphasized.

"These gentlemen in question were under contract at Boston College to teach philosophy and physics. They had been cautioned by me and others to stay within their own fields and leave theology to those who were adequately and competently prepared.

"They continued to speak in class and out of class on matters contrary to the traditional teaching of the Catholic Church, *ideas leading to bigotry and intolerance.*

"Their doctrine is erroneous and as such could not be tolerated at Boston College. They were informed that they must cease such teaching or leave the faculty."

The case of St. Benedict Center was not yet the so-called Boston Heresy Case, but it was now in the news. It would be for some time to come, as will be seen.

Before it is, we must look at the record of another conversation which took place in April, 1949. It was a conversation between Fr. Feeney and Fr. Vincent McCormick, S.J., an old teacher of Father Feeney at Woodstock and now the American Assistant to Fr. Janssens, the General of the Jesuits. It took place in the Provincial's Room at Boston College on April 1. Fr. Feeney wanted this meeting, hoping it would be a step towards a full-fledged hearing on himself, St. Benedict Center, and their defense of the dogma *extra ecclesiam nulla salus.* In fact, the meeting itself would be the nearest thing Fr. Feeney would ever have to a hearing. That is why we want to look at the record of it in its entirety.

It must be underlined that the account of the meeting which we have is one-sided. We do not know what was reported by Fr. McCormick to Fr. McEleney, the provincial, or to Fr. Janssens at the Gesu in Rome. That is because the Jesuits' files on the case of Fr. Feeney, like those in the archives of the Archdiocese of Boston, remain closed. Sr. Catherine includes the record of the talk in *The Loyolas and Cabots,* as does Pepper (much of it) in his sociological study. However, Pepper, quoting directly from the original text archived at the Abbey of St. Benedict in Still River, includes a passage omitted by Sr. Catherine. It is quoted here, and speculation offered as to why St. Catherine omitted it.

We are told by Sr. Catherine that Fr. Feeney was greeted cordially by Fr. McCormick, that the two clerics chatted about the older man's health, which was not very good just then, and that when Fr. McCormick said, "I have not as yet seen Fr. McEleney, I wanted to see you first and hear what you have to say," Fr. Feeney refrained from asking whether there had been contact by letter, telephone or delegate. Sr. Catherine also relates—she would have had to hear it from Fr. Feeney—that Fr. McCormick "was extremely nervous, and was biting his fingernails all during the interview."

Fr. McCormick: "I do not know anything that has caused so many people to be distressed as this unfortunate affair. I do not know anything ever that has evoked so many prayers from priests and nuns and even lay

107

people, as this situation. I am anxious to see it settled not only for the *good of the Society and your Province* but also for the salvation of your own soul. The only way it can be settled is by doing the will of God no matter how difficult or unjust or harsh it may seem to be. And the will of God as indicated to you is the voice of Father Provincial, which means that you must go to Holy Cross as you were told and leave everything else to the will of God—that is what is meant by obedience, as every good Jesuit understands when he makes his vows."

Fr. Feeney: "Well first, Father Assistant, I think you must agree that I have never been conspicuously hard to rule. I think I have been, if only by reason of temperament, a somewhat docile Jesuit."

Fr. McCormick: "That I agree—and that is why I expect you to be in this emergency the splendid Leonard Feeney we all know and love and admire. You have great talents, great gifts, and great charm; and I am sure there is much splendid work left for you to do provided you do the will of God as is clearly indicated to you now by the voice of your superior."

Fr. Feeney: "Do you realize how much it has cost me in suffering and misunderstanding and persecution not to do the 'will of God' as you call it in this matter? You know very well that instead of commanding me under holy obedience to obey his fraudulent order, Fr. McEleney has gone out of his way, by every arrangement possible, with everyone with whom I am associated, to try to ruin my morale and my reputation so that his tyrannical order could be obeyed."

Fr. McCormick: "Why do you call it tyrannical? Every order of obedience could be called tyrannical if you cared to term it so."

Fr. Feeney: "Father, I know that you know that this was the strangest order ever given by a Jesuit superior. If it were a clear mandate of obedience, why did Father Provincial not give it to me on status day, when the time for the yearly appointments was at hand? Why must he wait for the Archbishop and Bishop to be two days out at sea, why must he inform the Vicar General before he has informed me, and then hide behind him so as to make his order effective? Why would a Jesuit superior assume that he has no authority over his subject who has taken a vow of obedience until he has made a secret arrangement with the Archbishop, Bishop, and Vicar General as to how he can make it effective? Why was my obedience so suspected by Fr. McEleney even before he gave the order?"

Fr. McCormick: "Now, come, come. We can't go into all that. That is all involved and complicated and entirely beside the point. You are a subject, and a good subject must obey."

Fr. Feeney: "But Fr. McEleney is your subject. Why don't you insist that he rule decently?"

Fr. McCormick: "A superior does not have to tell his subjects why he does things. Fr. McEleney did not have to tell you why he moved you."

Fr. Feeney: "He did tell me why he moved me. He said it was by the bidding of higher authorities and for my doctrine."

Fr. McCormick: "Did he say that?"

Fr. Feeney: "Yes, he let that slip and then regretted he had said it. But even if he hadn't said it at all, I know that it was the reason. I also know the reason why Archbishop Cushing went to Lowell House, and Bishop Wright spoke at the Liberal Union."

Fr. McCormick: "You think Bishop Wright knew about this?"

Fr. Feeney: "I'm sure he did. It was even arranged that my dismissal should come exactly at the point when he and the Archbishop were on the high seas, and could not give me a hearing. I cabled to Archbishop Cushing. I cabled twice to Bishop Wright. It did me no good. Fr. McEleney tried to make my being pushed out of the diocese of Boston—which is the fact of the matter—seem as if I was merely being transferred to Holy Cross. The point of my being sent to Worcester is that it is out of this diocese, which is what Bishop Wright and Archbishop Cushing wanted. My whole vocation and priesthood and reputation are at stake, Father Assistant! If I am hitting back in strong fashion, it is because I terribly protest the type of vilification of my character which has been going on for seven solid months, in secret and sly ways, and by my Jesuit brothers and my Provincial. You know, and so does every superior in this Province, and in every house I have ever lived in, that this is the first time in my life I have ever attacked a fellow Jesuit. You can go through all the files in Rome, and you will not find one sentence of complaint by me against anyone."

Fr. McCormick: "That is true. And that is why I feel all this strong language does not represent your true character."

Fr. Feeney: "I believe that my reasons for staying at St. Benedict Center are loving ones, instead of resentful ones."

Fr. McCormick: "What possible reason can keep you there, against the will of your superior, which is a loving reason?"

Fr. Feeney: "Just as no one in Rome has ever heard a word of complaint from me about anyone, so I believe there is no one of a complaining nature that has not perhaps had something to tell you about me. In my writings at least, I have been something of a public character. I do not think there is priest or nun or Catholic school child who does not know some of my writings, and I know many converts have been helped into the Church by encouragement from some of the things I have written. I do not think I try to conceal my defects in my writing—and my defects are: that I use superlatives, that I raise my voice, that I gesticulate and make faces and push home a point too strongly, and that I am not overtactful in taking into account what non-Catholics will think when I talk. All these facts and general comments on my many defects are the property of all people who have ever heard me. And so I think I could say, almost better than any American Jesuit you will meet on your visitation, that I am not a saint. Now, while knowing this to be true, I still dare to say that it is Our Blessed Lady who is keeping me at St. Benedict Center. I hesitate to say this to you, because when I once said it to another priest, he spread the rumor around that I was claiming to have had a vision from Our Lady!"

Fr. McCormick: "If you think you are being changed for matters of doctrine, why did you not go to Holy Cross and then put in your appeal *in devolutivo?"*

Fr. Feeney: "First I wanted Fr. McEleney openly to state that was why he was changing me. He by accident admitted that it was the reason. I knew very well that it was the reason. But he did not want me to know that it was the reason, because then he would have to defend a heresy. Part of the whole horror of the heresy that has infected our Province, including the terribly incompetent professors in our seminaries, is contained in Fr. Philip Donnelly's attack on *From the Housetops*. Did you read Mr. Karam's article on 'Liberal Theology and Salvation' in the December issue?"

Fr. McCormick: "Yes, I looked at it. "

Fr. Feeney: "Didn't you agree with it?"

Fr. McCormick: "There were some things in it which were wrong."

Fr. Feeney: "What things?"

Fr. McCormick: "We can't go into that matter now."

Fr. Feeney: "You are putting yourself in my regard in the same position as Fr. McEleney. What Mr. Karam holds is what I hold. If what I hold is wrong, why not tell me where it is wrong? Why go sending me to Holy Cross College? I am going to teach the same doctrine up there. If what I am teaching is heresy, you owe it to the boys not to let me teach any more until I have mended my doctrine. Don't you think you ought to be solicitous for the dogmas of the Church?"

Fr. McCormick: "My solicitude for the dogmas of the Church I shall have to leave for another situation. My business now is *the good of the Society, the good of the Province,* and thereby the good of your soul."

Fr. Feeney: "Why not be good to all souls? I think it would be better for me to be a disobedient Jesuit than an heretical one. Don't you?"

Fr. McCormick: "You are supposed to obey your superior."

Fr. Feeney: "A decent superior giving decent commands does so with decent credentials—at appointment time, and not after deals with secular priests who are trying to control our Order. Everybody admits that Bishop Wright is trying to run our Order. I hope for a great deal from you. You know very well, Father Assistant, what havoc has been done to the Jesuit Order in the United States by the Visitors who have come over here as American Assistants. All they looked to was the political advantage of our Order and never for its blazing ideals as outlined by St. Ignatius. Please don't be a Visitor like that, and leave nothing but havoc behind you."

Fr. McCormick: "You are making a mistake in calling me a full-fledged Visitor. I am not a Father Visitor to the American Provinces. I am over here to take care of a certain number of problems, but not to be a Visitor in full jurisdiction."

Fr. Feeney: "Well, whatever you are, please tell Father General what I am trying to say. Did you hear from Father General about the letter written to him by the Boston College teachers?"

Fr. McCormick: "You mean accusing Boston College of teaching heresy?"

Fr. Feeney: "Yes."

Fr. McCormick: "I did. And that is utterly absurd. There is no heresy being taught at Boston College. "

Fr. Feeney: "Father Assistant, you are wrong. It is being taught at Boston College that there is salvation outside the Church. It is being taught at Boston College that the Church is the 'ordinary means' for salvation but that there is another and 'extraordinary means.' The dogma of no salvation outside the Church is so miserably explained in the religion classes that in one class you are flunked if you say there is no salvation outside the Church, and in another class you are passed for saying there is no salvation outside the Church provided you add an explanation to your admission of this dogma which undoes all its effect. Religion at Boston College is an absolute minor interest. Father Assistant, if you doubt that heresy is being taught at Boston College, I implore you to go over, I think it is the day after tomorrow, and listen to Fr. J. Franklin Ewing, S.J., lecture on evolution to the students. I think you have it on your conscience now to go, now that I have accused him of teaching heresy. If the General will not listen to the Boston College lay teachers, you certainly cannot refuse to listen to me. I have been your student; you know that I have not a too bad mind in Theology. I was offered an opportunity to study and teach it in our Society. I positively declare that Fr. Ewing and Fr. Doherty, in their anthropology classes, are teaching heresy, to the total undoing of the inspired book of Genesis and to making Catholic boys believe that the explanation of the origin of man is best derived not from Scripture or the definitions of the Church or the teaching of the 29 doctors, but from a blasphemously atheistic hypothesis, like Hooton of Harvard gives. Fr. Ewing is one of Mr. Hooton's leading disciples. Why not trust me in this emergency for which you say so many people are praying? Why not go once to a Fr. Ewing lecture, or call in some of the Weston fathers for a conference in theology, and then tell me if in conscience as Jesuit superior you can make arbitrary discipline your major interest and let Catholic doctrine go to the dogs?"

(Fr. Feeney's reference to Mr. Hooton was to Prof. Earnest A. Hooton, a teacher at Harvard since 1913 and author of numerous books on the theory of evolution—but not as a theory. An article in the January 6, 1950 editions of the *Boston Traveler,* "Prof. Hooton Backs 'Mercy Killer,'" shows him also as having been a sort of early-day Dr. Jack Kavorkian. "If 'thou shalt not kill' is a 'law of God' that convicts Dr. Sander of murder, let us have done with such a savage and sub-human deity and substitute a god of mercy and loving kindness!" he told the *Traveler*. "I hold the medical profession to be the noblest and most useful of human pursuits—not excluding religion... Laymen will have to be educated and liberated from the thralldom of religious superstition before proper enactments [i.e. legislation making euthanasia legal] can be made.")

Fr. McCormick: "Couldn't you have told all this to the General by letter from Holy Cross?"

Fr. Feeney: "No, I could not, and for many reasons. First of all, I had taken it for granted, due to Father Provincial's appointment at status time, that I was to be at St. Benedict Center for the year. I had made commitments to these students. In strict natural justice, Fr. McEleney owed it to me to give me and my students a hearing in view of the fact of my year's commitment. Every time one of my students or a committee of them tried to see him, he avoided them. He would not even answer a letter. He had already let it be known, through Fr. William FitzGerald, that they were a bunch of radicals, whom Fr. FitzGerald was going to take in hand and control. [Fr. FitzGerald was slated to be Fr. Feeney's replacement at the center, had Fr. Feeney moved to Holy Cross.] But even this point, strong as it is, is a minor one compared with the fact that I was being put out of St. Benedict Center because I held a dogma of the Faith. Subsequent events in every sector prove this, as well as Fr. McEleney's absolute refusal to give me a hearing so as to make a doctrinal defense. And, oh Father, I beseech you to watch the theologians who come from the Gregorian in Rome. They do not know their theology lovingly and devoutly. They absolutely snub our two great doctors, St. Peter Canisius and St. Robert Bellarmine. Their heroes are some second-rater, usually some liberal like De La Taille, Bainvel, or Teilhard de Chardin."

Fr. McCormick: "Teilhard de Chardin's works have been discarded."

Fr. Feeney: "Why did you not discard him when he came to Weston some years ago and taught his evolutionary theories to our theologians? The Gregorian theologians seem to be superficial specialists. I myself heard the canon law professor at Weston, whose legalism rules the Province in many affairs, state that the Athanasian Creed holds that *Pater est creans, et Filius est creans, et Spiritus Sanctus creans, sed non sunt tres creantes sed unus creans.* When I vehemently objected that the Athanasian Creed said nothing of the kind, but that what it did say was: *Pater est increatus, et Felius increatus, et Spiritus Sanctus increatus,* and that it was horrid to hear a professor of theology get the words *creans* and *increatus* mixed up, he merely put me down as a poet or possibly an excitable person who likes to make objections."

Fr. McCormick: "All this is beside the point. My duty here today is to ask you once and for all, 'Are you or are you not going to obey your Provincial?'"

Fr. Feeney: "Is it all over with me if I do not?"

Fr. McCormick: "I am afraid it is."

Fr. Feeney: "Is this final?"

Fr. McCormick:"Yes, this is final."

Fr. Feeney: "All right, Father. I cannot do what you ask me to do in conscience. I never had one doubt about my vocation all my years. I know I am doing what St. Ignatius would want me to do, and therefore I accept this as final. You can do what you care to."

Fr. McCormick then stood up and took Fr. Feeney by the hand. "Oh come now," he said. "That must never be. I came here to do a work and I failed. But I am still not going to give up hoping and praying that this will turn out as it should. I am going to hope and pray."

Fr. Feeney: "Thank you, Father. And I would like your blessing."

Fr. McCormick gave his blessing ("perfunctorily," says the *Log*) and then, again taking Fr. Feeney's hand, said, "Goodbye, goodbye."

Fr. Feeney: "Apart from all this, I still remember you as my teacher in theology, and the happy year I spent with you in the study of the Sacraments. I want you to know that my gratitude and admiration and affection for you as my teacher I shall always keep."

Fr. McCormick ("very quietly," says the *Log*): "Thank you."

The conversation had lasted an hour. Perhaps its most notable feature is that unlike others—Fr. Keleher, for example—the American Assistant to the General of the Jesuits, who, after all, represented Rome on this occasion, did not try to dodge or much less challenge it when Fr. Feeney spoke of "his doctrine," the Church's teaching *extra ecclesiam nulla salus*. He declined to discuss Raymond Karam's article, but of the dogma itself he did not say, "Let's not get into that" or "You have it wrong." As Fr. Feeney's old theology teacher, he certainly *could not* say, "I've never looked into the theology of that, so lets not discuss it ."

As to what Sr. Catherine omitted from the record of the conversation, we have to assume that she did not decide on the omission, or did not decide by herself. The conversation being the nearest thing to a hearing that Fr. Feeney ever had, publication of the record of it was simply too important for that Fr. Feeney would have decided on the omission, or at least Sr. Catherine and Fr. Feeney decided together.

Here is what was omitted. It comes early in the conversation. Fr. Feeney has just said, "Why should a Jesuit superior assume that he has no authority over his subject until he has made a secret deal with the Archbishop, Bishop and Vicar General as to how he can make it [i.e. an order] effective?"

Fr. McCormick then says (as can be seen above), "Now, come, come. We can't go into all that..." but Fr. Feeney continues: "The whole thing was managed at the instigation of Harvard University because I was embarrassing them by the boys I was attracting to the center and away from Harvard, in collusion with Bishop Wright because I was embarrassing him by the assertion that Protestants must become Catholics in order to be saved, in collusion with Fr. McEleney because I was embarrassing him by my definite although not outspoken disapproval of his letting Jesuit priests sit in the classes of atheists, Christ haters, Mary haters, Communists and sexual perverts."

Another passage of the conversation was not omitted, but somewhat rewritten for publication. In the original text cited by Pepper, when Fr. Feeney is asked, "You think Bishop Wright was behind this?" he answers: "I know he was. Much as Harvard wanted to get rid of me, and as much as McEleney wanted to get rid of me, neither could have done so without Bishop Wright. It was Bishop Wright who gave orders to Fr. McEleney to dismiss me exactly when he was on the high seas and could not give me a hearing." The version of Fr. Feeney's answer published in Sr. Catherine's book is much softer. It does not name Bishop Wright in the same way. We can conjecture that it does not because as logical as it was to deduce from the circumstances that it was Bishop Wright who gave the order for Fr. Feeney's removal from Boston, they had no "smoking gun" at the center, no documentary evidence to support the charge. So it was not made.

But why was the other passage simply omitted? I think it was because of Fr. Feeney's reference to Jesuit priests sitting docilely in the classes of sex perverts, among others, but above all, sex perverts. The conclusion can be drawn for several reasons. First, we want to remember that Leonard Feeney was so anxious to preserve purity, including his own, that he would not attend the theater even when he was working in New York City as a critic. Beyond that, in a conversation with the present writer, Bro. Leonard Mary, the M.I.C.M. brother in California who knew Fr. Feeney for a longer time than anyone else still living, allowed that the practice of sodomy was a sin that Fr. Feeney found especially abhorrent (old catechisms used to number it among the sins that "cry to Heaven").

Add something else to the picture. Francis Kelly, the retired Marine colonel who as a young lieutenant used to hear Fr. Feeney preach on Boston Common and who is quoted in Chapter One of this book, was a product of Catholic education. Among the contacts his background gave him was a distinguished Franciscan serving in Boston and residing in a house of his order when Kelly visited the city. Kelly still remembers having lunch with the priest one day and being the object of a confidence that shocked him. The priest, evidently filled with such disgust that he felt the need to unburden himself (and with whom better might one speak of such things than a Marine?), related that he was distressed by the number of his brothers in religion who were evidently homosexual. The house in which he lived was "full of them." We may surmise that if the Franciscans were already "full of them" by the 1950s, homosexuals would also have made their way into the Society of Jesus by then, and if Kelly's priest was scandalized and disgusted by the situation, so would have been Fr. Feeney.

Now, visibly homosexual priests are commonplace in the Church in the U.S. today. Which big-city diocese has not had at least several die from AIDS by now? But it was not so in 1949. Far from being inured to the practice of homosexuality by priests as are most Catholics today, most 45 years ago would have been scandalized—like Kelly's priest, Kelly himself and, we may suppose, Fr. Feeney.

All of this being so, I conclude that the passage with its reference to sex perverts was omitted because the clear implication of Jesuit priests being comfortable around homosexuals was that the priests themselves might be homosexual, and Fr. Feeney, badly treated though he was, did not want Sr. Catherine's book to give scandal to readers by suggesting that.

That is, Fr. Feeney's days among the Jesuits might be numbered— indeed, they were over by the time *The Loyolas and the Cabots* saw print—but he still clung to the ideal of the celibate priesthood and thought that for the good of the Church it was important for others—especially laypersons—to continue to believe the ideal was still being realized, as too many after him would not and do not. What ideal, after all, is there today?

There is the one that was first expressed as being "open" and "honest." In practice, it has come to mean: Parade your vice.

That Fr. Feeney's abhorrence of homosexuality and the possibility that he may have complained about its practice by priests could have strengthened the resolve of local Jesuit and diocesan authorities to get rid of him is not something we can explore because there is nothing in the record to allow for it—not in the available record.

Chapter Eight

Although it had tacked onto its conclusion a scrolled text that was offensive in its political correctness, *The Mission* remained one of the best English-language films made during the 1980s. Fictional in its details, it related in a way that was basically true the story of how one of history's most successful social undertakings, the civilizing of Paraguay's native population by Jesuits in the 18th century, was purposely undone in a futile effort to prevent the suppression of the Society of Jesus in Europe. The film only suggests how many souls may have been lost because of the undoing. Further, perhaps assuming a greater degree of historical knowledge on the part of the audience than was likely, the movie did not deal at all with the fact that the Jesuits were suppressed despite the actions taken in Paraguay.

The film is here recalled because of Fr. McCormick's repeated insistance to Fr. Feeney in their meeting of April 1, 1949, that Fr. Feeney was being ordered to leave St. Benedict Center "for the good of the Society." After all, it was supposedly for the good of the Society that the Jesuits' own missions in Paraguay were destroyed with the connivance of Jesuit superiors. Yet, the "good" was not attained. The Jesuits were suppressed, anyway.

In 1949, Fr. Feeney refused to collaborate in the destruction of his mission. The Jesuits were not then suppressed, nor have they been since, but who can deny that they are no longer regarded as an elite by anyone? Who can deny that they now are universally recognized as having been vital, if not supremely important, in leading the Church into her post-conciliar disarray and, as far as the general society is concerned, her negligibility (with the result that the Jesuits themselves are even more negligible)? Only, the Jesuits' process of self-destruction in this century and country did not begin at the end of Vatican II in Rome. A better date would be 1949, and the place was Boston.

There is a moral. Three decades ago, Americans watching television saw a Vietnamese village burned in order to "save" it. In 1949 at Provincial headquarters in Boston and maybe even at the Gesu in Rome, the thought may have been to "save" the religion by not upholding its teachings, but the truth is that must be as difficult a thing to accomplish as it is to save a village by burning all its dwellings.

The question is, how many souls have been lost since 1949?

We have seen that it was on April 14 of that year that St. Benedict Center made the news. That was after the four center members who taught at Boston College and Boston College High School were dismissed. By the next day, April 15, the story was on the front page of the *New York Times*. Also on the 15th, which was Good Friday, the Spring issue of

*Housetops,* the one carrying Raymond Karam's article, "Reply to a Liberal," was delivered by its printer and copies were taken by center members to be sold in the streets of Cambridge and Boston. One copy was put in the mail for Rome, addressed to Pope Pius XII. A cable, signed St. Benedict Center, was also dispatched to the pope.

"We beseech Your Holiness, in the name of our patron, St. Grignion de Montfort, to read the defense of Your Holiness' supremacy, for which doctrine we are being persecuted. We are sending this defense to Your Holiness by air mail. It is written by our spokesman, Raymond Karam.

"We are Your Holiness' loving children, in the Immaculate Heart of Mary."

The notion that the center members, now Slaves of the Immaculate Heart of Mary, might win deliverance from Pope Pius in far-off Rome may seem unrealistic today, but it is clear from talking with M.I.C.M. religious who were on the scene in 1949 that they genuinely hoped and even believed that it would be forthcoming. In part, that was due to their devotion to the papacy. How could Peter let them down when it was he they championed? All they needed to do was show him that is what they were doing. Beyond that, they thought they had some reason to believe that their case really was under examination at the Holy See. This is because their first communcation to Pius, the letter sent on February 11, received an answer, unlike the letters to Fr. McEleney and Archbishop Cushing.

Written in Rome on March 25 and received in Cambridge on April 5, the acknowledgement of the letter of February 11 said (emphasis added): "The Secretariat of State, at the gracious bidding of the Holy Father, acknowledges receipt of the document submitted to Him by Mr. Fakhri Maluf, and bearing the signatures of various Professors of Boston College High School and of St. Benedict's Center, and, while communicating that it has been forwarded to the Supreme Congregation of the Holy Office *for consideration and attention,* has pleasure in assuring the signatories that His Holiness, appreciating the Catholic sentiments which prompted their gesture, cordially imparts to them His paternal Apostolic Blessing."

Unlike the supposed decree of excommunication published against Fr. Feeney in 1953, the above letter was stamped with an official seal (that of the Secretariat of State). It was signed by the Pro-Secretary of State, Giovanni Battista Montini (the future Pope Paul VI).(We shall have occasion later to speak of letters like this one.)

Still speaking of events on April 15, the *Boston Herald* that hit the streets that morning featured a story headlined, "B.C. President says Teacher Issue Closed with Dismissals." The story's lead: "The issue involving four lay teachers who trespassed on the field of theology with preachments of rigorist doctrine which the Very Rev. William L. Keleher, S.J., characterized as 'contrary to the traditional teachings of the Catholic

Church' and 'ideas leading to bigotry and intolerance,' is closed with their dismissal, the Boston College president emphasized last night. However, the teachers, three from Boston College and the fourth from Boston College High School, expressed confidence that their appeal to Pope Pius XII soon would bring a pronouncement that would 'destroy the heresy of liberalism. "'

The four center members were wrong. No papal pronouncement then or since has "destroyed" liberalism. But Fr. Keleher was also wrong. The "issue" was not closed. It was really just opening.

When center members went into the streets on April 15 to sell *Housetops*—all of them were male members of the center—one of the things they did was position themselves in groups of two or three outside churches as worshippers came out from Good Friday afternoon services. They did this after checking City Ordinances and ascertaining that wares could be sold on the streets of Boston as long as a vendor did not stand still in one spot. He also had to carry on his person advertising necessary to explain his product. Consequently, the center's "vendors" carried placards reading, "No Salvation Outside the Church."

Their conformity to the ordinances did not matter. In each instance, police showed up at the various churches and hauled the center members to precinct stations for questioning. (All were released.) The *Boston Daily Globe* would the next day, April 16 (Holy Saturday), headline an article: "Churches Picketed in Controversy Over Ousted B.C. Teachers." Said the article itself: "A half dozen Catholic churches in Boston were picketed yesterday afternoon by men carrying placards which read, 'No Salvation Outside the Church,' in support of the doctrine of the three discharged Boston College teachers."

The article's use of the word "picketed" clearly suggested that center members were trying to prevent worshippers from attending Good Friday services, and Archbishop Cushing would seize on it.

(An amusing incident related by Sr. Catherine in her telling of the events of April 15 deserves to be repeated here. At one of the police stations, an officer who had arrested two of the students "remembered," apparently, his early Catholic teaching in the days when orthodoxy was the rule, rather than the exception. He took a copy of the *Housetops* from Temple Morgan, and opened it by accident at Donnelly's article [the entire text of it was printed in the center's review].

"'Look at this!' he said, pointing to the page. 'See this. It says here that there's salvation outside the Catholic Church. Anyone knows that's wrong. What's the matter with you fellows?'

"'We know that's wrong. Read the rest of it,' the boys begged him. But the officer was skeptical. He closed the book and led them to the 'man at the desk.'")

The *Boston Daily Globe* story of the 16th, which would be picked up by newspapers all around the country, reported: "Articles contained in the current issue of *From the Housetops* support the doctrine of no salvation outside the Catholic Church. The ousted Boston College professors charge they were fired because they were teaching this doctrine at the Heights." Nationally, the news of the "picketing" would include a statement from Archbishop Cushing. "I heard that they and a few misguided partisans had been picketing churches and otherwise scandalizing the community during Holy Week."

Archbishop Cushing would be featured in the main, front-page headline of the the *Boston Evening Globe* on Holy Saturday: "Archbishop to Rule on B.C., Says Vatican." There was a subhead: "Jurisdiction in 'Heresy' Dispute Left to Local Authority." The article itself was from the Associated Press and datelined Vatican City. "Jurisdiction in the Boston heresy controversy will be in the hands of Archbishop Richard J. Cushing of the archdiocese of Boston, Vatican sources said today.

"These sources said jurisdiction in such cases is always entrusted to local church authorities.

"Reports from Newton, Mass., earlier this week said four Catholic educators, dismissed from Boston College because they had accused the college of teaching heresy, had appealed their case to the Pope."

At St. Benedict Center it was understood that the "Vatican sources," whoever they were, probably had no way of knowing that the Boston Chancery was working in tandem with Fr. Keleher and Fr. McEleney, but the fired teachers and fellow center members were still dismayed that they were being turned over for judgment to Archbishop Cushing. Under the circumstances, Fr. Feeney decided to put the authority of his priestly office as well as his personal prestige and celebrity behind the center men in a public way. That Holy Saturday evening he wrote and released to the press a statement that made his position unequivocally clear. Unfortunately, it would not see print in the Boston papers until Monday morning—not that it necessarily would even have postponed, let alone stopped, the action about to be taken. But he truly had committed himself to the center and its young persons when he made his decision to remain with them in Cambridge. Here was the proof:

"I was very much surprised to learn from newspaper reports that Fr. Keleher had said that a profession—and where needed, an explanation—of the truths of our Holy Faith, which Fr. Keleher seems to have relegated to a specialist under the title of 'theology,' is forbidden any Catholic teacher speaking to Catholic students at a Catholic college. Inasmuch as very few—I might almost say a bare minimum—of the classes are directly concerned with religion and are in the hands of what the President calls 'competent theologians,' this procedure would leave the principles of our Holy Faith almost totally unmentioned for the greater part of the four-year course of a college boy's life.

"I know many erroneous things that have been uttered by irresponsible teachers in Catholic colleges, but why the three basic premises of Catholic life—the very direction signs by which one finds it—should be forbidden Professor Maluf, Professor Walsh, and Professor Ewaskio is beyond my competence to understand.

"As for my personal associations with these three men, and with their staunch associate, Professor Supple of the High School, I am very glad to state what I know to be their qualifications in the matter under which they have been disciplined.

"Charles Ewaskio and James Walsh are both excellent students of theology, to which subject I know they give all their leisure time. Charles Ewaskio is a very devoted student of Holy Scripture, which I know he reads and even memorizes and beautifully expounds, and James Walsh I have heard personally give talks on theological subjects that would do credit to the most trained theologian.

"David Supple, as everyone knows, is one of the most ardent lay apostles the Church has in Boston. His readings on the subject of the Faith have been enormous. There is almost no point of Catholic doctrine or program on which David has not a seasoned judgment, expressed with his inimitable grace and ease. Strong faith has a tradition in his family. His two uncles, Msgr. Supple and Dr. James Supple, are imperishable memories in the minds of all unequivocal Boston Catholics.

"As for Dr. Fakhri Maluf, I am at a loss to know how to praise him. There is no one who has ever met him who has not sensed in him a positive genius for the things of the spirit, especially in his brilliant theological defenses of Our Blessed Lady as an essential part of all sound dogmatic thinking. His discourses on the *Summa Theologica*, every one of which for the past five years I have attended at St. Benedict Center, puts him, in my measured judgment, as the most brilliant exponent of the true St. Thomas that our country possesses.

"Finally, I may mention Raymond Karam, who was not discharged from Boston College, but who voluntarily left there a month ago in protest against some of the liberal and unpenalized teaching. I do not think after reading his superb article in the current *Housetops*, the article entitled 'Reply to a Liberal,' that anyone will ever want again to excuse the laity from full competence in the field of theology as it is academically defended."

On Monday morning, April 18, when the *Boston Herald* published Fr. Feeney's statement under the headline "Father Feeney Defends Teachers B.C. Fired—Jesuit Deplores Faculty Curb," the newspaper commented: "The statement was expected to create a sensation in theological circles, not only because of the implied criticism of the alleged lack of religious teachings at Boston College but because of the open scoring of a famed Jesuit's educational and theological problems by another well-known priest."

On Easter Sunday morning, the day before Fr. Feeney's statement appeared in the local press, a center student reported that his mother had talked on the telephone with the chancellor of the archdiocese, Msgr. Walter J. Furlong. Msgr. Furlong had said to her that "the axe will fall on Monday."

The axe? What axe? How would it fall? On whom? Nobody at the center was thinking beyond the four fired teachers, and in light of what the newspapers reported on Holy Saturday and the new, ominous talk of an "axe," the four cabled the Holy Office in Rome (it is now the Congregation for the Doctrine of the Faith) and released a statement to the press on Easter Sunday evening:

"We are appealing directly to His Holiness, the Pope, and to the Holy Office, concerning the doctrinal issue between us and Boston College, because we were led to believe that Fr. Keleher was acting in constant contact with the local authorities all through the case. We cannot conceive Fr. Keleher taking it upon himself without trial and investigation to pronounce our doctrine contrary to the traditional doctrine of the Church, and summarily firing us, without having consulted His Excellency, the Archbishop.

"We wish to stress the fact that our future and the livelihood of our families are in jeopardy, and we have to act in the quickest and most direct way. His Excellency, the Archbishop, knows from the statements of Fr. Keleher to the press, and from the theological document by Fr. Philip Donnelly, what doctrine Boston College is teaching. We have submitted Fr. Donnelly's document, with our reply, written by Mr. Raymond Karam, to His Excellency for his consideration. Our refusal to conform with the doctrine in Fr. Donnelly's document is the cause of our expulsion from Boston College.

"His Excellency's custody of the Faith and his concern about orthodoxy would justify his taking the initiative against Boston College even without our appeal to him."

The cable to the Holy Office said: "For refusing to conform with the following three doctrines taught at Boston College, 1) that there may be salvation outside the Catholic Church; 2) that a man may be saved without confessing that the Roman Church is supreme among all the churches; 3) that a man may be saved without submission to the Pope, Fr. Keleher, President of Boston College, pronounced that we hold a position which is contrary to the traditional teachings of the Church and which leads to bigotry and intolerance, and has expelled us from our teaching positions. We appeal to your Holy Office this judgment, and request a speedy reply."

"Easter Sunday passed," Sr. Catherine writes in *The Loyolas and the Cabots*. "The next day, Monday, April 18th, proved to be the longest and saddest day in our lives." It began with a survey of the morning press, including the *Boston Herald* story we have already looked at. Then the morning was spent fielding phone calls, receiving telegrams, special delivery letters and opening the ordinary mail. "Many people seemed to be for us, and as many more against us," Sr. Catherine says. At some point in the morning, the four fired teachers conferred among themselves and decided to call on Archbishop Cushing at his residence. They left the center at 11:50 and returned at 2:30 in the afternoon. Their report of their meeting with the archbishop was entered into the center *Log*. Considering the archbishop's general demeanor at his meeting with the four teachers, Catholics without much experience of dealing with bishops may be shocked, and even appalled, by what else His Excellency did on the 18th.

"We spoke to His Excellency of the grave injustice done to us by Boston College in placing our future and the livelihood of our families in jeopardy, and in treating us as if we were in heresy, without any process of law or any opportunity for self-defense. We brought to his attention the document written by the Rev. Philip Donnelly, S.J., which gave unmistakable expression to the liberal theology taught at Boston College, and we also called attention to our reply to this article of Fr. Donnelly's by Mr. Raymond Karam. We entreated His Excellency, in the interest of souls, to look into the doctrines taught at Boston College, and to take measures on his own for the protection of the Faith. The Archbishop was utterly noncommittal on the doctrinal issue. Although His Excellency told us that he had seen Fr. Donnelly's article and Mr. Karam's reply to it, he was unwilling to make any statement.

"When we saw that the Archbishop would not assume responsibility himself, we asked him to present to the Holy See our plea for a clarification of the doctrine, and to advise the Holy Father that a decision on it was urgently needed. The Archbishop merely kept repeating to us that Rome was very slow in deciding such issues. We then reminded His Excellency that the doctrines we were defending had already been defined by the Church, and that the only points in question were the so-called interpretations and additions made by the liberal theologians, which we claimed were in contradiction to the teachings of the Church. If the theologians of Boston College were merely interpreting the dogma that there is no salvation outside the Catholic Church, we asked, why should we be persecuted for professing the dogma? His Excellency did not reply.

"Our interview with the Archbishop was most unsatisfactory. At no point in the discussion did he give us the slightest hint of his feelings with regard to us. We had opened our hearts to him, presenting our grievances as loyal children of the Church to their father. He did say to us several times, 'What do you want me to do? I'll do anything I can for you. But I'm just one poor man.'

"'No, you're not, Your Excellency', we told him.' You are the Archbishop. The jurisdiction of this case rests with you.'

"'Well, what would you have me do? I'm willing to do anything I can for you.'

"'Either take the matter into your own hands, Your Excellency, or entreat the Holy Father for an *ex cathedra* pronouncement,' we pleaded with him.

"'I can't do that,' he answered us. 'Sometimes these things drag on for years.'

"'But, Your Excellency, there has been an injustice done. We've been fired from our jobs, our reputation is ruined, and our families are dependent upon us for support. Over and above all that, there is to be considered the faith of thousands who have been thrown into complete confusion. This is not a matter that can wait for years. Could you promise us, Your Excellency, that you will bring this matter before Rome? Would you ask the Pope to reconvene the Vatican Council, if necessary, or to give us an infallible pronouncement?'

"'Well, we will see, we will see. We will see how it will work out. I don't want to hurt anybody.'

"The Archbishop looked very uneasy throughout the entire interview. He kept pacing the floor, constantly going to a half-open door in the room and looking out. We definitely got the impression that our conversation was being heard by someone else.

"We knelt for the blessing of the Archbishop, which he seemed happy to give us, and we kissed his ring. Then we left."

When the men returned to St. Benedict Center from the Archbishop's residence, they were silent, even solemn, and were asked about it, Sr. Catherine tells us.

"Why are you all miserable? You say the Archbishop was friendly?"

"Yes," they answered. "And he gave us his blessing. And while he did not tell us where he stood on the doctrine, he did seem to wish to be of help."

"Well, isn't all that good?"

"Yes," they admitted, "we suppose it is. But we all have the same feeling of uneasiness about it, somehow. It was a strange interview."

There was a news conference at the center at 4:30 on the afternoon of the 18th. It was explained that the center wanted to sponsor a movement in the Catholic world to appeal to the pope to reconvene the Vatican Council to pronounce on the issues involved in what was already being called the "Boston heresy controversy." (The council that is now known as Vatican Council I had been cut short by the outbreak of the Franco-Prussian War.) The four fired professors related that they had met with Archbishop Cushing that day and laid the proposal for a reconvened council before him. Most of all, Fr. Feeney wanted to reconfirm to the press his support of the four teachers. It was also announced that a copy of *Housetops* with Karam's article was being mailed to every cardinal, bishop, patriarch and metropolitan bishop in the Church.

"This is a strange way to move into heresy," Fr. Feeney said to the reporters, "if that is what we are supposed to be doing—to lay our case at the feet of every orthodox person listed in the Church's directory, and to await for one word of reproof on anything we have said."

He was obviously looking to strike a note of irony when he said that, but his language was probably unfortunate. After all, the "Boston Heresy Case" began with the four teachers from the center charging heresy against Boston College Jesuits, and when Fr. Keleher responded with his statement, he did not use the word, he did not speak of heresy when he spoke of the center members. He said "their doctrine is erroneous" and that they promoted "ideas leading to bigotry and intolerance." Fr. Feeney's ironic use of the term may have been the first step in a process that ended with the public believing that it was he and center members who were guilty of heresy.

Of course the working of the process was made easier after the event that capped Monday, April 18, 1949. Sr. Catherine received word of it in a phone call to her home from Fakhri Maluf. He called near midnight. This was after center members had heard reference to their appeal for reconvening the Vatican Council on the 8 o'clock radio news, and then all departed for their homes at about 10:30.

"You did not hear the late news? You did not see the late papers?"

"No," Sr. Catherine answered. "Was there something about us?"

"Yes," came the answer. "Archbishop Cushing has *silenced Father*. He has put the center under interdict."

"Silenced Father! But you saw him, just today. He didn't say anything about it. Where did he silence Father?"

"In the newspapers. D.D. Supple saw the headlines on the way home and telephoned us. Peter Embree [a Harvard student] saw them, too, and telephoned us also."

The axe had fallen. Clearly, in order for the text of Archbishop Cushing's decree against Fr. Feeney and the center to make it into newspapers printed on the evening of the 18th, it was already being swung even as the prelate met that afternoon with the four center members and assured them he "did not want to hurt anybody."

The decree, published in all the Boston papers, read as follows: "Rev. Leonard Feeney, S.J., because of grave offense against the laws of the Catholic Church has lost the right to perform any priestly function, including preaching and teaching of religion.

"Any Catholics who frequent St. Benedict's Center, or who in any way take part in or assist its activities forfeit the right to receive the Sacrament of Penance and Holy Eucharist.

"Given at Boston on the 18th day of April, 1949."

Some of the newspaper headlines that accompanied publication of the decree: "Archbishop Silences Priest"; "Father Feeney Silenced by Abp. Cushing"; "Priest Silenced"; "Archbishop Sternly Disciplines Jesuit in Ruling on B.C. Dispute"; "Catholics are Barred From St. Benedict's Directed by Father Feeney"; "Abp. Cushing Endorses College Action on Ousted Instructors"; "Prelate Acts Due to Jesuit's Support of 3 Fired at B.C."; "St. Benedict Youth Center Is Under Ban." None of the newspapers reported that under Canon Law a priest censured as had been Fr. Feeney was to receive at least three formal warnings beforehand. Fr. Feeney had not been warned even once.

At the center, reporters, including representatives of the wire services, began arriving with questions as early as 6:30 in the morning on April 19. Fr. Feeney, who spent the night sleepless, had prepared a statement to give them.

"The reason I am being silenced is because I believe there is no salvation outside the Catholic Church and without personal submission to our Holy Father, the Pope, and Archbishop Cushing believes that there is. The reason I am being silenced is because I believe there is no salvation outside the Church or without personal submission to our Holy Father, the Pope, and Bishop John Wright believes that there is.

"The reason I was told to leave the diocese seven months ago is because I believe there is no salvation outside the Catholic Church or without submission to our Holy Father, the Pope, and Archbishop Cushing and Bishop Wright, then in Europe and managing the affair through others to dismiss me, believe that there is. I cabled twice to Bishop Wright in Europe and once to Archbishop Cushing in Europe and asked for a hearing. That hearing I never received. They have not contacted me at St. Benedict Center during these seven painful months when, in the face of all sorts of gossip and misunderstanding, I remained here at the earnest plea of my students until this doctrinal issue was settled. IT WAS AND IS A MATTER OF CONSCIENCE to me in the sanctity of my priesthood, as I openly declared to every superior I could contact.

"I believe my removal in view of the facts is invalid; the taking away of my faculties was invalid; and I believe the present silencing of me is totally invalid. What humiliation my priesthood, and sympathetically the priesthood of my two brothers, will take because of this brutal action, when I sought to protect four brave Catholic boys in a profession of faith similar to my own, Our Blessed Lady alone knows. I also believe the beautiful Catholics of Boston somehow understand.

"I thank God that a copy of *From the Housetops* was to reach Our Holy Father, every Cardinal in the world, and every Bishop in the United States before Archbishop Cushing and Bishop Wright managed to disgrace me."

In a one-on-one interview with a reporter from the *Providence Journal-Bulletin,* Fr. Feeney declared: "It may take a little time. But, I know the only way to reach this country and it is not by the Christophers, and liberalism and all this Boy Scoutism. The only way is to come out and preach the authoritative, exclusive, visible road to heaven governed by that man [Fr. Feeney gestured to the portrait of Pius XII which adorned the text of the Apostolic Blessing which the pope had bestowed on St. Benedict Center]. I don't suppose there is a portion of the world that was given so much of a chance to become Catholic as the New World."

He went on to say, "What is really cruel is to deny others the knowledge of where salvation is. When we say that there is no salvation outside the Church, what we are really saying is that there is salvation inside the Church."

*Life* magazine, perhaps at the instigation of Mrs. Luce, did a spread on the action taken against the center. That article quoted Fr. Feeney saying, "I don't care what happens to me after this. The only one who can clarify our Faith and preserve it for posterity is the Holy Father. Christianity is not a lot of vague ideas. You cannot preach Catholicism without enthusiasm."

Of all the press coverage of Archbishop Cushing's interdict of the center and silencing of Fr. Feeney, Sr. Catherine selected one piece for reproduction in her book, *The Loyolas and the Cabots*. It appeared in the *Boston Daily Globe* on April 19.

"Rev. Leonard Feeney, S.J., whose presentation of religious subjects has made him a widely read author and poet, was born in Lynn. He is the son of Mr. and Mrs. Thomas B. Feeney of 73 Lewis St., Lynn. Mr. Feeney is in the insurance business.

"While still a student at the Jesuit House in Weston in 1928, Fr. Feeney's works of prose and poetry presaged for him a brilliant future as a writer.

"His book, *Fish on Friday,* a humorous dissertation why Catholics eat fish on fast days, was acclaimed in the publishing world in 1934. It was gay reading, according to critics.

"Fr. Feeney admits he has fun writing. His books of verse, *In Towns and Little Towns* and *Riddle and Reverie,* were done in the same spirit.

"'That's the way I like to write—for the joy of it,' he said.

"Fr. Feeney comes from a family of priests. Two of his brothers are clergymen—Rev. Thomas Butler Feeney, S.J., a professor of English and French at Boston College, and Rev. John Feeney, who is assigned to a Keene, N.H. parish.

"Fr. Feeney's literary works reflected his interests in everyday occurrences of the ordinary people around him. His sense of humor attracted many friends in all walks of life. One of his staunchest friends was the late Gov. Alfred E. Smith of New York, whose Presidential candidacy was considerably enlivened in the nation's press by a letter written by Fr. Feeney concerning Smith's famous brown derby.

"The priest was for many years an editor of *America,* the Jesuit weekly publication, and one of its most prolific contributors.

"When Fr. Feeney's *Fish on Friday* won public acclaim for its witticisms, he commented:

"'So many people have the utterly false impression that religious writers or writers on religious subjects must have a long face and a solemn, sorrowful approach. That's not the Catholic conception of religion at all.'"

Having reproduced the *Globe* article, Sr. Catherine wrote, "This same Fr. Feeney who, even while he had lured the Catholics of America to laughter with his humor and had shared with them his joy, had also led them to love God and His Mother, was now forced to listen through the seemingly endless day of April 19th, to radio announcers proclaiming the withdrawal of his priestly functions, and the banning of his Center.

"'At least,' Father said in the late afternoon, 'the doctrine gets out each time. Maybe that is what Our Lady wants. And though it is made to look as if I am the only priest in the world who holds it, it is the truth, and the Holy Ghost can fructify it. Many souls will remember it before they die, and many may be saved. We can thank God for that. '

"At some time during the day, Father's superior, Fr. Louis Gallagher, S.J., telephoned, to say that this whole thing must be lifted right away. All Father had to do was to go to Holy Cross College at once, and all the censure would be removed. Father was amazed. Going to Holy Cross now would be even more of an admission to the world that the doctrine for which he had fought so hard was wrong. And he would be abandoning now, more than ever, his people who in conscience held the same doctrine.

"Center friends dropped in throughout the day. Toward the end of the afternoon, Father requested all who were not registered in the Center School to abide by the ruling of the Archbishop, and not come to the Center any more. He assured them that we would hold them in our hearts and our prayers always. The Center as such was to be closed. Only the School would remain open."

There is something Sr. Catherine does not tell in regard to the center's closing. It is another piece of irony, one that connects to the horror felt at the center when the atom bomb was dropped on Hiroshima and Nagasaki. It also relates to Harvard, the university "nobody should attend," according to Sr. Catherine when she met Fr. Feeney for the first time.

During World War II, President Franklin Roosevelt named Harvard's president, James B. Conant, to head the National Defense Research Committee. The committee was the body in charge of secretly developing the atomic bomb, and the week the center was closed, the *Saturday Evening Post,* then one of the most widely circulated and influential magazines in the U.S., published an article lauding Conant for the "crucial decision" in the development.

(Late in 1993, an entire book—one 948 pages long!—was published by Knopf on the subject of the Harvard president and the bomb, *James B. Conant: Harvard to Hiroshima and the Making of the Nuclear Age.*)

Chapter Nine

In one of his first lectures at the center school after Fr. Feeney was censured and the center interdicted, Bro. Francis (Fakhri Maluf) declared: "The Church has always held that the doctrine that there is no salvation outside the Church is incontestable. We are trying to prove it *is* being contested when we are willing to continue to suffer because of it."

It cannot be doubted that Fr. Feeney, Sr. Catherine and the center students did suffer. There was material privation which resulted from young students being cut off from their families on account of their loyalty to Fr. Feeney and dedication to the defense of historical Church teaching. There was a degree of emotional suffering from the knowledge that however just their cause, in the eyes of many they must be wrong if they incurred the censure and interdict. Perhaps worst of all, they had lived in hope and even confident expectation that Rome would vindicate them, but weeks went by with no word from the Eternal City, despite the urgency of the appeals they had launched in that direction. Finally, on May 28, 1949, Fr. Feeney penned another one, addressing it to Pope Pius XII. Sr. Catherine did not reproduce the letter in *The Loyolas and the Cabots*, presumably because in 1950, when the book came out, Fr. Feeney was still hoping for an answer. The appeal said, in part:

"Your Holiness must believe me when I tell you that the condition of the Church in the United States of America in the matter of doctrine is utterly deplorable. There is no doubt about it that we are slowly becoming a National Church, controlled not in the least by Your Holiness, but by the National Catholic Welfare Conference of Washington, D.C. [now the National Conference of Catholic Bishops with the United States Catholic Conference as its civil arm]. Americans are not being taught the Catholic Faith as it is contained in the writings of the Fathers and the Doctors and in the definitions of the Councils of the Church. They are being taught what a committee of extremely deficient American theologians think will interest the American mind without ever embarrassing or challenging it.

"I am writing this letter to Your Holiness simply, and as a child. Your Holiness may see already that it is not a legally organized document. It is a cry of anguish from my priestly heart. In order not to tire you with too many details, may I tell you in brief statement what is the fundamental heresy universally taught by Catholics, priests and teachers, in the United States of America? This is the doctrine which American Catholics are being taught.

"'The way to be saved is by being sincere to your convictions and living a good life. If one of your convictions happens to be that the Roman Catholic Church is the true Church of Christ, then you are obliged to join it. If you do not sincerely think it is the one way to salvation, then you are invincibly ignorant and God will save you, apart from the Church. You are then said to belong to the soul of the Church, and whatever you desire for yourself in the way of salvation, Catholic theologians are prepared to call "Baptism of Desire." Were you to sincerely think that the Roman Catholic Church is not the true Church of Christ, it would be a sin for you to join it.'

"Your Holiness, I assure you in all my honor, in the sanctity of my Sacrament and whatever voice I have to be heard in profession of Faith, that the above statement is the substance of what is being taught all Americans as the means of eternal salvation. I am bold enough to say that you know what I am telling you is the truth. There is no Pope in history who has been as close to the American mind as you have been. I personally heard you speak in New York City when I was one of the editors of *America,* and I know that this is true. Every day you defer calling a halt to the wild Liberalism of the American hierarchy, a Liberalism which pays not the slightest attention to Your messages against Interfaith movements and against exposing our Catholics to the dangers of heretical perversion, the more will grow the spirit of indifference and apostasy in our land, and ten years from now will be too late to save it. I know along with this challenge which I offer to Your Holiness, while prostrate at your feet in reverence and love, there go thousands of graces to enable you as Christ's Vicar to save this world for our Holy Faith. Unless you are the thundering leader of the world, other thunderers will take your place, be they the Hitlers, the Mussolinis, the Stalins or the Roosevelts, who have already so confused the world that is waiting for Our Pontiff to speak."

In the meeting he had with Fr. McCormick, the American Assistant to the General of the Jesuits, on April 1, Fr. Feeney accused himself of defects—using superlatives, raising his voice, "pushing home a point too strongly." In a word, he admitted that sometimes he was given to exaggeration. Reread his May 28 letter to Pius and see, in the light of all that has transpired since, if he was exaggerating then. The Catholicism that he described in 1949 as coming in the U.S. is the Catholicism that now is—and not merely in the U.S. Yet, though he wrote to the pope that the situation would be in ten years beyond saving, we know that he, Sr. Catherine and the others must already have been looking past the decade then facing them. They had to be looking farther than to save the situation, the one they foresaw and in which we now live, else Sr. Catherine would not have written that when they transformed themselves into a religious order it was because they realized the battle lying ahead was not so much for the preservation of the Church's sacred dogmas, "but actually for their restoration."

It remains, in 1949 and during the immediate years to come, the Slaves of the Immaculate Heart of Mary had many trials to bear. Some have just been mentioned. There were others. As soon as Archbishop Cushing promulgated his interdict, malicious rumors about them, and especially about Fr. Feeney, began to spread. The origin of some was traced to members of the Society of Jesus, as Sr. Catherine recounts. One rumor, that Fr. Feeney was mentally or emotionally unbalanced, began to be picked up and given further currency by the episcopally-controlled Catholic press. This was also when stories began to circulate that Fr. Feeney supposedly had a "problem" with alcohol. We have already looked at that rumor, and discounted it, in the Introduction to this book, but it might be mentioned here that for a long period in his life, mainly during the years when he wrote a great deal and when he was living in New York City, Fr. Feeney was a heavy smoker. At some point before he became involved with St. Benedict Center, he gave up the habit, and after the Slaves of the Immaculate Heart of Mary came into being, he encouraged its smoking members to emulate his example.

(I have never seen an M.I.C.M. religious light up, but as a group they seem disinclined to have their house rules dictated by federal bureaucrats in the matter of smoking. When I interviewed Bro. Thomas Augustine in his office in Still River he asked another brother to fetch me an ashtray so I could smoke. As my supply of cigarettes was running low, the same brother obligingly bought a couple of packs for me when he ran into town on an errand. At St. Benedict Center West in Los Angeles, I filled a large ashtray twice while interviewing Bro. Leonard Mary. At St. Benedict Abbey in Still River they restrict smoking to the T.V. room in the main guest house, but that is likely due to their being a retreat center, which means many visit the premises who will not be ready to tolerale the presence of tobacco smoke. As is well known, most of U.S. society, having been told that if it avoids smoke it will live longer the only life in which it really believes anymore, is not tolerant. If M.I.C.M. religious do tolerate it, they are not encouraging vice. They are giving evidence that freedom is not merely a slogan among them, and that they know there are more important things in this life than clinging to it for as long as doctors now like to claim you may if you will but follow their prescriptions, including the one not to smoke.

(I have not talked to any of them about it, but Christian as they are and the general society is not, I also expect M.I.C.M. religious may have a decent respect for smoking *and* drinking on account of their being pleasures of the poor man. Rich men, after all, indulge themselves with yachting, horse-breeding and buying sports teams. I know that at least some M.I.C.M. brothers drink. The brothers in California, for instance, take wine with their meals, something that is routine in European religious houses, but rare in the U.S.—as if the pope himself is without wine on his table. All of the M.I.C.M. religious seem to eat well, simply, but well. The one meal I had at St. Ann's House in Still River was especially good, perhaps because the sisters grow most of their own vegetables and fruit, which they also sell at a roadside stand for some extra income. The sisters also serve wine, at least when they have a guest. Such things tell us something. Since the first pope in history who may not have wine on his table will likely be the first one elected from this country, these practices of the M.I.C.M. religious tell us that in more ways than one they are not guilty of Americanism.)

Before we go further in tracing the life led at St. Benedict Center and the battle waged from there after the center was interdicted, the parenthetical reference just made to Americanism gives us the opportunity to put both the life and the battle in the context which was seen by the Slaves of the Immaculate Heart of Mary themselves. We can do that by citing a passage of *Testem Benevolentiae,* Pope Leo XIII's apostolic letter condemning the heresy of Americanism. This is a passage different from the ones we have quoted elsewhere in these pages. This one is also cited by Sr. Catherine. She fingers it after speculating whether Fr. Keleher, the Boston College president, might hold "in his heart, the defined dogma of the Church on salvation, but at the same time feels that it is, religiously or politically, not expedient to confess it at this time."

Here is the passage (Pope Leo is describing Americanists): "They contend that it is opportune, in order to work in a more attractive way upon the wills of those who are not in accord with us, to pass over certain heads of doctrines, as if of lesser moment, or to so soften them that they may not have the same meaning which the Church has invariably held. Now, Beloved Son [the pope is addressing Cardinal Gibbons], few words are needed to show how reprehensible is the plan that is thus conceived, if we but consider the character and origin of the doctrine which the Church hands down to us. On that point the Vatican Council [i.e. Vatican I] says: 'The doctrine of faith which God revealed is not proposed like a theory of philosophy which is to be elaborated by the human understanding, but as a divine deposit delivered to the Spouse of Christ to be faithfully guarded and infallibly declared.... That sense of the sacred dogmas is to be faithfully kept which Holy Mother Church has once declared, and is not to be departed from under the specious pretext of a more profound understanding.' (Const. de Fid, cath.c.iv.)... Far be it, then, for any one to diminish or for any reason whatever to pass over anything of this divinely delivered doctrine; whosoever would do so, would rather wish to alienate Catholics from the Church than to bring over to the Church those who dissent from it. Let them return; indeed, nothing is nearer to Our heart; let all those who are wandering far from the sheepfold of Christ return; but let it not be by any other road than that which Christ has pointed out."

The road which Christ has pointed out. There is only the one. Most of the Catholic world, not to speak of all of the larger one, no longer believes on the eve of the Third Millennium that there is no other. But in 1949, much of the Church in the U.S., following the lead of prelates like Archbishop Cushing, was already coming to unbelief.

No matter, said the men and women of St. Benedict Center to one another. If Catholics were ever again to believe in only the one road, and thus be fully Catholic, belief in it had to be kept alive *now*. If Archbishop Cushing and other prelates would not keep it alive, they would. How? It certainly would not be by hiding the belief in their hearts, by passing over it, by softening it or presenting it as a philosophical theory to whomever would listen. No, they would *proclaim* the belief—"from the housetops." This was the task the Slaves of the Immaculate Heart of Mary set themselves, and it is the one they are still about a half-century later, though by now it is most of the Catholic world which no longer believes instead of merely much of it. Watching them begin their work is what we now want to do. We shall even see them make a couple of terrible mistakes.

They became a kind of novitiate. This term, like so many others, is not widely understood among Catholics nowadays, especially younger ones. Strictly speaking, it refers to a period of time, usually a year, during which a candidate for entrance into a religious order tries out the life of the order in circumstances somewhat more relaxed than will be the case if he perseveres and actually joins the community. In effect, a novitiate is the apprenticeship of a religious. We say that St. Benedict Center became a kind of one because the rules regulating its life, at least at first, had to be even less rigorous than those of a normal novitiate.

That was inevitable. The members had their slavery to Mary's Immaculate Heart, their doctrinal crusade, and they took that vow of obedience of which we have already spoken, but they were also living in a major metropolis, not in rustic seclusion; numerous of them were married and had children; and most everyone—single persons as well as married men—had to go to jobs during the day in order to make money. That is unless they were full-time students at the center school, like the 14 veterans attending its lectures on the G.I. Bill. (In all, there were 75 students.)

Fr. Feeney was compelled to leave the Jesuit house in which he had long resided. With several unmarried center men he moved into a house a few steps from the center.

They named their house Sacred Heart Hall. It was there that Fr. Feeney heard confessions and daily celebrated the Holy Sacrifice of the Mass for the community. Another house was secured for unmarried female Slaves of the Immaculate Heart of Mary and called Immaculate Heart Hall. A house for married couples was named St. Joseph Hall. (Later, it served as the community's infirmary.) The center itself was moved a few doors from 23 Arrow St. to 12 Bow St.

The Slaves of the Immaculate Heart of Mary having been organized as an unincorporated religious society under the general laws of the Commonwealth of Massachusetts, they were able to operate with all the privileges of a corporation. Thus, they did not rent, but purchased, the structures they occupied in Cambridge. By the time they moved to Still River in January, 1958, there would be 12 buildings. A number of them being adjacent to one another, a fence was built, forming a small compound.

A uniform was also adopted: black suits with white shirts and black neckties for the men, black skirts and jackets with white blouses for the women. (The women also adopted a veil, but not until after the death of Sr. Catherine in 1968. Some sisters, notably those of the community headed by Bro. Thomas Augustine, now wear a full-length habit.) On the lapels of their jackets, they would eventually wear a medal. One side shows the Blessed Virgin Mary and says, "Sweet Heart of Mary, Be My Salvation." The other has our Lord Jesus Christ and says, "Sweet Heart of Jesus, Have Mercy on Us."

As the Slaves of the Immaculate Heart of Mary began more and more to live like a religious order, they would add vows of poverty and chastity to their original simple one of obedience. This had its repercussions, for there were by then 12 married couples with 39 children among the group. A decision was made to rear the children communally. As will be seen, the decison was a fateful one.

Meantime, on account of the fence, the dark clothing and the discipline in which they visibly lived (even though it was not as rigid as that of many other orders), neighbors took to referring to the compound and other buildings occupied by the Slaves of the Immaculate Heart of Mary as "Quaker Village."

On June 6, 1950, "Quaker Village"—not that it was quite yet that—was struck a blow. The Commonwealth of Massachusetts had granted state authorization for the operation of St. Benedict Center School on June 29, 1949. The authorization was to expire on June 6, 1950, and the center was notified it would not be renewed. Unable to persuade Commonwealth Education Commissioner John J. Desmond to reverse the decision, which the center people were certain had politics behind it, Fr. Feeney managed to arrange a meeting with Massachusetts' governor, Paul Dever, and he, Bro. Francis and other center men drove to the State House in Boston for the appointment. The matter was one of extreme importance to the center school because without the state authorization, the veterans attending courses on the G.I. Bill would not be able to continue to do so.

After being told by Gov. Dever that there was nothing he could do, Fr. Feeney said to him, "There is an obvious injustice. I will take our case to the people."

That is according to Bro. Francis, who goes on to relate that after Fr. Feeney and the men returned to their car, he, Bro. Francis, asked Father what he now proposed to do.

What did Bro. Francis mean?

"Well," Bro. Francis says he explained, "you told the governor you will take our case to the people. You cannot say a thing like that and now not do it."

They sat in silence for a time. Then it was, still according to Bro. Francis, that he suggested that Fr. Feeney go into Boston Common on Sunday and make the case there. Fr. Feeney instantly began rubbing his hands together in a way he had of showing relish. "Yes, yes, yes!" he said. Thus would begin his Sunday afternoon preaching on the Common.

The Sunday afternoons in the park commenced at three o'clock with the procession described by *Life* magazine in 1953. The M.I.C.M. religious walked behind a banner of Our Lady of Guadalupe. This was after they drove from Cambridge into the heart of Boston in a cavalcade of gray Oldsmobiles provided by a sympathetic auto dealer. By the time Fr. Feeney started to speak, M.I.C.M. brothers would have warmed up the crowd with talks of their own. The numbers who gathered to hear the talks were not great the first few times that the Slaves of the Immaculate Heart of Mary made their witness on the Common, but that soon changed. Newspaper coverage of Fr. Feeney's appearances saw to that. The priest was preaching hatred, said the papers, and on occasion he did say things that could be construed that way, as we have already seen. All a reporter had to do was listen for the right sort of quote and remove it from its context—or rely on the rewrite desk back at the office to do so.

For instance, in the midst of a sermon on the Blessed Virgin Mary and why men should love her as their own mother, for she is the Mother of God, a heckler interrupted Fr. Feeney to ask if he loved Protestants and Jews.

"No!" he shot back, but did not leave it at that. The press the next day could report him saying: "I hate all Mary-haters, and will hate them until they learn to love Mary and enter the Catholic Church. Only then can I give them the privilege of my love."

With statements like that being reported, the size of the crowds on the Common was bound to grow, and the Catholics be outnumbered. By train and bus from New York and all over New England, Protestants and Jews flocked to Boston to hear for themselves if Fr. Feeney was really talking about them as the newspapers said.

It was easy for them usually to hear what they wanted, and they developed a taunting chant that often drowned out the speakers: "Mary-cult! Mary-cult! Totalitarian system!"

But whatever the crowds thought they were hearing, what are we to make of Fr. Feeney's "preaching of hatred"? Verses 21 and 22 of *Psalm 138* in the *Old Testament* will help us, especially if we read them in the copiously footnoted Haydock edition of the Catholic Douay-Rheims version of Holy Scripture.

"Have I not hated them, O Lord, that hated thee: and pined away because of thy enemies?

"I have hated them with a perfect hatred: and they are become enemies to me."

If we consult the footnote for the last verse, we are advised: "Christ commands, 'Love *your* enemies,' and not those who hate God."

To be sure, we are not to hate even the enemies of God with the sort of unreasonable, undifferentiating, all-consuming kind of hatred that would corrode our soul. It is as St. Augustine says in the same footnote: "We must love in them what God loves, and detest what he condemns." The idea is completed by the 18th-century French Jesuit Guillaume-Francois Berthier, the object of more than one attack by Voltaire, tutor of the Dauphin's sons, and translator in eight volumes (with notes) of the *Psalms:* "Fervent zeal against God's enemies is commendable."

It was anything but that in the view of the *Harvard Crimson*, official campus newspaper of St. Benedict Center's powerful academic neighbor. In December, 1951, the paper ran an article, "Father Feeney, Rebel from Church, Preaches Hate, Own Brand of Dogma to All Comers." According to the article, "His harangues have gotten more biting and vitriolic every Sunday, and his audience larger. His 'cause' is to 'rid our city of every coward liberal Catholic, Jew dog, Protestant brute, and Thirty-third Degree Mason who is trying to suck the soul from good Catholics and sell the true faith for greenbacks.'"

The article was certainly correct in reporting that Fr. Feeney's audience was growing larger. Apart from that, the day after the article appeared somebody smashed the front window of St. Benedict Center with a rock.

It was not the only violence. Bro. Francis—Fakhri Maluf, an ethnic Arab who looked it—was often a target on Sunday afternoon. On one occasion he felt obliged to run—for his life as far as he could tell from the cries of the mob chasing him. The driver of a passing truck, a big man, rescued him.

Scenes like that went on for years, despite the presence of the police surrounding the speakers. Bro. Leonard Mary remembers a Jewish heckler spitting on the banner of Our Lady of Guadalupe 24 times. "That had to be diabolic," he says. "No normal human being who is not possessed can spit that much."

The *Boston Record* headlined on September 12, 1955: "500 Jeering Youths Break Up Feeney Talk." The "youths" were Brandeis University students and according to the newspaper's own account they punched M.I.C.M. religious, ripped their clothes, drenched their white shirts with ink and black suits with bleach and then pursued the Slaves of the Immaculate Heart of Mary back into Cambridge in a car chase, all because Fr. Feeney had spoken out against a plan—one backed by Archbishop Cushing—to build a Catholic chapel (along with a Protestant one) on the campus of the Jewish university. To build the chapel, Fr. Feeney said, would be to "place the One True Faith, the Mass, and the Holy Eucharist on a par with heretical persuasions and even with Jewish perfidy."

The last phrase is apt to strike the contemporary ear especially harshly. After all, it is a number of years since the reference to "perfidious Jews" was excised from the Good Friday Scripture Readings (except in the Byzantine Rite). However, if the rhetoric seems extreme—"Jew dog" was more so, even inexcusably, even if hurled at someone who spit on the image of Our Lady and if the term was actually used, as reported by the *Harvard Crimson*—we want to remember that in his conversation with Fr. McCormick and on other occasions Fr. Feeney admitted to a weakness for being carried away, of "pushing home a point too strongly." Most of the time—nearly all the time when he was not being baited by hostile hecklers—he expressed himself quite temperately when speaking. This can be seen in the book *Bread of Life*, which is a collection in print-form of some of his lectures, but all of them delivered to his own young men and women in the calm of St. Benedict Center—not on the Common shouting over the jeers of a mob. In calmer circumstances he would speak of Interfaith relations, his subject when the Brandeis students broke up his talk, in such terms as these: "An Interfaith meeting is a place where a Jewish rabbi, who does not believe in the divinity of Christ, and a Protestant minister who doubts it, get together with a Catholic Priest, who agrees to forget it for the evening."

In *The Loyolas and the Cabots*, Sr. Catherine has her own remarks to offer concerning Interfaith. "St. Benedict Center's policy with regard to it," she writes, "follows of necessity from its adherence to the defined doctrine of No Salvation Outside the Church. For a Catholic to encourage his fellow-man to think that there are numerous ways of getting to heaven is, to our way of thinking, dishonest. We have no quarrel with Protestants and Jews getting together to discuss religion; that is none of our affair. But we feel that Catholics have no right to be there. There are legitimate ways for Catholics, in their everyday association with Protestants and Jews, to express personal friendliness, one to the other, in a social way. To enter the religious field for this purpose is to compromise the Faith, to dilute it, on the one hand, and to mislead people on the other. It is to pull the Faith down from its position as the perfect service of God, and to make it serve the social, political, economic ends of Liberal Catholicism."

Nearly a half century after those words were written, it may be observed that all these past decades of ecumenical activity (as Interfaith came to be known) have led to nothing, except precisely to the dilution of the Faith, as Sr. Catherine said. That is, the Protestants and Jews have not become Catholic, but no one will seriously argue that we have not become more like them. In any event, it is unfortunate that St. Benedict Center speakers and writers did not on every occasion express their views in the kind of measured tones we have just heard, for the truth being told by Fr. Feeney and Sr. Catherine needed telling. Proclaiming it from the housetops was one thing. Lapsing into invective was another.

But lapse is all it ever was. You find no invective in *The Point*. This was a monthly paper launched by St. Benedict Center in February, 1952, *Housetops* having ceased publication with the spring issue of 1949. Until March, 1959, when they stopped bringing it out, it was in *The Point* that center writers dealt most directly and most often with the subject of the Jews and how their influence was helping make Christendom ex-Christendom. Doubtless it was already difficult to write about Jewish influence in the fifties. Today, it is politically incorrect to the extent of being virtually forbidden. (President Truman could describe the U.S. in a letter to the pope as "a Christian nation." When governor Fornice of Mississippi said the same thing in 1993, he came under a firestorm of criticism. He soon apologized and announced his agreement that the national heritage is "Judeo-Christian.") Perhaps because the subject was difficult, much of *The Point's* writing on it, while not lapsing into invective, is satiric. Indeed, that was the general tone of much of the writing on every subject. It is a style that does not lend itself readily to quotation, especially since many of the targets of *The Point's* biting humor—personalities and events of nearly five decades ago—are now unfamiliar. As to who did the writing, it was most anybody at the center with something to say, including Fr. Feeney. No particular individual was ever named editor.

The title of the publication was not the best possible one. The proof is that it had to be explained in the first issue. "What are we here for?" it was asked. "Where are we going? What is the point of it all? If there is any adjective that describes American life today, it is 'pointless.' Our particular concern, though, is that Catholics are living in this general regime of pointlessness." In a word, *The Point* was meant to counter the pointlessness of life in American society.

It was said some pages ago that St. Benedict Center was struck a blow in June, 1950, when its school lost the authorization of the Commonwealth of Massachusetts. It is fair to speculate that the authorization would not have been lost save for another blow struck nine months earlier. That was on September 3, 1949, when *The Pilot*, the newspaper of the Archdiocese of Boston, published portions of a letter supposedly written at the Holy Office in Rome the previous August 8. The selectively chosen portions of the letter were included in an article headlined: "Holy Office Condemns Teachings and Actions of St. Benedict Center."

Before we read the *Pilot* article, a curious fact must be noted and even emphasized. It is that the "Letter of the Holy Office," presented, after all, by *The Pilot* as an official condemnation of St. Benedict Center, never appeared in the *Acta Apostolicae Sedis*, the Vatican publication which is equivalent to the U.S. government's *Federal Register*. That is, the A.A.S. (*The Acts of the Apostolic See*, in Engish) is the publication in which all of the truly official acts of the Church's government are registered. If an act is not registered in the A.A.S. it simply does not exist officially anymore than an act of the U.S. government would have official existence if it did not appear in the *Federal Register*.

Now, governments, or branches of them, do undertake acts, especially clandestine ones, which lack an official character. This allows the government to deny responsibility for the act. For instance, it now seems clear that early in John Kennedy's administration, the CIA undertook to assassinate Fidel Castro, but that was not official and it is not clear if President Kennedy was informed. Most CIA-watchers probably believe he was not, simply in order to keep any planned attempts on Castro's life from becoming official to any degree. We can only conjecture as to why the "Letter of the Holy Office to the Archdiocese of Boston" was kept unofficial. Most probably it was because it was understood in Rome that what was being done might be wanted by Archbishop Cushing for reasons of local and even national political expediency, but on account of what the Church historically held by way of teaching it could not have an official character, no more than an attempted assassination of Castro could be official for the reason that international order will break down if heads of government officially authorize the killing of other heads of government.

In 1963 the "Letter of the Holy Office" was published in the authoritative *Enchiridion Symbolorum*, commonly referred to as "Denzinger" for the name of its pubisher, somewhat as the authoritative Directory of the Church in the U.S. is commonly called the "Kennedy Directory" for its publisher. In 1963, the editor of Denzinger was Rev. Karl Rahner, S.J., author of the post-Vatican II theory of the "anonymous Christian"—i.e. the notion of someone being Christian without knowing it. Being unable to cite the *Acta* as the source for the "Letter," because it never appeared there, Fr. Rahner reached for *The American Ecclesiastical Review* of October, 1952, as his source. Nothing appearing in the *Review* would have official standing, of course.

As for the *Pilot's* article of September 3, 1949, it reported: "An official letter has been received by Archbishop Cushing from the Supreme Sacred Congregation of the Holy Office, through the Apostolic Delegate in Washington, the Most Rev. Amleto G. Cicognani, answering what are called 'the opinions and contentions' of the followers of Saint Benedict's Center in Cambridge. Included in this group are four young professsors who accused the faculty of Boston College of teaching heresy, and two students of Emmanuel College who resigned from the institution on the eve of Commencement last Spring. The letter from Rome bears the signature of His Eminence Cardinal Marchetti-Selvaggiani.

"The Holy Office, over which the Pope himself presides, is the Congregation which safeguards the teaching of faith and morals. The Roman pronouncement reveals that this Sacred Congregation met in plenary session on Wednesday, July 27, 1949, and that the decisions set forth in this letter were approved by His Holiness, Pope Pius XII, in an audience on the following day.

"The Office declares: 'This Sacred Congregation is convinced that the unfortunate dispute is due to an insufficient study and understanding of the well known dictum "*Extra Ecclesiam nulla salus*," and that the dispute has been rendered more acrimonious because of the serious disturbance of discipline occasioned by the refusal of some members of the aforementioned group to revere and obey duly constituted authority.' The Sacred Congregation refers to the axiom as 'an incontestable principle,' but continues: 'However, this doctrine must be understood in the sense in which the Church herself understands it. Surely it is not to private judgment that Our Savior committed for exposition the deposit of faith, but to the teaching of the Church.'

"The Roman letter points out that the teachings of Saint Benedict's Center are inconsistent with pronouncements of His Holiness Pope Pius XII concerning the relationship to the Church of those who are not of the Fold. The Holy Office condemns the teaching of the Cambridge group in these terms: 'From all the foregoing it is clear that the doctrine presented by the periodical *From the Housetops* (Vol. 3) as genuine Catholic teaching, is far from being such, and can do nothing but grave harm both to those who are in the Church and to those outside it.'

"With regard to recent actions of the Center leaders, the Holy Office employed severe terms of censure, declaring it 'beyond understanding how St. Benedict's Center can consistently claim to be a Catholic school, and desire to be called such, while actually refusing to conform to the prescriptions of Canon Law, and while functioning as a source of discord and revolt against Church authority, and as a cause of great upset to many consciences.'

"The letter singled out by name the sole priest associated with the Center and declared: 'Similarly it is beyond understanding how a member of a religious society, namely Father Feeney, can present himself as a "defender of the faith," and at the same time not hesitate to attack the catechetical teaching proposed by legitimate authorities, and not even fear to bring upon himself the weighty sanctions of Canon Law leveled against his grave violations of duty as a religious, as a priest, and as an ordinary member of the Church.'

"The Sacred Congregation reproved the publishing activities of Saint Benedict Center, saying:'...it is nowise to be borne that Catholics should arrogate to themselves the right to publish a magazine for spreading theological doctrines without that permission of competent Church authority which is called an "imprimatur," and which is exacted by Canon Law.'

"Center spokesmen have repeatedly declared that they would be content only with a pronouncement of the Holy See itself. The letter from the Holy Office points out that now 'Rome has spoken,' and ends with a solemn warning to the dissident group 'at the peril of their souls' immediately to return to Church unity in belief and practice."

The *Pilot's* reference to the letter employing the ancient formula, "Rome has spoken," is notable because the day came when Archbishop Cushing made his own striking use of it. This was in 1968 after Pope Paul VI published *Humanae Vitae*, his encyclical condemning artificial contraception. Meeting with reporters, Cushing, who had been made a cardinal by Pope John XXIII on December 15, 1958, said: "Gentlemen, we have a phrase in the Church which says, 'Roma locuta est, causa finita est.' Now that's Latin, and what it means is this. Rome has spoken. The case has ended—at least for the moment." The cardinal's remark was published in all the Boston newspapers, and in many beyond Boston.

Even so, the papers in September, 1949, picked up on the *Pilot* article. "Pope Assails Feeney Group—Censures St. Benedict's Center As Source of Discord and Revolt," headlined the *Boston Daily Record*. The *Boston Daily Globe* said: "Vatican Condemns Cambridge Center."

Of course the pope himself "assailed" no one. More ominous than that misrepresentation, however, was the way the *Globe's* story was written: "The Vatican has condemned the teachings of the St. Benedict Center, Cambridge, and has warned Rev. Leonard Feeney, S.J., four discharged Boston College professors and their followers at the Center that they remain outside the authority of the Catholic Church 'at the peril of their souls,' it was revealed last night." The line about "remaining outside the authority of the Catholic Church" made it sound as if everybody was excommunicated.

To be sure, Fr. Feeney put out a statement, and some papers quoted it: "It is reported by *The Pilot* in the letter from the Holy Office, which it partially quotes and partially composes, that 'the decisions set forth in this letter were approved by His Holiness, Pope Pius XII, *in an audience*' (Italics ours). St. Benedict Center still knows that it has had no answer on its doctrinal crusade and its appeal for an *ex cathedra pronouncement* from the Holy Father. IS THERE SALVATION OUTSIDE THE CATHOLIC CHURCH, or IS THERE NOT? If we have said something inconsistent with Catholic doctrine, we would like to know what it is from the Holy See and in clear, definite statement.

"The one unmistakable statement from the Holy Office that got through the censorship of *The Pilot* is the reaffirmation of the fact that the doctrine that there is no salvation outside the Church 'is an incontestable principle.' This is exactly the principle which Archbishop Cushing, Bishop

Wright and Boston College have contested, and the principle for which we have been suffering for a solid year. *The Pilot* advises us to 'return to the unity of the Church at the peril of our souls.' That we are outside the unity of the Church we deny."

The statement was a counter-attack, but its vigor did not prevent the *Worcester Telegram* from heading an article: "Vatican Rules Against Hub Dissidents; Holds No Salvation Outside Church Doctrine to Be False."

Sr. Catherine wrote of the *Telegram's* headline: "There it was, plain as day. The Vatican holds No Salvation Outside the Church to be a *false* doctrine. No one could deny that this was one wolf the shepherds had let into the sheepfold. That the *Worcester Telegram* should draw this conclusion is not surprising. It would have been surprising if someone had not drawn it."

Meantime, *The Boston Traveler*, in contradiction to the *Globe*, decided the center members were not outside the Church after all, but might soon be. Under the headline, "Church May Oust Priest, Four Others," it ran a UP dispatch from Vatican City. "An unimpeachable Vatican source said today that a Jesuit priest and four discharged Catholic college professors may be excommunicated if they persist in their 'obstinate ways.'...

"The source implied that Archbishop Richard J. Cushing of Boston would decide on the matter....

"'After they have been deprived of the sacraments, they may even be excommunicated. It is absolutely out of the question that the Pontiff will say anything after the action of Archbishop Cushing and the Sacred Congregation of the Holy Office. Now it is only a matter of procedure according to canon law. There is no further need for Vatican action because their Archbishop has full jurisdiction, authority and guidance.'"

Such was the line of the unnamed "Vatican source." Fr. Feeney immediately let it be known he was challenging it. Said the *New York Times* on Sunday, September 4, 1949: "Feeney Will Appeal To Vatican If Banned." The newspaper's article said, in part: "Commenting on a report that he faces possible excommunication, the Rev. Leonard Feeney said today that he would appeal any such action to the Pope in person.

"An unofficial Vatican source has been quoted as saying that Father Feeney and four of his adherents may be excommunicated if they persist in their 'obstinate' ways.

"Father Feeney, head of St. Benedict's Center in Cambridge, has not receded from his contention that there is no salvation outside the Catholic Church....

"His appeal to the Vatican would have 'the backing of thousands of Greater Boston Catholics who are ready to support me in an emergency,' Father Feeney said. He added that he was sure that the Pope would want to hear 'the true story' of the controversy, 'which has never been presented to him by Auxiliary Bishop John J. Wright and his political friends in Rome.'

"The noted Jesuit author and lecturer insisted that, even though excommunicated, 'I will never withdraw my allegiance to the holy Catholic faith or to the Holy Father.'"

On September 17, 1949, Fr. Feeney wrote to Cardinal Marchetti-Selvaggiani, Secretary of the Holy Office (the original was in Latin): "It is now being proclaimed everywhere in American newspapers, both secular and Catholic, that the Holy Office edited an official decree, signed by you, and approved by the Roman Pontiff, and partially quoted by the official newspaper of the diocese of Boston, *The Pilot*, in which decree it is announced that the dogma of the Church 'Outside the Church there is no salvation' we must now interpret according to the norms of American liberalism according to which salvation is bestowed on everyone on account of his own sincerity."

The cardinal did not respond to Fr. Feeney's letter, but there was a message from Rome. It came on August 21, 1950, in the form of Pope Pius XII's encyclical *Humani Generis*. Sr. Catherine writes about that day in her book, *Gate of Heaven*:

"The *New York Times* telephoned and asked for Father Feeney.

"'We have the translation of the Pope's encyclical, *Humani Generis*,' the *Times* man said,' and we have checked his pronouncement on no salvation outside the Church with the release you gave us when you were silenced. In that release you said theologians today are making the doctrines of the church absolutely meaningless. Did you know the Pope says the same thing in his new encylical? He says, "Some reduce to a meaningless formula the necessity of belonging to the True Church in order to gain salvation." Will you give us a statement?'

"The editions of the *New York Times* for the next day carried Father Feeney's statement, and newspapers all over the United States printed the United Press release of Father's story of his joy and relief—for the salvation of souls—at the Holy Father's confirmation of the Church's solemn doctrine."

M.I.C.M. Bro. Thomas Mary Sennott, in his book, *They Fought the Good Fight*, reports that he was present when the call from the *New York Times* came in. "It was Sister Catherine's birthday," he writes, "and when Father Feeney announced the news, there was wild cheering for several minutes. Father then made a little speech which began, 'Now that we've won, we don't want to lose our high ideals...' We all thought at the time that it was all over—little did we know."

How little will be seen. Before it is, it is worth noting, if only in passing, that on January 12, 1953, Pope Pius XII would name a number of new cardinals, including Archbishop James McIntyre of Los Angeles, the first shepherd of that see to be made a cardinal. With William O' Connell, Boston had a cardinal for decades, beginning with his elevation to the purple in 1911 and until his death in 1944, but Cushing was not made one—not by Pius. We have already seen that Richard Cushing had to wait until 1958 when it was John XXIII, the pope who convened Vatican Council II, who made him a cardinal. In other words, Pius may have given his consent to the Holy Office sending its letter of August, 1949, to Archbishop Cushing (though obviously not to its publication in the A.A.S. as an official act of the Apostolic See), but in a matter over which he had direct control, the distribution of red hats, he did not give one to Boston.

(Something else to be noted: Pius' cardinal, McIntyre, was the sole American prelate at Vatican II who did not sign the *Declaration on Religious Liberty.*)

We have said that publication of *Humani Generis* ended nothing for Fr. Feeney, St. Benedict Center and the Slaves of the Immaculate Heart of Mary. For one thing, without the kind of formal, *ex cathedra* definition for which Fr. Feeney longed, liberals felt able to interpret the pertinent passage of the encyclical as freely as they did the formula *extra ecclesiam nulla salus* itself, or to ignore it, as one day, following the lead of such as Cardinal Cushing, they would ignore *all* of *Humanae Vitae*. Alas, the liberals were not confined to these shores. From Rome herself, if not from Pius XII, would emanate language leaving open, or opening again, the doctrinal question that we may suppose (as they supposed at the center) the pope believed he had closed. Very notably, the Vatican II document, *Lumen Gentium*, would contain language which must be read very carefully. On a following page we shall want to read it for ourselves, but with some guidance. It is fitting to observe at this juncture, however, that *Lumen Gentium* references "Letter of the Holy Office to the Archbishop of Boston" in a footnote.

It was on October 10, 1949, a little more than a month after portions of the "Letter" were published by *The Pilot*, that Fr. Feeney and St. Benedict Center were struck their next hard blow. It was especially the priest who was hit, for that October 10 he was expelled from the Society of Jesus. The letter notifying him of his expulsion and signed by John Baptist Jenssens, General of the Society, is preserved in the St. Benedict Center Archives in Still River. The operative parts of it read (translated from the Latin):

"Fr. Leonard Feeney, solemnly professed and a member of the New England Province of the Society of Jesus, received an order under Holy Obedience on the 21st day of April 1949 from the Superior of his Province which was given in the city of Cambridge, Massachusetts (U.S.A.) where he was residing, that he proceed within twenty-four hours to the College of the Holy Cross in Worcester...

"Considering the obstinacy involved the following questions officially proposed must be answered by this final sentence:

"1. Whether it is certain that there is a crime of serious and permanent

143

disobedience, after virtually three warnings in this case.

"2) Whether the failure of amendment is certain.

"3) Whether Fr. Leonard Feeney should be dismissed from the Society of Jesus...

"To the first AFFIRMATIVE...

"To the second AFFIRMATIVE...

"To the third AFFIRMATIVE...

"Wherefore by the authority which the Sacred Canons give us, we declare Fr. Leonard Feeney dismissed from the Society of Jesus."

Of course his expulsion was really inevitable from the day Fr. Feeney met with his old teacher, Fr. McCormick, and of course his preaching *extra ecclesiam nulla salus* was really behind it, but it has to be underlined that when the action finally was taken the Jesuits seized on a disciplinary matter, his remaining at St. Benedict Center instead of going to Holy Cross. He was not officially expelled from the Society for doctrinal reasons, no more than the Jesuits or other Church authorities ever granted him a hearing on doctrine. That last point has already often been made in these pages, but it must be reiterated. Simply nobody in authority wanted to talk with Fr. Feeney about doctrine. More precisely, nobody in authority wanted to have to answer him when he made his case, so he was never given the opportunity to make it. That is the only logical conclusion to be drawn from the steadfast refusal of the Jesuits and others to give him a doctrinal hearing.

Years after Fr. Feeney was expelled from the Jesuits, Frank Sheed, who published some of the priest's books and who was his friend (though no champion of *extra ecclesiam nulla salus*) wrote in his autobiography, *The Church and I*, about there not being a hearing.

"He was condemned but not answered," said Sheed. "When Boniface VIII said in the bull *Unam Sanctam* that it was' altogether necessary for salvation for every human creature to be subject to the Roman Pontiff,' he seemed to be saying not only what Father Feeney was condemned for saying, but what a vast number of yesterday's Catholics had grown up believing. Everybody would have been helped by a full-length discussion."

On September 4, 1952, on which day Archbishop Cushing wrote a letter to Fr. Feeney and had it delivered to him, it became clearer that there would be no discussion. It should be mentioned that even before then, and in addition to Fr. Feeney' s appearances on the Common, the production of *The Point*, the continuation of some classes at the center school and the development of the religious life of the M.I.C.M. men and women, St. Benedict Center became embroiled in two legal cases. One involved the center's effort to have restored the financial support its veterans received under the G.I. Bill prior to the Commonwealth of Massachusetts' withdrawal of authorization of the center school. The case made it to the Supreme Court of Massachusetts and was there lost. In the other case, the

144

center was brought before Cambridge Criminal Court after a Cambridge woman filed a complaint charging that city safety and sanitation codes were being violated at Sacred Heart Hall, the house where Fr. Feeney lived, and also that the premises were used for religious services. The neighbors were becoming hostile to "Quaker Village."

As for the letter sent to Fr. Feeney by Archbishop Cushing on September 4, 1952, the short of it was that the prelate therein threatened to reduce the priest to the lay state. The threat came after Fr. Feeney was told to appear before the archbishop and "to make explicit profession of your submission to the local Ordinary and the Apostolic See." His Excellency said he was extending this "invitation" "by direction of the Supreme Sacred Congregation of the Holy Office, with the complete approval of His Holiness, Pope Pius XII," but he offered no evidence of that, such as enclosing a copy of the directive. Fr. Feeney was to appear "on or before" October 4. "If unfortunately, you should refuse to do so, the same Congreagtion, with the full approval of the Holy Father, has ordered me to tell you at this time that you will be reduced to the lay state."

The letter went on: "By direction of the same Sacred Congregation, again with the full approval of the Holy Father, you are also warned to desist immediately from your activities as leader of the St. Benedict Center movement, under threat of still graver punishments to be determined by the Sacred Congregation.

"The Holy Office, with the full approval of the Holy Father, has placed St. Benedict Center under local interdict and yourself under personal interdict. The local interdict applies to all properties owned and controlled by St. Benedict or its members. As you know, it forbids 'divine office, or sacred rite,' for example, the celebration of Mass, administration of the Sacraments, preaching, etc. These interdicts are in force immediately, but their existence will not be published at the present time. I am praying and hoping that you will submit voluntarily to the wishes of the Sacred Congregation and of the Holy Father. If you do not do so, however, it will be necessary to publish these interdicts, after October 4th, 1952."

The letter continued with the archbishop's announcement that he would soon publish, again supposedly at the direction of the Holy Office and with the pope's approval, the full text of the letter sent to him on August 8, 1949, by Cardinal Marchetti-Selvaggiani.

Archbishop Cushing concluded by saying the Holy Office had "ordered the withdrawal from circulation of the book *Gate of Heaven*."

More likely, the archbishop himself was ordering the withdrawal since the book, Sr. Catherine's defense of the doctrinal position of St. Benedict Center, had only recently been published. No competent authority in Rome would yet have had time to examine it. (To the present writer's thinking, *Gate of Heaven*, written for the understanding of ordinary readers, is the clearest and best exposition of the center's stand so far to see print. After it could not be sold in bookstores around Cambridge and Boston, it would reach most of its audience when M.I.C.M. religious began selling it and other literature.)

The full text of "Letter of the Holy Office to the Archbishop of Boston" was published in *The Pilot* on September 6, 1952. Again, the ambiguous document never was published in the *Acta Apostolicae Sedis*. In light of its own declaration that *extra ecclesiam nulla salus* was "an incontestable principle," there were two paragraphs of the "Letter" that Fr. Feeney found especially objectionable. In time, we shall look at them, along with the related passages that appear in Vatican II's *Lumen Gentium* and also Raymond Karam's article, "Reply to a Liberal"

For now, we need to consider an appeal—another and most solemn one—that was sent on September 24, 1952, by "The Slaves of the Immaculate Heart of Mary of Saint Benedict Center in the Archdiocese of Boston to: The Sovereign Pontiff, Pius XII, Gloriously Reigning over the Universal Church." The appeal was entitled: "Notification to Your Holiness in the External Forum of the Existence of the Disability of Excommunication for Heresy Incurred by Richard Cushing, Archbishop of Boston, Under the Provisions of Canon 2314 of the Sacred Code of Canon Law and Petition for Further Relief Against the Same."

The appeal, replete with newspaper clippings and citations from Canon Law, was very long. It is here presented much shortened. As we read it, there is a scene to have before our mind's eye. It is of something that happened on September 26, two days after the appeal's dispatch to Rome. That was when twenty-five center men drove from Boston to Washington, D.C., in four cars and confronted the apostolic delegate of the day, Archbishop Amleto Cicognani, in his office on Massachusetts Avenue.

"Confronted" is the only word. The men had been told by underlings of the archbishop that they needed an appointment, that His Excellency was busy, and even that he had just left. A group of them went upstairs and into His Excellency's office anyway. Italian and diplomat that he was, the archbishop seems to have handled the situation with considerable grace.

Hugh MacIsaac, a big, burly man who became one of Fr. Feeney's unofficial M.I.C.M. bodyguards on the Sunday afternoons in Boston Common, blurted out that Archbishop Cushing was threatening to reduce Fr. Feeney to the lay state and that he said he was taking his instructions from Archbishop Cicognani.

"Did he say that?" the prelate asked. (Any instructions to Cushing from the Holy Office or anyone in Rome would routinely reach Boston via the apostolic delegate.)

One of the M.I.C.M. brothers asked another question. "Is Fr. Feeney excommunicated?" It was a fair question given the tone and substance of

Archbishop Cushing's September 4 letter.

The answer came back unequivocally. "No."

After some further exchange, the center men left peacefully and began the long drive back to New England.

The scene in Washington described, here is the edited text of the center's appeal to Pius XII wherein Archbishop Cushing is charged with heresy:

"On April 18, 1949, Richard Cushing, Archbishop of Boston, without previous notice or hearing, and through the public press, issued a decree suspending Father Leonard Feeney by depriving him of his right to exercise his priestly faculties in the Archdiocese of Boston and censuring the members of Saint Benedict Center by depriving them of the Sacraments of Penance and Holy Eucharist. Later, by oral order of the Chancellor, Msgr. Walter J. Furlong, in a telephone conversation, the scope of the decree was extended to include the Sacrament of Matrimony. By its own terms, the decree stated that the censures which it imposed were for grave offenses against the Catholic Church. The issuance of this decree was the direct result of the public defense made by the Reverend Leonard Feeney of four professors who were discharged from Boston College, a Catholic institution in the Archdiocese of Boston conducted by the Society of Jesus, for holding and teaching that there can be no salvation outside the Catholic Church. For the holding and teaching of this doctrine these professors were accused by the rector of that institution, Rev. William Lane Keleher, S.J. of disseminating ideas which lead to 'bigotry and intolerance.'

"Although all the parties affected thereby have questioned the canonical validity of this decree, they have since observed its provisions in order to avoid public scandal to the extent that they have been able to do so without compromising the doctrines of the Faith....

"This action of the Archbishop in the midst of a controversy concerning the doctrine that 'there is no salvation outside the Catholic Church' has had the substantial effect of denying and calling into doubt this doctrine and has been the direct occasion of propagating and disseminating heresy. On several occasions it has been stated in the press; and consequently, the impression has been created in the public mind that the Archbishop of Boston holds that there can be salvation outside the Catholic Church. The said Richard Cushing, Archbishop of Boston, has never taken any action to dispel such an impression. His failure to do so in a matter that is the subject of public controversy on a doctrine of the Faith indicated his assent to the doctrinal holdings attributed to him....

"On August 8, 1949, the Supreme Congregation of the Holy Office issued a document which is Protocol No. 122/49 of that Congregation [this is a reference to "Letter of the Holy Office to the Archbishop of Boston"]. This Protocol is substantially defective in that it contains heresy insofar as it states that one can be saved under certain conditions outside the Roman Catholic Church and without personal submission to the Roman Pontiff. It is formally defective in that it was never published in the *Acta Apostolicae Sedis* and consequently is without any binding effect as an Act of the Holy See. This Protocol, which contained heresy, was published in part in the *Pilot*, the official organ of the Archdiocese of Boston on September 3, 1949. On September 6, 1952, the full text of the same Protocol was published in the aforementioned *Boston Pilot* at the direction of the said Richard Cushing, Archbishop of Boston, who signed his name to the published letter authorizing the publication of the Protocol....

"For the aforementioned publication of the said Protocol No. 122/49 of the Supreme Congregation of the Holy Office which heretically states that under certain conditions one can be saved outside the Catholic Church and without submission to the Roman Pontiff and for the consequent dissemination of its substance throughout the secular and Catholic press of the United States of America with disastrous consequences to the integrity of the Faith and the salvation of souls, we accuse the said Richard Cushing, Archbishop of Boston, of the crime of heresy as defined by Canon 1325 of the Sacred Code of Canon Law....

"The order of September 4, 1952 of the said Richard Cushing, Archbishop of Boston, exacts compliance on the part of the Reverend Leonard Feeney under the threat of reducing him to the 'lay state.' The purpose of such threat is to create in the public mind the impression that the sublime dignity of the priesthood does not have the indelible character of a sacrament but is a simple office that can be given or taken away. Such contemplated action is explicitly forbidden under the penalties for heresy by a decree of the Holy Council of Trent....

"(Canon 4. 'If anyone shall say that through this sacred order the Holy Spirit is not given, and that therefore in vain do the bishops say "receive the Holy Spirit;" or that through it a character is not impressed or that he, who was once a priest, can again be made a layman, let him be anathema.')

"In this dark hour when the plague of heresy has paralyzed the very government of the Church, we the members of Saint Benedict Center have consecrated ourselves to the religious life as the Slaves of the Immaculate Heart of Mary for our own sanctification and for the preservation and propagation of the Faith. We place our little religious community under the personal protection of Your Holiness and we pray that the Immaculate Mother of God, the Destroyer of All Heresy, will give you the courage to grant us relief against the heretical bishop who rules the Church of Boston."

Again, it is difficult to know at this remove in time the extent to which it was seriously believed at St. Benedict Center that "relief" would or could be obtained by such an appeal. It is true that in the summer of 1993, the Congregation for the Doctrine of the Faith (as the former Holy

Office is now known) declared null and void a decree of excommunication promulgated by Honolulu's Bishop Joseph Ferrario against six Hawaii Catholics for the ostensible reason that they worshipped at Masses celebrated by priests belonging to the Society of St. Pius X, the religious association founded by Archbishop Marcel Lefebvre. However, it is a rare occurrence, even in better times than these, when Rome reverses the action of a local ordinary or takes the part of someone against whom he is acting. The presumption is usually, if not always, in the bishop's favor. Moreover, in the instance of the center's appeal, the bishop in question was actually being accused by them of heresy!

(In the Hawaii case, there was reason to believe that Bishop Ferrario had come under a cloud in Rome's eyes, and in fact he soon resigned, announcing that it was for "reasons of health." The case was also interesting inasmuch as evidence eventually emerged of collusion between Ferrario and Archbishop Cacciavillan, the pro-nuncio in Washington. That was to the degree that the archbishop had implied in an official letter that the six should be placed under interdict by Ferrario even if they were not truly excommunicated. The decree of the Congregation in favor of the six said nothing like that, and the archbishop was finally obliged to admit to one of them that what he had written "was simply intended as a reflection and suggestion to the Bishop.")

We could speculate today as to whether there was ever positive collusion between Archbishops Cicognani and Cushing or between the latter and parties in Rome other than Pius XII, but after nearly five decades, and especially with relevant files still being kept sealed, there is no way of ascertaining it for sure. As will be seen presently, Fr. Feeney at one point did raise the question of whether some purportedly official communications from Rome were in fact forged.

In any event, Fr. Feeney, being himself a cleric, must have known that the odds of obtaining "relief" were not great. If he may have hoped against hope in 1949, by September, 1952, he surely could not anymore. Equally surely, he must have communicated this at least to Sr. Catherine. It seems likely, therefore, that the appeal of September, 1952, and other documents subsequently produced at the center and sent to Rome, formed part of a center strategy to put their position on record against some future day when their cause, if never Fr. Feeney himself in his lifetime, might win a hearing. In a word, the center people were maneuvering as best they could.

They had not much room for it, nor much time. As soon as October 25, a mere month after the center sent its appeal to Pius, Fr. Feeney was summoned to Rome for a "hearing." This was not to be a hearing in the sense of one that the embattled priest sought all along. This was to be a hearing in the sense of a trial, as when we speak of somebody having to appear before Judge So-and-So for a hearing.

Something else to be borne in mind when we read letters like the following one from Giuseppi Cardinal Pizzardo, Cardinal Marchetti-Selvaggiani's successor as secretary of the Holy Office, is that the government of the Church is an absolute monarchy (the only one left in ex-Christendom). Accordingly, all acts of the Apostolic See are performed in the pope's name and he is ritualistically invoked even as in Great Britain, whose monarchy is not absolute, acts of the British government are performed in the name of the queen. Indeed, the government is called Her Majesty's Government, and official documents employ formulas like, "By the grace of Her Majesty the Queen," without Elizabeth II being the least directly involved in the government's doing.

When it comes to the pope, you may write him, but without the letter ever reaching his desk or even that of one of his private secretaries, it will be shunted off to the Secretariat of State. If you receive an answer, and you usually will, the functionary who signs it will tell you that His Holiness imparts his Apostolic Blessing, though the pope has no idea you ever wrote. This is here being explained because we simply can have no idea of the degree to which Pius XII may have personally interested himself in the so-called Boston Heresy Case. Cardinal Wright would tell a story about the pontiff's direct involvement, as will be seen, but Pius was dead when he told it and, as he related it, there was no one else in the room besides himself to witness what was done. Anyone who knew Cardinal Wright can testify that he was a tremendous story-teller.

Whatever the case, when Cardinal Pizzardo wrote to Fr. Feeney on October 25, 1952, it was in these terms: "The Supreme Sacred Congregation of the Holy Office has been obliged repeatedly to make your teaching and conduct in the Church the object of its special care and attention, and recently, after having again carefully examined and calmly weighed all the evidence collected in your cause, it has found it necessary to bring this question to a conclusion.

"However, His Holiness, Pope Pius XII, in His tender regard and paternal solicitude for the eternal welfare of souls committed to His supreme charge, has decreed that, before any other measure be carried into effect, you be summoned to Rome for a hearing. Therefore, in accordance with the express bidding and by the special authority of the Supreme Pontiff, you are hereby ordered to proceed to Rome forthwith and there to appear before the Authorities of the Supreme Sacred Congregation of the Holy Office as soon as possible."

Although no brother cleric felt able to defend Fr. Feeney in a public way after he came under Archbishop Cushing's censure, M.I.C.M. religious relate today that numerous of them went to the priest privately to encourage him and to express agreement with his doctrinal stand. They came "like Nicodemus in the night," the religious say, referring to the one member of the Sanhedrin who was not against Jesus. One or more of these clerics may have been expert in Canon Law. We already know that Fr.

Feeney had the advice of a canonist in the matter of safeguarding his faculty to hear confessions. Therefore, it is almost certain that he had advice when he replied to Cardinal Pizzardo on October 30, as surely as he also had it on other occasions. The language of this letter, like others, is too lawyerly for Leonard Feeney, published poet and literary essayist.

"I have just received a letter from the Holy Office, written in English and signed with Your Eminence's name. It is dated October 25, 1952. This is the first official notification I have received of the existence of a cause, judicially cognizable, in which I am an interested party. Your letter not only informs me that such a cause exists but also that there is to be a hearing for its disposition. A hearing or trial presupposes some formal complaint or accusation which serves as a legal basis for the proceedings and which also informs the accused of the charge against him so that he can prepare to defend himself. Before I can participate in a trial I would like to know with more adequate particularity what I am to be tried for."

There is another paragraph in which Fr. Feeney makes reference to the appeal sent to Pope Pius the month before. Clearly, he wondered what had happened to it.

He was not told in the next letter sent him by Cardinal Pizzardo. It was written on November 22. In this short and very stiff note, His Eminence speaks of the priest "evading the issue," an assertion that can seem baffling only under the assumption that authorities intended to do something other than totally, once-and-for-good silence Fr. Feeney. After all, the priest had written on October 30 to find out exactly what was the "issue," not to evade it.

The complete text of Cardinal Pizzardo's second letter: "Your letter of the 30th October clearly shows that you are evading the issue, instead of obeying promptly the order which was given you in the name of His Holiness, as was clearly expressed in my letter of the 25th of October.

"You are to come to Rome immediately where you will be informed of the charges lodged against you.

"I wish to inform you that if you do not present yourself at the Congregation of the Holy Office before the 31st December this act of disobedience will be made public together with the canonical penalties."

There was a postscript: "The Apostolic Delegate has been authorised to provide for the expenses of your journey."

It is probable that after receipt of Cardinal Pizzardo's second letter, Fr. Feeney felt himself in something of a quandary. Whatever he may have thought about the cardinal's orthodoxy, he certainly recognized the prelate's authority. He simply would have ignored the summons, were it otherwise. Instead, he wrote to Rome again, and again probably with the the advice of a canonist. But to what degree did he consider complying with the summons? Any at all? Was consideration given to sending an emissary in an effort to ascertain what charges were being lodged against him and to show that Cardinal Pizzardo's authority was recognized? Bro. Francis says he urged Fr. Feeney to go to Rome. Other M.I.C.M. religious who were on the scene in 1952 think the priest might have made the trip save for Sr. Catherine urging the contrary, and in his book *They Fought the Good Fight*, Bro. Thomas Mary Sennot offers the opinion that an emissary should have been sent. He does not say if that was actually considered at the time. On the other hand, he went into print with the flat-out statement, "Father Feeney himself did want to go to Rome, but was prevented by some of his more over-protective disciples."

Be that the case or not, the priest's next letter to Cardinal Pizzardo was written on December 2, 1952. "Your Eminence seems to have misconstrued my motives in replying to your letter of October 25, 1952," he begins. "I had presumed that your first letter was to serve as a canonical citation to appear before your Sacred Tribunal. As a citation, however, it is fatally defective under the norms of Canon 1715 especially in that it did not inform me of the charges against me. This canon requires that the citation contain at least a general statement of the charges. Under the norms of Canon 1723 any proceedings based on a citation so substantially defective are subject to a complaint of nullity.

"While under Canon 1555 the Supreme Sacred Congregation of the Holy Office may judge causes according to its own proper custom, I do not think that these customs dispense with the substantial requirements of justice of the 'Ius Communale' of the Church. In this way the law of the Church gives effect to the Apostolic injunction that no priest shall be condemned except by the universally accepted modes of judicial proceedings.

"'Against a priest receive not an accusation, but under two or three witnesses...Then that sin reprove before all; that the rest may have fear.' (1 Tim. 5:19-20.)

"This text gives Scriptural authority to the establishment of the external forum for the purpose of judging causes according to the basic requirements of justice for the conduct of legal proceedings. See Bellarmine, *De Romano Pontifice*, Liber Quartus, Caput XVI: 'Probatur testimonis verbi Dei posse pontifices veras leges condere.'

"I am concerned at the suggestion in Your Eminence's letter of the imposition of vindictive penalties without the formalities of a trial. Canon 1959 would seem to prevent this. I can see no grounds for proceedings against me 'ex informata conscienta.' My offense, if any, is not occult. On the contrary, it is a notorious public fact that I am in the anomalous position of being under censure for holding and teaching the Catholic doctrine that there can be no salvation outside the Catholic Church, nor without submission to Our Holy Father, the Pope.

"I am at a loss to understand why Your Eminence should threaten me with the penalties for contumely when there is no indication of it on my part. I have no intention of being contumacious of the authority of your most Sacred Tribunal. The questions, however, which I have raised in this letter, and in my previous one, are legitimate under Canons 1842 and 1843 These questions are: 1) What are the charges against me; and 2) What is the nature of the proceedings to which I have been summoned? Under Canon 1715 a description of the charges and the nature of the proceedings should be in the citation, for its validity.

"I am also unfamiliar with the procedures proper to the Holy Office under Canon 1555. Since such procedures are to govern the conduct of the proceedings, I would like to have them made available to me so that I can familiarize myself with them in order to protect my rights under them. I would also like to know whether in this instance under Canon 247, your Supreme Sacred Congregation is acting as a court of the first instance or as a court of appeal from the actions of the Archbishop of Boston. Your Eminence must admit that proceedings before your Supreme Sacred Tribunal, whether original or appellate, even by special provision of the Code, are so extraordinary in their nature that neither a priest nor a canonist can be expected to have a ready familiarity with them.

"There is also the question as to whether, for the sake of convenience, the jurisdiction of your Supreme Tribunal can be exercised by either a delegated tribunal or by delegated judges in this country. Furthermore, since the issue of orthodoxy is immediately involved, it is also possible that questions of recusation might be raised."

Fr. Feeney moved on in his letter to speak of the religious association, the Slaves of the Immaculate Heart of Mary, which by now had nearly 100 members. "The rumor has falsely and maliciously been circulated and countenanced by ecclesiastical authorities, that I and the members of my Congregation are excommunicated and are no longer members of the Catholic Church. My spiritual children suffer this because they hold and preach that there is no salvation outside the Catholic Church, nor without personal submission to our Holy Father, the Pope.

"Because I am immediately responsible in such extraordinary circumstances for their spiritual welfare, I am reluctant to leave the country readily, if other provisions are either feasible or convenient under Canon 1555 as proper to the Holy Office. I fear for my spiritual children lest my absence from the country be seized on by my enemies as an opportunity to persecute them still further:

"'I will strike the shepherd, and the sheep shall be dispersed.' (Mark 14:27.)

"The extraordinary situation in which I and my spiritual children find ourselves has been brought to the attention of the Sovereign Pontiff, in accordance with the provisions of Canon 218. This was done informally in a letter to His Holiness, dated May 28, 1949, and formally by a document, dated on the Feast of Our Lady of Ransom, September 24, 1952. This latter document was called to Your Eminence's attention in my letter to you of October 30, 1952.

"The document of the Feast of our Lady of Ransom was a petition to His Holiness that he give us the protections in this situation which are ours as of right under Canon 2232. A copy of the document was also transmitted to the Cardinal Archbishop of New York. [That was Francis Cardinal Spellman, known to be no great friend of Archbishop Cushing.]

"The state of the Faith existing in the Archdiocese of Boston as recounted in this document is most grave. For example, it has even reached the point where, in a predominantly Catholic city, a heretical minister, on the occasion of the definition of the Assumption of the Most Blessed Virgin Mary [November 1, 1950], publicly attacked her virginity by a paid advertisement in every secular newspaper in the city, without any public protest by either the ordinary or the clergy. I am the only priest in the Archdiocese of Boston who has attempted to remedy this situation by my public utterances and by proper recourse to the Holy See.

"Because of the direct and indirect responsibility I have for the care of souls in this deplorable situation, which approximates conditions under which the See is embarrassed under Canon 429, I hope that some way can be found in which the necessary preliminary questions can be settled without imposing on me, and those dependent on my pastoral care, the unnecessary burden of my absence from the country."

A fair and unbiased reading of Fr. Feeney's letter must lead to the conclusion that he sought nothing unreasonable. He wanted information on three points that any Catholic in his position, lay or cleric, would want, and it was information to which he was entitled under provisions of Canon Law. 1) With what was he being charged? 2) What was to be the nature of the proceedings against him? 3) Was it possible that the proceedings could be conducted in the U.S., at least in their preliminary stage? It was reasonable for him to seek the information not simply because he was entitled to it by Canon Law and the rules of ordinary justice. Though he nowhere says it in so many words, if his case—whatever it consisted of—was sufficiently important for the Church's highest tribunal to be concerned, it ought to be important enough for that tribunal to take the time and make the effort to spell out what was going on. That is, it ought to be *if* justice was intended by the tribunal as well as sought by him.

Evidently it was not. The next communication from Rome, another (and last) letter from Cardinal Pizzardo, was dated January 3, 1953. It said: "In reply to your letter of the 2nd Dec. 1952 asking for further explanations, the Supreme Sacred Congregation of the Holy Office communicates to you herewith the orders received from His Holiness, that you are to present yourself to this Congregation before the 31st January 1953, under pain of excommunication incurred automatically (ipso facto.) in case of failure to present yourself on the date indicated. This decision of

His Holiness has been made after the arrival of the latest documents from St. Benedict Center."

There it was in black and white. The threat of excommunication. After it was no longer merely a threat Fr. Feeney would always contend, as his supporters still do, that he was never truly excommunicated, arguing that no one could be for professing a dogma of the Faith. The horror—that is what it must have seemed to the priest and everybody at St. Benedict Center—was that although his profession of *extra ecclesiam nulla salus* was the real reason Church officials were acting against him, when he was pronounced excommunicated it would be on account of his not going to Rome when summoned. In other words, by not going he would provide the officials with a pretext for acting against him. They would not have to pronounce him excommunicated, as they truly could not, for professing a dogma.

Doubtless the horror was made worse by the thought that too many ordinary Catholics, unaccustomed to questioning the actions of Church officials, would never understand or even listen to Fr. Feeney's argument that no one could be excommunicated for professing a dogma. They would see him as cast out of the Church, and cast out exactly because of his profession of *extra ecclesiam nulla salus*. The press would help make it seem so, and as far as the thinking of these ordinary Catholics would go, the dogma professed by Fr. Feeney was evidently changed or abandoned. Fr. Feeney and the Slaves of the Immaculate Heart of Mary would spend the coming years trying to correct this misapprehension, but that effort lay in the future. For now, Fr. Feeney decided he would not accept "excommunication" quietly and without protest. He wrote one last time to Cardinal Pizzardo. It was on January 13, 1953, and he took the occasion to make some charges of his own—serious ones. Why not? What was there to lose now? A felt need to put things on record is also obvious.

"I have received your letter of January 3, 1953. I have been in communication with your Eminence since October 25, 1952. I was under the impression that all bona fide communications from your most Sacred Tribunal, acting as the Inquisitors-General of the Holy Roman Church, were protected by the 'secrecy of the Holy Office,' which, if violated, is punishable by the penalty of automatic excommunication—absolution from which is reserved to the Sovereign Pontiff. It is most irregular that the substance of your communications to me was divulged both publicly and privately on several different occasions by several persons.

"These instances are as follows:

"1) On Sunday, November 16, 1952, a Mrs. Weiler of Boston, Massachusetts, in collaboration with a Mr. and Mrs. Joseph Uberti of Waltham, Massachusetts, called out to me, 'Why don't you go to Rome as they have asked you to? They'll give you the money now.'

"2) On Sunday, November 23, 1952, this same person, under identical circumstances, again called to me, 'Why don't you go to Rome as they have asked you to? They will give you the money now.'

"3) On Wednesday, January 7, 1953, the Very Reverend William E. Fitzgerald, the Provincial of the New England Province of the Society of Jesus, asked my brother, the Reverend Thomas B. Feeney, S.J., why I didn't go to Rome as ordered by the Holy Office. He further said, 'All these delays, excuses and subterfuges with which he is carrying on are a scandal.'

"4) On Thursday, January 8, 1953, George Croft, a reporter for the *Boston Globe*, a secular newspaper, came to Saint Benedict Center, on instructions from his paper, to seek out information on a story that 'Father Feeney was to go to Rome.' Mr. Croft said that he had been sent by his superior, Mr. William R. Callahan, who is the Catholic religious editor of the *Boston Globe*.

"5) On Friday, January 9, both Mr. Callahan and Mr. Haviland, the Managing Editor of the *Boston Globe*, confirmed the report that they had received information to the effect that Father Feeney was to go to Rome.

"Such divulgence of my communications with the Holy Office, together with your threat to publicize my failure to be in Rome, whether or not such failure is justified, indicates that our correspondence is not subject to the 'secrecy of the Holy Office.' It further indicates that your purpose is not to inflict spiritual penalties for any crime of which I might be found guilty, but to intimidate me by threats of 'smearing' in the public press. This is an unconscionable use of documents of the Holy See for the purposes of intimidation, for which you, under the provisions of Canon 2333, incur the same penalty with which you threaten me—automatic excommunication.

"Your letter of January 3, 1953, states that if I do not appear in Rome on or before January 31, 1953, I incur *automatic excommunication* (excommunication *ipso facto*). The most diligent search of the Sacred Canons fails to indicate any authority for this, and your letter is equally obscure on this point. Once more your letter threatens the imposition of a penalty without stating the crime for which it is imposed, in violation of Canon 2225.

"I hope that you are not implying that my repeated efforts to determine this controversy were in bad faith. My correspondence with you will stand in the archives of the Church, and before the whole Catholic world, to show that I have been firm in my respect for ecclesiastical authority, as well as adamant in my refusal to compromise the Sacred Dogma of our Faith, that there is No Salvation Outside the Catholic Church, nor without personal submission to the Pope. Your threat to impose penalties without either accusations or proceedings, as required by the Sacred Canons and the *ius communale* of the Church, is outrageous and barbarous.

"You know as well as I do that the action which you threaten is subject to the Complaint of Nullity under Canon 1680. The Cardinals of the Supreme Sacred Congregation of the Holy Office, as the Inquisitors-General of the Holy Roman Church, are bound by the decree which Fourth Lateran or Twelfth Ecumenical Council applies to all proceedings before inquisitors.

"'The accused shall be informed of the charges preferred against him, that an opportunity may be given him of defending himself. His accusers shall be made known to him, and he himself shall have a hearing before his judges.'

"The fact that the Sacred Code makes provision for the excommunication of those who would forge or tamper with documents of the Holy See (Canon 2360) indicates that it is a practice that is not beyond the realm of possibility. [Numerous historians have believed that Galileo was condemned in 1633 on the strength of a document earlier forged and placed in the Vatican archive by a hostile curial official.] This suspicion is further confirmed by the fact that one of your previous letters on this controversy (Protocol 122/49) has been disseminated as a doctrinal pronouncement of the Holy See and it was never published in the *Acta Apostolicae Sedis*. ["Letter of the Holy Office to the Archbishop of Boston" did not come from Cardinal Pizzardo, of course, but purported to come from the Holy Office and the signature it bore was supposedly that of Cardinal Marchetti-Selvaggianni.]

"I want to again protest Protocol Letter 122/49 of August 8, 1949, to the Archbishop of Boston. *This heretical letter says that there can be salvation outside the Catholic Church.* There has been a diabolical plan to convey to the minds of the people that this protocol Letter of the Holy Office is, in effect, an infallible pronouncement of the Pope *ex certa scientia, motu proprio*, presuming to abrogate the 'Solemn judgment of the Church,' as expressed in the following infallible pronouncements:

"1) The Decree of the Jacobites, of the Council of Florence;

"2) The Decree against the Albigenses, of the Fourth Lateran Council;

"3) The Bull, *Unam Sanctam*.

"All of these pronouncements have infallibly declared that there is No Salvation Outside the Catholic Church, nor without personal submission to the Pope.

"This pernicious Protocol Letter has been circulated throughout both the secular and Catholic press of the United States of America as the doctrine of the Church. What is more deplorable is that there are provable instances where Catholics have been threatened with ecclesiastical penalties for not assenting to the heretical contents of this letter.

"I very seriously question both the good faith and the validity of any attempt to excommunicate me because I dared to call the substance of this decree to your attention, and because I dared to insist on my rights under it

157

in both my letters of October 30 and December 2, 1952."

On February 13, 1953, a month to the day after the above letter was written, Fr. Feeney was "excommunicated." A decree declaring it appeared on page 100 of the *Acta Apostolicae Sedis* for February 16. It said (translated from the Latin): "Since the priest Leonard Feeney, a resident of Boston (Saint Benedict Center), who for a long time has been suspended from his priestly duties on account of grave disobedience of Church Authority, being unmoved by repeated warnings and threats of incurring excommunication ipso facto, has not submitted, the Most Eminent and Reverend Fathers, charged with safeguarding matters of faith and morals, in a Plenary Session held on Wednesday 4 February 1953, declared him excommunicated with all the effects of the law.

"On Thursday, 12 February 1953, Our Most Holy Lord Pius XII, by Divine Providence Pope, approved and confirmed the decree of the Most Eminent Fathers, and ordered that it be made a matter of public law.

"Given at Rome, at the Headquarters of the Holy Office, 13 February 1953."

The first most striking feature of the document as it appeared in the AAS is that it bore the signature of no "Eminent Father." Cardinal Pizzardo did not sign it. Much less did the pope. The only signature is that of Marius Crovini, Notary. According to canonists expert in Vatican procedure, no other was technically necessary. It remains that the absence of a signature of someone with weightier authority than a notary is almost as striking as another feature of the document: It lacked the seal of the Holy Office. In fact, it bore no seal at all. This is striking insofar as the purpose of a seal is to attest to the genuineness of a document and its contents. Indubitably, pubication of the decree in the *AAS* gave it an official character. One still has the sense that parties within the Church may have wanted to be able in 1953 *to say* that Fr. Feeney was excommunicated, but things might be left a bit vague, a little irregularity might be in order, in case it someday proved desirable to be able to say, well, he was not excommunicated after all. And how could he be? As long as he upheld Church teaching it could not be for doctrinal reasons, which is exactly why none were cited. As for disobedience as the grounds, they might be cited, but the lack of due process—all the irregularities cited by Fr. Feeney in his correspondence to the Vatican—made them (and thus the "excommunication" itself) dubious, to say the least. In any event, the question of Fr. Feeney's "excommunication" would become legally moot in 1972 when he was "reconciled."

That does not mean the decree, such as it was, lacked effect. As far as the world was concerned, Leonard Feeney had been excommunicated. Indeed, much of the public mistakenly supposed that since Archbishop Cushing's interdict and the partial publication in *The Pilot* of "Letter of the Holy Office to the Archbishop of Boston" back in 1949, thanks mainly to the way the developments were covered by the press. No doubt that helps explain why coverage of the "excommunication," when it finally came, was not nearly as extensive or given as prominent play as the reporting on the earlier developments. It was not needed, the more so since Fr. Feeney's preaching on Boston Common had also by now made him the "hate priest." A majority saw Feeney and the "Feeneyites" in the Outer Pale. So much was that the case, in his 1978 book, *Seven American Catholics*, author John Deedy, no friend of Fr. Feeney, characterized the "excommunication" as "over-kill."

We saw Fr. Feeney in his last letter to Cardinal Pizzardo raise the possibility of the forgery of "Letter of the Holy Office to the Archbishop of Boston". M.I.C.M. religious relate that the priest wondered whether other documents received from Rome might be forged. Also, he seems to suggest the possibility in his letter to Cardinal Pizzardo of October 30, 1952. If the suspicion of forgery existed in his mind it was because the letters received in Boston did not always bear a seal, their language was sometimes surprisingly informal, and they were written in Engish, instead of Latin. (The latter is still the official language of the Church, but forty years ago its use was more common than today, at least in Rome and elsewhere in Europe, Latin America and Asia, if not in the Church in the U.S.)

Forgery would explain a number of anomalies, especially as regards the "Letter of the Holy Office to the Archbishop of Boston" never being published in the *Acta Apostolicae Sedis*. That is, it would explain them at least as well as the reason conjectured earlier in these pages. Perhaps it will be remembered, however, that we said Cardinal Wright had a story to tell after Pope Pius XII was dead. The story was about the "Letter". It was told in an article His Eminence wrote about his personal memories of Pius. (The pope died in 1958.) The article originally appeared in the English-language edition of the Vatican's newspaper, *L' Osservatore Romano*, in March, 1976. Not surprisingly, given the story Wright told in it, the piece was reprinted in *The Pilot* that same month. The mass-circulation *Reader's Digest* also picked it up. The passage of the article which interests us:

"It was suggested that I should make a trip to Rome to answer certain questions about the movement [i.e. St. Benedict Center and the Slaves of the Immaculate Heart of Mary] in the mind of the astonished Supreme Pontiff. The 'Boston Heresy' was inevitably condemned by the then Holy Office over the signature of Cardinal Marchetti-Selvaggiani, but the Pope personally wished to supervise and, indeed, *make* the official English translation which would be sent to the Archbishop of Boston for promulgation in the battle zone. As a result I spent three hours one sunny morning in the Holy Father's study at Castelgandolfo while he personally, with infinite care, reviewed and revised a document which would mean so much to the peace of mind of thousands.

"I shall never forget how painstaking, precise and scholarly was the Chief Shepherd of Christendom as he labored on a document designed to restore peace to a relatively small corner of the Christian world.... When the work of translation was done to his satisfaction he read it through with great silence and, again, great solicitude. I remember that he closed his eyes as if in prayer when he had finished the reading of the English version and then with a gesture of finality, he put it to one side."

We shall not here consider the real likelihood of Pius spending three hours with a junior auxiliary bishop personally working on a problem involving (to use Wright's own words) "a relatively small corner of the Christian world." After all, in 1949 the Communists in China, where there were more Catholics than in the Republic of Ireland today, were on the verge of winning a bloody civil war, and the Church in that land would face certain persecution when they did. In Argentina, the most Catholic nation in Spanish America, tensions were building between the Church and the government of General Juan Peron. In Hungary, Cardinal Mindszenty was in prison. So was Cardinal Stepinac in Yugoslavia. Cardinal Wyszynski soon would be in Poland. In Italy itself, Communism was such a threat that in that very year, 1949, Pius was obliged to decree that anyone joining the Party or voting for its candidates was subject to excommunication. With all that and more on his plate, we are to believe the pope, solicitous of souls as he may have been, spent three hours on the "Boston Heresy," which thing, though Wright characterizes it invidiously, was simply a priest and a hundred others militantly upholding the dogma *extra ecclesiam nulla salus*? Further, we are to believe the same pope, after taking so much personal trouble with the document, did not then see to its publication in the *Acta Apostolicae Sedis* so that it would become truly official?

No, let us not consider that. It is easier to believe that the "Letter" was a forgery. It becomes still easier when we remember it was this very pope who, in his encyclical *Humani Generis*, condemned those who "reduce to a meaningless formula the necessity of belonging to the True Church in order to gain salvation." Is it likely this same pope would approve and even "make" a document like the "Letter," or at least these two paragraphs of it:

"12. That one may obtain eternal salvation, it is not always required that he be incorporated into the Church actually as a member, but it is necessary that at least he be united to her by desire and longing.

"13. However, this desire need not always be explicit, as it is in catechumens; but when a person is involved in invincible ignorance, God accepts also an implicit desire, so called because it is included in that good disposition of soul whereby a person wishes his will to be conformed to the will of God."

Apart from those paragraphs reducing to meaninglessness the "Letter's" own statement that *extra ecclesiam nulla salus* is "an incontestable principle," they are in clear contradiction to *Humani Generis*. Of course, in recent years the faithful have become used to papal self-contradiction. An example was the 1994 decision on the use of altar girls. However, such inconsistency was not a pattern with Pius XII.

Yes, "Letter of the Holy Office to the Archbishop of Boston" with the two paragraphs would be cited by footnote in Vatican II's *Lumen Gentium*. Yes, fifteen years before then Archbishop Cushing and Bishop Wright held the view expressed in "Letter." Yes, by now most Catholics probably do not believe it is necessary to be a baptized member of the Church in order to gain salvation. Clearly, when something no longer is taught it does not take long for persons to fall into such unbelief that the opposite of the thing can be held. In this instance, the mass of Catholics went from the conviction that no one but members of the Church reached Heaven to the belief that anyone can and even that everybody does, and the notion is confirmed in the so-called *Catechism of the Catholic Church*, and this took but two generations. What Cardinal Wright's 1976 article proposes is that Pope Pius moved in the opposite direction, that he thought in the way of the "Letter" in 1949 but had come to belief in *extra ecclesiam nulla salus* a year later when he published *Humani Generis*. How *is that* to be believed?

There are other questions. Did Pius spend even fifteen minutes, let alone three hours, on the "Letter"? Was it the document in its final form that he saw? Were the paragraphs contradicting his own encyclical, which was probably already in the works, a part of the text put before him? That they may not have been would be an explanation of why the "Letter" was never published in *Acta Apostolicae Sedis*. I.e. Cardinal Marchetti-Selvaggiani or someone else—someone possibly working in tandem with the Boston prelates—might use the "Letter" to introduce new doctrine but not be bold enough to present it as official, as it would become if published in *Acta Apostolicae Sedis*. This possibility conforms to our own earlier speculation based on the known practice of heads of government sometimes being kept in ignorance of their governments' unofficial acts. Did Pius see what had happened and was he trying to rectify the situation by assuring that *Humani Generis* condemned those who reduce *extra ecclesiam nulla salus* to a "meaningless formula"? Alas, the questions here being raised may never have clear answers, not even when and if all the archives on the "Boston Heresy" are opened.

However, in terms of the "Letter" contradicting Pope Pius' encyclical, it needs to be observed that the document contradicted much else. In that regard, one of the most interesting newspaper articles published on the "Boston Heresy Case" when the storm over St. Benedict Center first broke appeared in the *New York Times* on May 2, 1949. It was headlined "Papal Bull Quoted On Salvation Issue." The article's subhead: "Word of Boniface

VIII in 1302 Held by Dr. Bonnell to Back Ousted Catholic Teachers." The article said, in part:

"A papal bull, 'Unam Sanctam,' issued by Pope Boniface VIII in 1302, was quoted yesterday morning in a holy communion meditation by the Rev. Dr. John Sutherland Bonnell at the Fifth Avenue Presbyterian Church at Fifty-fifth Street, as apparently supporting the position of the Roman Catholic lay teachers dismissed recently at Boston College.

"Three were members of the college's faculty and a fourth taught in an affiliated high school. The Very Rev. William L. Keleher, S.J., president of the college, declared that they had been teaching 'ideas leading to bigotry and intolerance.'

"The teachers said they had objected to having students at the college taught that there may be salvation outside the Roman Catholic Church and that a man may be saved without submission to the Pope and without acknowledging the supremacy of the Roman Catholic Church among churches.

"The papal Bull quoted by Dr. Bonnell as 'one of the most important of all papal declarations,' reads:

"'Now, therefore, we declare, say, determine and pronounce that for every human creature it is necessary for salvation to be subject to the authority of the Roman Pontiff.'

"'This papal Bull, so explicit, so definitive, has been made a part of the Roman Catholic canon law,' Dr. Bonnell said. 'And, in the light of this declaration, it seems that the dismissed lay teachers have some very powerful documents to quote on their side.'"

The newspaper quoted the Protestant cleric as going on to say (and it is significant): "Protestants are especially impressed by the explanation given by Father Keleher, president of Boston College.

"'Discussions within the Roman Catholic Church as to who can be saved outside its boundaries, are, of course, of interest to Protestants, since we compose the majority of the people concerning whom the controversy has arisen.

"'Protestant interest in this question is largely theoretical, however, since millions who profess the Reformed faith will sleep just as soundly in their beds at night, even if it had been decided by the Roman Catholic hierarchy that they are all doomed to utter darkness.'"

That Protestants slept soundly, beginning with the original "Reformers" who first decided membership in the Church was not necessary for salvation and accordingly left, was not to be doubted. That they should not sleep soundly, and that it was not true charity to allow it, was Fr. Feeney's contention. The April 30, 1949, issue of his old magazine, *America*, published an editorial about him. Therein the magazine's editor, Rev. Robert C. Hartnett, S.J., presented what he termed the "Church's teaching" on *extra ecclesiam nulla salus*. In a lecture at St. Benedict

Center, Fr. Feeney spoke about the editorial. He said:

"There is not an informed Protestant living who, in his heart, does not look upon Father Hartnett's interpretation of the dogma No Salvation Outside the Church, as anything but sheer casuistry and subterfuge.

"All the 'Christianity' of the dogma seems to come from Father Hartnett's kindly presentation of it, for the sake of well-meaning Americans. The 'bigotry' and 'intolerance' of the doctrine is made to come from the way it was originally devised and phrased by the Church. All Protestants in the United States know very well that the Liberal Catholic clergy they are lately reading and listening to, particularly the Liberal Jesuits, are phrasing the teachings of the Church differently for American ears than they were once phrased for European ears by the saints and the doctors of the Church.

"Father Hartnett's method of off-setting the challenge of the dogma: No Salvation Outside the Catholic Church, by means of arbitrary and softly-phrased evasions, is the one method monotonously employed by every Liberal apologete of our day. The Liberal first admits the dogma to be true, calls it a 'basic principle,' an 'incontestable axiom,' an 'ancient truth,' or some such phrase. He then proceeds to present the dogma in a sense that makes the form in which it was originally phrased utterly meaningless. This is what is called the 'charitable' presentation of doctrine, or the adaptation of it to the modern mind. What this dishonesty really does is to kill off the chastity of truth, by reason of the promiscuous manner in which it is presented. This is intellectual license of the wildest kind, and every churchman in the United States knows this to be so."

Chapter Ten

"Fanatic" is how Fr. Feeney and the Slaves of the Immaculate Heart of Mary were usually described in the 1950s. It is the adjective the press invariably attached to them after St. Benedict Center was interdicted and during the seven-and-a-half years Fr. Feeney preached on Boston Common. It remains the case to this day when they are written about.

The adjective would probably have been mouthed even by persons who never went to the Common to hear Fr. Feeney and to see the young men and women in their black garb who accompanied him. It is probable because most persons in U.S. society have been accustomed for a long time to think in the terms provided them by the mass media. Anyone who has ever worked for a newspaper or broadcast station and who is honest can testify that the media know it, too. It is why they never use some words. They know most persons would think far different than they do about certain things if vagrants were not "homeless," carriers of AIDS not "victims," and baby-killing was not a matter of "choice."

Zealous could have been the word used to describe the men and women on the Common, but that would not have had the same pejorative connotation as "fanatic," or at least not in the 1950s. (It is not very "cool" to be zealous today. No one is supposed to believe that much in anything, and, indeed, why should he? The man who still deeply believed in the things to which this society held fast after forgetting God—limitless material prosperity, progress, the glories of freedom and democracy— would be a fool.)

If the young men and women of St. Benedict Center were seen as fanatics, Fr. Feeney was viewed as the chief one. Indisputably, he was the center's leading light. It is interesting, however, that from the perspective of today, M.I.C.M. religious who were young forty years ago remember Fr. Feeney (and Sr. Catherine) as the great moderating influence at the center, even the restraining one. It is easy to understand why they would have been. Both Fr. Feeney and Sr. Catherine were in their fifties by then. Most everyone else at the center was in his twenties, with a few in their thirties.

One evening in September, 1992, when in Still River the present writer dined at St. Ann's House with its superior, Mother Teresa, and some of her sisters, I asked if they had contact with the sisters belonging to Brother Thomas Augustine's next-door community, all of whom, save one, were under the age of 30.

"We see them," Mother answered.

"I am impressed with them," I volunteered. "Aren't you?"

There was a short pause. A somewhat wry smile came to Mother's lips. "We used to be full of zeal, too," she said.

It was age—very becoming age—paying homage to youth. It was also maturity with its first-hand knowledge of the price to be paid, the sacrifices to be made, and the mistakes that can be committed when the good race St. Paul talked about is being run to the end. Today we speak of the race when we talk about "keeping the faith." Start it too fast and you may flag before the end is reached, you may not keep the faith all the way.

That their young men and women would not flag must always have been of great concern to Fr. Feeney and Sr. Catherine, and the reason for their acting to moderate zeal or even restrain it when they did. Yet, mistakes are committed by the older and wiser as well as the younger and less experienced. It is the more likely to happen if the maturer person has resisted against his spirit growing as old as his years, and who is more likely to do that than a poet? The older man who has remained young in spirit, a man of poetic temperament, an *Irishman*, may on occasion even be caught up—despite his maturer judgment—by the enthusiasm and zeal of the younger persons about him.

There was one possible example of that if in fact, as Bro. Thomas Mary Sennott has it, Fr. Feeney let himself be persuaded by the "overprotectiveness" of the center's young members not to go to Rome when he was summoned. If that is why he stayed in Boston, it surely is arguable it was a mistake, for not merely did his decision not to go to Rome bring down on him his "excommunication." It precluded his ever having the hearing he sought.

Be that as it may, it certainly was a mistake, one that certainly produced unfortunate consequences for the center (as we shall see presently), when Fr. Feeney let himself be persuaded that the center's married couples should live apart and that the children of the center should be raised communally.

The only good thing about the decision heard by the present writer from anyone during the preparation of this book was said by Bro. Francis. When I asked him about it, he replied, "I wouldn't do it today, but I think that at the time, it may have been the only thing that kept us together."

We shall come to the decision, how it was made, and its consequences in due course. Before then, we want to take another glance at the life of the Slaves of the Immaculate Heart of Mary while they still lived in "Quaker Village" in Cambridge, and then see them move from there to Still River.

On Sunday afternoons they made their regular appearance on Boston Common. Sometimes they would be physically attacked and have to defend themselves, as during the period (and as we have seen) when Fr. Feeney was protesting the erection of a Catholic chapel (and the presence of the Eucharist) on the campus of Brandeis University, a Jewish school. More than once, a brick or rock was thrown through a window of St. Benedict Center or one of the residences of "Quaker Village." On occasion the parents of a center student would show up, demanding of their child that he or she sever all links with Fr. Feeney and return to Ohio, or wherever. It also came to pass that center members—those who worked at jobs—found it hard to keep employed, or find another job when they lost one. There were fewer newspaper stories about the center as time went by, but when one appeared it would be hostile, or contemptuous. There were always references to Fr. Feeney as the "hate priest" and to the "bigotry" and "intolerance" of center members. And, of course, all during these years they lived under Archbishop Cushing's interdict, outcasts, men and women with whom other Catholics were to have no dealings. They tried to keep their lives going according to a routine: daily Mass, regular confession, the Rosary, other prayer, lectures, reading, study, and the many mundane things that mark the quotidian round whether in a suburban home or a religious community: shopping, preparing meals, washing dishes, doing laundry, maintaining their properties, caring for anyone among them who fell ill, and on and on. Still, keeping to the daily round was not sufficient distraction to prevent their coming to feel beleagured, to feel under siege. There was no public support for them from any quarter, no hand of friendship extended in their direction.

All we are trying to do, they said among themselves, is uphold a fundamental dogma of the Church, and persecution is the result.

After Sr. Catherine's book, *Gate of Heaven*, was ordered "withdrawn" by Archbishop Cushing, none of the Cambridge or Boston bookstores would carry it. As a consequence, the Slaves of the Immaculate Heart of Mary took to selling it themselves, as also *The Loyolas and the Cabots*. After a time, they added other pieces of literature to their sales list. They did not sell these things in the street. They entered into shops and stores and into office buildings. Nor did they limit their sales effort to Boston and its environs. They were soon selling in other eastern-seaboard cities. After that, they began to move out into the Midwest. By 1955, selling books was the center's principal means of income as well as a vehicle for evangelization, but the early years of it were rough.

(How well *Gate of Heaven* sold could not be determined for the present book. However, all 10,000 copies of the first edition of *The Loyolas and the Cabots* sold out at $3.50 each, and by 1955 125,000 copies of Fr. Feeney's *Bread of Life* had sold at $1. These figures are according to Bro. Leonard Mary. Clearly, the public of the day had some interest in learning the center's side in the so-called Boston Heresy Case.)

It was not simply that the sales teams usually lacked the money for much eating and often found themselves sleeping on some floor, head to feet, feet to head. In town after town, there were also arrests, many of them. The charge was usually trespassing or vending without a license. The M.I.C.M. brothers would spend a night in jail—in those days, only the brothers went on the sales trips—and in the morning they would be released and told to get out of town.

Most of the branches of St. Benedict Center still sell books today. As reported in the Introduction to this one, Bro. Leonard Mary estimates that a half-million pieces of literature have been sold by all of them over the years. During the present writing, one team of M.I.C.M. sisters made a foray as far from their eastern base as Hawaii. It remains that back in the early days of this effort, the police surveillance, the arrests, the nights spent in jail and mornings having to beat it out of town, deepened the sense of beleaguredness in Cambridge.

The sense of being persecuted and beleaguered lingered for years after the Slaves of the Immaculate Heart of Mary left Cambridge for Still River, and it still exists to a degree, especially among some older members with their memory of times past. Was it, is it, irrational? In 1968, at *Triumph* magazine, we received the unsolicited manuscript of an article from a doctor of veterinary medicine in Massachusetts. His name was Dr. Lambert. We published the article that May. I learned while preparing this book that Dr. Lambert, a gentleman who really lived and who lent his name for the purpose, was actually Bro. Leonard Mary. They were not sure in Still River that we would accept the article if we knew its author's true identity. I cannot say for certain, but as the only Catholic magazine in the U.S. then expressing the prayerful hope that Pope Paul VI would hold the line on contraception, as he would do that summer with the promulgation of *Humanae Vitae*, we were already stirring plenty of controversy. It is possible we might not have wanted to add to it by accepting an article from a known "Feeneyite." The fact we were close to certain bishops, including John Wright, by then the Bishop of Pittsburgh, could also have made it difficult, if not impossible. The question arises, if *Triumph* would have turned a cold shoulder to the "Feeneyites," who would not?

Whatever, if men are beleaguered for very long, one of two things will happen. Either they will give up, or they resolve to resist still harder—at least if they feel their cause to be right and just. If their resolve is to keep resisting, the resistance must entail further sacrifice than they have already made. In the instance of the Slaves of the Immaculate Heart of Mary, it seems to have been the willingness to make additional sacrifice which led to chastity being added to the simple vow they had already taken. It is known, in any event, that one married couple in particular spent months persuading Fr. Feeney that they wished to make the "sacrifice" (it was the word they used) of their conjugal rights. That couple was eventually joined by others, and then by all, in this petition. What needs underlining, and this is by all accounts (published and unpublished), is that the addition of the vow of chastity for the married couples as well as the single men and women was not instigated by Fr. Feeney and Sr. Catherine.

By itself, the addition of that vow might not have been fateful. There is a long history of Catholic married couples, many of them now canonized saints, undertaking to live as brother and sister with the aim of attaining a greater degree of spiritual perfection. It was another, related decision, that the children of the married couples would be raised communally, which was fateful.

It is not clear now if it was made before or after the idea first arose of moving the center from Cambridge. As far as that goes, it is not clear in whose mind the idea of moving originated or how long it percolated before it was translated into action. Certainly the addition of the vow of chastity made the Slaves of the Immaculate Heart of Mary more like most religious associations or orders. As that happened, it also became desirable for them to lead a more regular religious life. In other words, it was not simply the oppressiveness of Archbishop Cushing's interdict and the fact it effectively prevented the center from pursuing its original purpose, reaching out to students and others, which accounted for the move made in January, 1958. The nature of the Slaves' vocation was also developing in a new direction. They had begun by wanting to preach "from the housetops," and their book sales teams would continue to do that. However, the cultivation of their own interior lives now was becoming more important. They were becoming more contemplative, and throughout the course of Catholic history men and women seeking the contemplative life have tended to do it apart from the city, beginning with the early desert fathers.

It is to anticipate later developments in the story of St. Benedict Center, but that eight branches of it eventually came into being was due in part to a certain creative tension that arose between center members inclined to contemplativeness, some of them even becoming full-fledged Benedictines, and others who preferred for themselves a more activist apostolate.

Such tension is not new in the history of Catholic religious orders. Even within the one order of the Benedictines, there has been an historical division between communities which concerned themselves with life outside the enclosure and others which were more purely contemplative. But even in past ages when some great Benedictine houses actually formed dioceses, the monks still returned to the community at nightfall. In France today, where Benedictine life flourishes as in no other land, two traditional monasteries epitomize the historical division. On the one hand is Fontgombault and its daughter houses of Randol and Trior. They are contemplative. On the other hand is Le Barroux. Its monks spend the usual time in choir, but its founder and current abbot, Dom Gerard, has said in print that the community intends to be, and sees itself as, "the center of a small Christian society." So there are the two approaches to religious life within one religious order.

In the history of the Slaves of the Immaculate Heart of Mary, which will be 50 years old in 1999, three phases may be seen. First, there was the preaching "from the housetops." Second, there was the withdrawal to Still River for a more contemplative life. Finally, after the deaths of Sr. Catherine and Fr. Feeney, there came a division similar to the one that has always marked the Benedictines. There were M.I.C.M. religious who wished to remain contemplative, and other ones who wished to return to the more activist apostolate of publishing, running schools, picketing abortion mills, witnessing to the Gospel in the public forum. The two tendencies are visible today within the one town of Still River.

At one site, the original St. Benedict Center in Still River, is the Abbey of St. Benedict, a monastery pure and simple (although some of the monks do go out to sell books). Down the road and at the other end of the pole is the branch of St. Benedict Center whose superior is Bro. Thomas Augustine. They put out publications, run a school with more than 80 students, and welcome a couple of hundred worshippers to Mass in their chapel every Sunday. In between, at least geographically, are the M.I.C.M. sisters of St. Ann's House, serving as the official Tridentine Mass center for the Diocese of Worcester but no longer operating a school.

There was still but the one branch of St. Benedict Center in 1957 when a 300-year-old farm went on the real-estate market in Still River, which was technically part of the town of Harvard. The place is 30 miles from the university of the same name. (In today's traffic, it takes an hour to drive there.) The farm, which was a working one, featured a large main house, parts of which were as old as the property itself, and satellite buildings. The main house had many rooms and would be named by the Slaves for St. Therese, the saint popularly known in the U.S. (but not in France) as the Little Flower. Today, as in 1958, the farm's fields slope gently down to a wooded valley. Mount Wachusett can be seen across the way during the day. At night, and although Boston has grown considerably during the past forty years, stars can still be seen out there, and the silence will keep awake a visitor used to the urban sounds which are the background to sleep in a big city.

Apparently, the farm—or, more precisely, its main house—had been considered by a religious order or other body of the Church as a possible treatment facility for alcoholic priests when Sr. Catherine heard about it. Whether it was still under consideration when she looked at the property is not known, but she liked the place. So did Fr. Feeney and other center members when they looked at it. It was decided they would buy. The purchase was made possible by the sale of the center's properties in Cambridge. That the move out to Still River would also move the center out of Richard Cushing's archdiocese was doubtless a welcome aspect of the undertaking to the Slaves of the Immaculate Heart of Mary, but it was incidental. The farm in the country was seen as a place where they could more easily lead their life in religion, which was essentially based on the Rule of St. Benedict.

They were a hundred strong, including a dozen married couples with 39 children between them. If anyone in the company had much prior experience of farming, or any at all, it is not part of the "Feeneyite" folklore today. The dairying and fairly large-scale vegetable gardening to which they turned their hand after the move to Still River could not have been easy for them at the beginning, and perhaps never became more than onerous. Originally started with an aim at self-sufficiency and the production of some income in addition to what the book-selling brought in, the effort was eventually discontinued. Of the three branches of St. Benedict Center located in Still River today, only the sisters at St. Ann's House still grow anything. Bro. Thomas Augustine's community and the monks at the Abbey of St. Benedict get their food in institutional quantities from delivery trucks and their milk from cardboard cartons. Neither is anything grown at Bro. Francis' community in Richmond, N.H. In fact, their hilly, forested property would not allow for it. Computer consoles and desk-top publishing are the mode today, not milking-machines and rototillers.

(In France, at Le Barroux as well as Fontgombault, there is still considerable, labor-intensive agriculture. At Fontgombault, there is even enough of a vineyard for limited wine production. The hours spent outdoors seem to make a nice balance for the monks with the hours they spend in the choir stalls and the solitude of their cells. At Bro. Thomas Augustine's community in Still River and Bro. Francis' in Richmond something of the same balance has probably been achieved as the brothers busy themselves erecting buildings, but how it will continue to be so when all building needs are met could be problematic. This is not a trivial matter. We are physical as well as spiritual creatures, men are more physical than women, and younger men are especially physical. A young man who retires for the night with too much energy or who grows prematurely soft is likely not to be altogether healthy in either body or spirit.)

Besides their farming, another of the Slaves' main activities after the move to Still River was the rearing of the community's children. The decision to raise them communally was made while everyone still lived in Cambridge. Although the center's married couples wished to live more like religious and could possibly do so by living as brother and sister as long as children were not involved, how could they when in fact they had children to raise? The decision to raise the children communally was the solution to that problem, it is what lay behind the decision. It also launched the Slaves into uncharted waters. In modern times, no Catholic religious association has attempted anything like it. If someone in the historical past has tried it, the example does not come to mind—apart from heretical movements like the Cathars. In any event, once the zeal and earnestness of the married couples and other younger center members prevailed over the caution of Fr. Feeney and Sr. Catherine, some procedure had to be adopted.

Inasmuch as it was of Mary's Immaculate Heart that they were slaves, the center members let themselves be guided by Catholic tradition regarding her. According to one tradition, Our Lady's parents, Sts. Joachim and Anne, took her when she was three to the Temple, and trusting in God, they turned her over to the priests for rearing. Repairing to that tradition, the center members determined that as each center child reached the age of three, he or she would be put into the care of the community.

Further details of exactly how the system worked are unnecessary to our account of life at St. Benedict Center, although they are interesting from a sociological point of view, and one is in fact surprised that the lone sociologist to study the center, George Pepper, did not spend more time on them in his book. Ignoring the details, there are but three matters that interest us:

1) The academic education afforded the youngsters was excellent, as the later performance of several of them at college would attest.

2) The children's parents effectively ceased to exist as parents to the children, and more so as a child grew from three to five to ten and older. Care was taken that the children had no direct or special contact with their parents, save on a half-dozen major feast days during each year when the entire community would gather for socializing. On these occasions the children might chat with their parents, but after a certain time, the parents were seen by the children as scarcely more than another Big Brother or Big Sister. That is by most accounts given by the children themselves in later years. We shall come shortly to the major exception, but even that person, when he related his story as an adult, allowed that while still a child he did not much view his parents as his parents.

3) Discipline was strict, and it included corporal punishment. This is a point on which we want to dilate, because in today's social atmosphere it is bound to be a touchy one.

Today, after all, things have gone so far as there being talk of a child's "right" to "divorce" his parents. There has even been at least one court case in the U.S. in which such a "right" was upheld. Overseas, in Sweden, there is a law that allows a child to sue his parents if they mete out corporal punishment.

The situation was far different in the 1950s. It was not merely center children who were strictly disciplined. Children in general were subject to much more discipline than today. Even public school teachers were permitted in most states to inflict corporal punishment *in loco parentis*. The present writer vividly remembers his sixth-grade public school teacher, a man in his thirties, sternly reading the relevant empowering paragraphs from the state code to the class. However, in my elementary school corporal punishment was usually administered by the principal, who was also a male, at least when it came to the punishment of boys. The principal used a wooden paddle about the size and heft of a cricket bat. You dropped your trousers and bent over the principal's desk, and there was no talk about "this hurts me more than it does you." Parents were informed of such punishment *ex post facto*. This was in the state of

California, which was already priding itself on its progressiveness.

I have heard from cradle Catholics who attended parochial school at the same time I was in a public one that the sisters of various congregations were able to command a pupil's attention with the ungentle slap of a ruler across outstretched palms. At boys' Catholic schools run by male orders like the Jesuits and Christian Brothers, punishment could be considerably severer. It was more like what we had in public school, but probably more frequent.

The punishments meted out to the children at St. Benedict Center were described in detail in a book which appeared in 1979. The background of the book needs to be known.

Briefly, among the married couples who lived apart in Still River was one named Collopy. (The father, Robert, was mentioned in Chapter Seven.) They had five children, all sons, being raised by the community. During 1963-64, fully five years after the Slaves of the Immaculate Heart of Mary moved to the country, Robert decided that the separation from his wife and the communal care of his sons was wrong. He approached his wife and asked her to leave with him and the boys. She refused. He left anyway, but only after shocking the community by announcing his opposition to the course the center had taken a half-decade before.

Something like this was probably bound to happen—the post-Vatican II religious of most orders would soon be abandoning their vows by the hundreds and then the thousands—but Robert Collopy did not merely leave the center and the Slaves of the Immaculate Heart of Mary. Without money or other resources, he appealed for help from the local ordinary, the Bishop of Worcester, Bernard J. Flanagan. Thanks to His Excellency's offices, he obtained legal counsel and went to court, seeking custody of his sons. It was awarded to him in January, 1965. By that time, the case had brought another wave of bad publicity crashing down on the center. ("A Father's Dilemma: Can He Win Love of His Brainwashed Children?" was a headline in the January 10, 1965, editions of the *Boston Herald.*

The story was not yet done. Collopy took his sons to live with him in the Midwest, but eventually returned the two oldest ones to the center after their rebelliousness proved too much for him to handle. (Subsequently, he was able to have his marriage declared invalid by Church authorities on the grounds that the priest who officiated at the wedding, Fr. Feeney, was without faculties. He then remarried and became a lawyer.) It is ironic that one of the sons who returned to Still River would generate still another wave of bad publicity, perhaps the worst of all.

This was the eldest son. Under the name of Robert Connor, it was he who published in 1979 a book with the lurid title, *Walled In: The True Story of a Cult.* A copy of the book is hard to come by today because it was never published in hardcover. Although it never enjoyed anything but paperback publication, it drew enough attention to itself, appearing as it did at the time of the mass-suicide at Jonestown, Guyana, that the present writer looked for and bought a copy when it was available in drugstores throughout the nation.

"Connor" somewhat undercuts himself by his admission that "I had lived my life under strict discipline for the first twenty-one years, and when I finally left, that self-discipline helped me to make the adjustment. The habit of hard work and single-mindedness enabled me to graduate from MIT, complete a master's degree at Stanford (in electrical engineering) and land a job with a large electronics corporation." (He did not mention that his MIT tuition was paid by the center.)

Unquestionably, his book offers a picture—probably a fairly accurate one—of some of the difficulties likely to arise when the communal upbringing of children is attempted by any group. Beyond that, and after his descriptions of the corporal punishment meted out to center children, "Connor's "real subject is the emotional deprivation felt by a child separated from his natural parents and the difficulties that can produce in later life. Any child of divorce ought to be able to sympathize, and that raises a question. As unwise as may have been the decision to raise the center children communally, did the children suffer to a degree appreciably greater than do the very many ones now being brought up by a single parent or a succession of stepparents—and they are very many. Illigitimacy abounds. Nationwide, one of two marriages end in divorce. It has been the rate for a number of years, and in some parts of the U.S. (California, for instance) it is higher. It is possible to believe that the center children, even raised communally (but in a stable environment), could actually have enjoyed greater emotional security than a bride with six fathers (her natural one and five stepfathers) in attendance at her wedding. The present writer has attended such a wedding, and was not surprised when the young woman ran off with an older man a few months later.

It must also be noted that former center children who live today within driving distance of Still River have taken to gathering there for an annual reunion. In 1994 they had their third. Like persons who gather for any reunion, the former center children share memories as well as catch up with one another's current news. It does not seem probable that they would do so if the memories they have are ugly ones, or that they would gather at the very place where such memories were formed. Further, besides the academic success Robert "Connor" had, other center children did very well in college and later life. One of them, John M. MacGovern, went on to play a key leadership role as a Massachusetts state legislator, which is not something to be expected of any member of a group supposedly made emotionally unfit by a warped childhood.

In any event, by the time *Walled In* appeared in 1979, Fr. Feeney as well as Sr. Catherine had passed away and St. Benedict Center had already effectively divided into two branches.

In regard to that division, and other subsequent ones, we want to recall a point registered in this book's Introduction: Other religious orders have known as much or far greater turbulence than the Slaves of the Immaculate Heart of Mary in their first five decades. The early history of the Franciscans and Redemptorists is illustrative. In the instance of the M.I.C.M. religious, we have already noted that a certain tension existed between those given to contemplativeness and the brothers and sisters inclined toward a more activist apostolate. That tension had a part in the center's first division, but there might have been none without the death of Sr. Catherine in 1968.

Though Fr. Feeney was always the center's spiritual director, Sr. Catherine was the recognized administrator and also the unifier. She had a gift for conciliation that many women possess, if to a lesser degree, and especially mothers. Not simply must a mother conciliate differences between her children for the sake of the family. On occasion she may need to conciliate a difference between the children and her husband. We want to remember in this regard that Sr. Catherine was a mother and wife as well as co-founder of the Slaves of the Immaculate Heart of Mary. Her time was divided between her own home in Waltham, Massachusetts, and St. Benedict Center in Still River. Her two adopted children were not interviewed for this book, but those who know them say the brother and sister enjoyed a happy home life. Sr. Catherine always managed to be available to them when she was needed. What she succeeded in doing at home and even in her own life—reconciling her role of wife and mother with her role as an M.I.C.M. religious—she simply did on a somewhat larger scale at St. Benedict Center; the gifts she employed with her own family she employed with the bigger one at Still River.

When Hodgkins Disease, a form of cancer, carried her away, there was no person on the scene who had her gifts to the same extent. Fr. Feeney could not fill the breach. Even before the community moved from Cambridge, his health, which was never robust, began to fail. Now he was showing symptoms of Parkinson's Disease. Besides, great priest though he might be, no one ever accused the poet of being an able administrator, or the lover of argument of being a conciliator.

By 1971, St. Benedict Center was still but one corporation legally, but the question of the children's future had become an issue on which existing tensions could feed, as also had the question of Holy Mass. Was it to be celebrated according to the historical rite, the so-called Tridentine, or according to the new one promulgated by Pope Paul VI in 1969? Those and other questions may have been hotly debated by M.l.C.M. religious at the time, but they are not of much interest to us more than two decades later, no more than would be the passing squabbles of a regular family. To outsiders, and especially if they are considering the facts years later, such squabbles can look unimportant and even positively silly. To be sure, they can produce pain when they take place, and sometimes they leave scars, but it is interesting that twenty years later, the M.I.C.M. brothers and sisters who were doing the squabbling, and including the ones who became Benedictines, are extremely discreet. An occasional trace of bitterness may be heard from one or another, but no real recriminations. There is no finger pointing or name-calling. Further, as long as Fr. Feeney was still alive, all M.I.C.M. religious, whatever their differences, looked to the aging and ailing priest as their superior, even as all of them, including the monks of the Abbey of St. Benedict, now preserve the memory of him.

It remains that in the summer of 1978, following the death of Fr. Feeney, a judge directed that there be elected a single new superior of the Slaves of the Immaculate Heart of Mary, and he further ordered that outsiders supervise the election to ensure fairness. William Gibbs, then known as Bro. Gabriel, was elected, and the judge thereupon empowered him to decide whether center property was to be divided and how. Seeing that some center members were indeed determined on a separate existence, he agreed to it and there was a legal division of property.

It is the division that accounts for the sisters of St. Ann's House having that property today even as the building once known as St. Therese House is now the core of the Abbey of St. Benedict. The legal division was amicable enough when it came that the sisters did not take with them everything that was theirs.

In that regard, there is no moment of a visit to the Abbey of St. Benedict that is more awesome than when you step into the downstairs living room of the main house (formerly St. Therese House).

In that room, neatly arranged on shelves on all four walls, are more than 600 first-class relics of saints. Collected mostly by Fr. Thomas Feeney, they include relics of Sts. Anne and Joachim, all of the Apostles, all of the Fathers of the Church, all of the Doctors of the Church, and every canonized male saint with Mary in his name. It is a detail that there stands in the same room the statue of the Infant of Prague dedicated by center students in Archbishop Cushing's garden back in 1948. "The relics are really ours," Mother Teresa will tell you at St. Ann's House. "We just leave them over there."

We have said that most of the issues that began to divide the Slaves of the Immaculate Heart of Mary beginning in the early 1970s were such that it would be inappropriate, and for readers tedious, to dwell on them here. Yet, there was one issue of substance that divided M.I.C.M. religious twenty years ago and about which the various branches of St. Benedict Center still differ today. It is the issue of reconciliation, and we want to consider it, although not so much as a question that was divisive as in terms of how it came about that Fr. Feeney and some of his spiritual children were "reconciled." (The word is being put in quotation marks because of the doubtfulness of Fr. Feeney's "excommunication." How can someone be reconciled if he has not truly been apart?)

Even as we consider it, it has to be acknowledged that the time of St. Benedict Center's division into various branches, for whatever reasons, was an unhappy one, and nobody was made more unhappy by it than everyone's spiritual father, Leonard Feeney. We said that even petty disputes can produce pain, and in her biographical sketch of Fr. Feeney that is the introduction to the 1980 edition of *Survival Till Seventeen*, from which we have already quoted, Sr. Mary Clare offers a terribly sad picture of the priest when things were at their worst in Still River.

"Berated and blamed by certain members for not taking sides, the elderly priest would often break down like a child and weep. Incredibly this only engendered hostility. A victim of Parkinson's Disease, his health steadily declining, he continued to be pulled apart, caught between all groups. He loved every one of his followers, and he tried to unite them, but his efforts came to naught. Groping pathetically for answers he couldn't find, the old man would give up and sit helplessly by the hour, staring in a solitary, silent grief."

The initiative to "reconcile" Fr. Feeney and other center members did not originate with the center. It was undertaken by Humberto S. Medeiros in 1971, less than a year after he succeeded Richard Cushing as Archbishop of Boston. We have seen that as a young seminarian Cardinal Medeiros (he was elevated to the purple in 1973) used to attend Fr. Feeney's lectures at St. Benedict Center in Cambridge. Cooperating with the Boston ordinary was Bishop Flanagan of Worcester. As their first go-between, the two prelates commissioned Dr. David O'Toole, a Boston-area physician who provided his services to Fr. Feeney and other center members in Still River.

In May, 1971, a brother of Dr. O'Toole was installed as the head of the U.S. Navy Academy's research and development center, and the physician at that time made his opening approach to Bro. Gabriel, who was also in Annapolis for the installation ceremony. His message was that Archbishop Medeiros and Bishop Flanagan would seek the removal of all censures imposed on Fr. Feeney and the center without Fr. Feeney or other center members having to retract their position on *extra ecclesiam nulla salus*. In exchange, they asked for the center to stop trying to win an official hearing on the validity of Fr. Feeney's "excommunication," which hearing was sought on the basis of canonical irregularities, including some cited by Fr. Feeney himself in documents we have seen. Bro. Gabriel and other center members found the terms agreeable, and in June, just weeks after the Annapolis contact, Rev. Richard J. Shmaruk arrived at St. Therese House, announcing himself to be the representative of Archbishop Medeiros (he was also delegated by Bishop Flanagan).

Cardinal Medeiros died in 1983. We cannot say for sure what it was that moved him to want to close the rift between Fr. Feeney and the hierarchical Church, but we have already recounted that on at least one of his visits to Still River, he knelt and asked for the priest's blessing. His veneration of him must have been deep—deep enough to wish for the old priest to be able to spend his last days free of the stain, at least in the public mind, of supposed excommunication.

(If much of the public did not and never has heard about the "reconciliation" and the fact that Fr. Feeney was required to retract nothing, it was not the cardinal's fault. When the facts became publicly known, they simply were not reported by the media as widely as had been the supposed excommunication. Of course Fr. Feeney and his reputation have not suffered in this way uniquely. Others also have done. Few Catholics have been as high in U.S. public service or acted as ably while in office as Raymond J. Donovan, Ronald Reagan's first Secretary of Labor. Accused of criminal wrongdoing amid a storm of publicity, he was obliged to resign from the cabinet in order to fight the charges against him. When he was eventually totally exonerated, the media gave it one day's "play" and many never heard the news.)

If we cannot know the exact motivation of Cardinal Medeiros, Fr. Shmaruk claims some credit for inspiring it. That is according to notes on the "reconciliation" process kept by him at the time and which he provided to sociologist George Pepper when the latter was preparing his book on the so-called Boston Heresy Case. Having grown up in Lynn, Massachusetts, Fr. Feeney's home town, and an admirer of the priest's writings since his boyhood, Fr. Shmaruk had an additional reason for being interested in Fr. Feeney in 1971. He was assigned at that time to St. Paul's Church in Cambridge, the one that is across the way from the original site of St. Benedict Center.

Since Vatican II "we had gone out to heal divisions with other Christian churches," Fr. Shmaruk says he told Archbishop Medeiros, "but nothing was being done about that scandalous rift that exists with one of our very own"—meaning Fr. Feeney.

As to why he urged that the "excommunication" be lifted unconditionally, he says: "I feared one day critics and historians might accuse the Church of taking advantage of this old man in his dotage against his will. Not only would this seem very cruel and inhumane, it would leave the Church vulnerable to the accusation that deceit and trickery were employed in the process."

Fr. Shmaruk's statements are very "pastoral" in tone and in the same sense that Vatican II was called a "pastoral" council rather than solemn one (as had been every general council before it). His last statement is especially striking. In truth, it is quite singular. That is insofar as the history of the Church, search it as we may, reveals no instance of similar "pastoral" concern being shown for any real heretic. No emissaries were sent to Luther, Calvin, Zwingli or even Henry VIII late in their lives to offer a "reconciliation" that would not seem "cruel and inhumane" or otherwise trespass on their "dotage." Real heretics depart from orthodoxy, and there they stay (in most cases). Luther railed against Rome and the papacy to the end. So did Henry VIII. Fr. Feeney did not. He was their champion, and Cardinal Medeiros clearly did not see him as a heretic.

There are many details of the "reconciliation" process worked out by Fr. Shmaruk and center members that are interesting but which will here be ignored. Most of them have to do with keeping the process secret from the minority of center members opposed to "reconciliation," or opposed to it at that time.

It must be related, however, that during the period of the process, there were unplanned contacts between Boston clergy and Fr. Feeney, including a chance meeting with Auxiliary Bishop Lawrence Riley. During these encounters, the priests were invited to Still River, as was Bishop Riley. The clerics and the bishop were all received cordially, and none of the visitors showed anything to Fr. Feeney except respect. These unplanned contacts and cordial visits fortified the "reconciliation" process. They also led to visits between Archbishop Medeiros and Fr. Feeney, the first one, in January, 1972, taking place at the home of a family friendly to both the priest and the prelate. (A son of this family, Fr. Peter Connelly, is today a priest at the Abbey of St. Benedict in Still River.) That meeting and the archbishop's subsequent visits to St. Therese House could not have been friendlier by all accounts.

Soon after the first meeting Archbishop Medeiros had with Fr. Feeney, another line was opened for facilitating the eventual "reconciliation." It was to John Wright, now in Rome and the first American ever named to the papal curia. Cardinal Wright visited Boston in April, 1972, had a meeting with Archbishop Medeiros and Bishop Flanagan for the purpose of discussing Fr. Feeney's case, and whatever transpired in the past, offered at this time to make an approach to the Congregations for Religious and the Doctrine of the Faith on behalf of the "excommunicated" priest. The result of the offer was a letter received by Archbishop Medeiros in May from the Congregation for the Doctrine of the Faith in which a desire for Fr. Feeney's "reconciliation" was expressed. Rome herself was now behind the process.

With the process so far advanced, there was a consultation by phone with the head of the Canon Law Department at the Catholic University of America, Rev. Frederick R. McManus. Fr. Shmaruk wanted to know if canon law required special prayers or a ritual or a public abjuration of errors for lifting a ban of excommunication. Fr. McManus answered that there was no such requirement, especially not in the case of Fr. Feeney because it was not clear that he was really excommunicated.

Archbishop Medeiros now asked Bishop Riley to join directly in the process with Fr. Shmaruk. After some further discussion between these two and center members, it was agreed that all that would be required of Fr. Feeney for "reconciliation" would be for the priest to make a profession of faith. It was arranged for Bishop Riley and Fr. Shmaruk to witness this profession in Still River on the evening of August 23, 1972. The business was done with a certain casualness, in fact more or less conversationally. The bishop and priest took to discussing with Fr. Feeney the Church's various approved professions of faith, notably the Apostles' Creed, the Nicene Creed, and the Athanasian Creed. Fr. Feeney could recite them all, and did so enthusiastically, including the Athanasian Creed. As all Catholics know, or should, it begins: "Whoever wishes to be saved must, above all, keep the Catholic faith; for unless a person keeps this faith whole and entire he will undoubtedly be lost forever."

The next day, August 24, Bishop Riley and Fr. Shmaruk signed a letter attesting to Fr. Feeney's profession of faith. It went to Archbishop Medeiros. Bishop Riley also wrote notification to Bishop Flanagan, as well as the Holy See via the Apostolic Delegation in Washington, D.C.

That something like "reconciliation" had taken place was immediately suspected by center members opposed to it, and on August 31, Bro. Hugh McIsaac called on Fr. Shmaruk to find out if a "settlement" had been reached with Bro. Gabriel's group. Fr. Shmaruk explained what had happened, emphasizing that the well-being of Fr. Feeney was the only concern of Archbishop Medeiros and Bishop Flanagan. There had been no larger "settlement".

Bro. Hugh also called on Archbishop Medeiros. The interview somewhat alarmed the archbishop, who wondered if Bro. Hugh could be more representative of Fr. Feeney's views than Bro. Gabriel and the center members associated with him, but Fr. Shmaruk was able to still the prelate's misgivings with a review of the terms of the "reconciliation."

It remained actually to lift the ban of Fr. Feeney's supposed excommunication. This would be accomplished effectively simply by telling the priest that Church authorities saw him as "reconciled." It was up to Bishop Flanagan, as the ordinary of the diocese in which Fr. Feeney resided, to do this, and at a meeting on November 5, 1972, His Excellency delegated to Fr. Shmaruk the faculties for it.

Privacy was desirable. It was decided that Fr. Feeney should be taken to a place familiar to him and where a meeting with a priest he knew would not seem unusual to anyone. The place would be the Thomas More Bookstore in Cambridge. Everyone at the center was used to seeing Fr. Feeney be taken for a drive, usually by Bro. Leonard Mary. It was a regular part of the center routine.

It was on November 22, 1972, that Brother drove Fr. Feeney into Cambridge for the encounter with Fr. Shmaruk, which took place on the sidewalk in front of the bookstore. Bro. Leonard Mary remained across the street with the car, so he did not hear what transpired. After Fr. Feeney's death, Fr. Shmaruk wrote an account of the meeting that appeared in the Catholic press. Fr. Feeney had to be reminded of the younger priest's name but recognized him as someone who had been to Still River. That settled, and during the course of an otherwise inconsequential sidewalk conversation, Fr. Shmaruk told him that he was now "reconciled" with the Church and should feel at peace. Fr. Feeney thanked Fr. Shmaruk for telling him this.

Some at St. Therese House doubted that Fr. Feeney fully realized what had happened, but their doubt was dispelled when the Kennedy Church Directory for the new year reached Still River. Fr. Feeney checked it out and was disappointed not to find his name listed. (The "reconciliation" had taken place too late in 1972 for his name's inclusion.)

On June 7, 1973, Fr. Shmaruk informed Bishop Flanagan that the center brothers of St. Therese House were interested in "reconciliation." The bishop greeted this news with elation and offered that the same procedure employed with Fr. Feeney could be used with the brothers. Cardinal Wright's help in Rome was again sought, and Fr. Gilbert Graham, O.P., the American Assistant to the Superior General of the Dominicans, was also of assistance. (When the brothers at St. Therese House were thinking of which direction they should go as religious, the Dominicans asked them to consider joining their order.)

At about the time Rome was being contacted, Bro. Francis (Fakhri Maluf) drew up a statement saying that Fr. Feeney never retracted his position on *extra ecclesiam nulla salus*, and Fr. Feeney signed it. The statement was released by Bro. Francis and published in some newspapers. For a moment, that threatened the process of the brothers' "recociliation." Although Fr. Feeney did not in truth retract his position on *extra ecclesiam nulla salus*, and was not asked to do so, there were numerous parties in Rome as well as the U.S. who did not want the fact publicized. Fr. Shmaruk saved the day by pointing out to Cardinal Medeiros that the brothers of St. Therese never said they represented Fr. Feeney, and that a report sent to Rome stated as much, so no one in the Eternal City should feel misled.

On October 6, 1973, Fr. Shmaruk met with Bro. Gabriel and they went over the material that would be sent to the Congregation for the Doctrine of the Faith. It included two letters signed by Fr. Feeney meant to neutralize Bro. Francis' statement. Both were dated September 17, 1973. One stated that he believed there is no salvation outside the Church, but that he was also a loyal subject of the Church's hierarchy. The other said that he had met with Cardinal Medeiros and Bishop Riley, and that he had authorized no other party to speak for him.

On November 25, Bishop Flanagan wrote to Franjo Cardinal Seper, Prefect of the Congregation for the Doctrine of the Faith. His letter was in support of the petition of the 29 Slaves of the Immaculate Heart of Mary of

St. Therese House for absolution from censures.

Less that two months later, on January 23, 1974, Cardinal Seper wrote to Bishop Flanagan:

"The Cardinals of this Congregation presented to the Holy Father who approved it, the decree favorable to the reconciliation of the group of Brother Gabriel may take place not as a group but as individual persons who, after making the profession of faith before the Bishop (or his delegate) or their pastor, may receive absolution from censures and may be readmitted to full communion with the Church."

By March 19, 1974, the Slaves of the Immaculate Heart of Mary—29 of them, at least—could issue a press release announcing their "reconciliation." The release also reported that neither Fr. Feeney nor the 29 Slaves were asked to retract their position on *extra ecclesiam nulla salus*.

On January 30, 1978, somewhat more than five years after his "reconciliation," Fr. Feeney went to sleep in the arms of the Lord. He was 80-years-old. His remains were laid to rest, as had been those of Sr. Catherine, in a garden adjacent to St. Therese House. (The remains of Sr. Catherine's husband, "Hank" Clarke, are also buried there.) On the marble slab which covers Fr. Feeney's grave are engraved the words: EXTRA ECCLESIAM NULLA SALUS.

Ten years after the passing of Fr. Feeney, the 14 sisters of St. Ann's House were "regularized" (the word had replaced "reconciled"). That was in February, 1988. Soon after, a member of Bro. Francis' community in Richmond, N.H., Mr. Douglas Bersaw, wrote to Bernard Cardinal Law, Archbishop of Boston, about the regularization. Rev. John B. McCormack, Secretary for Ministerial Personnel for the Archdiocese of Boston, answered Mr. Bersaw's letter on behalf of Cardinal Law. When Mother Teresa of St. Ann's House learned of Fr. McCormack's answer, she communicated with Rev. Lawrence A. Deery, Vicar for Canonical Affairs and Judicial Vicar of the Diocese of Worcester. Fr. Deery thereupon wrote a letter to Fr. McCormack. We have earlier quoted a portion of the letter. Here it is in its entirety (it is dated May 4, 1988):

"I write to clarify some aspects of the regularization which took place at St. Ann's House in Still River this past February.

"Mother Teresa, Superior of the community, has expressed concern about your letter of 7 March 1988 to Mr. Douglas Bersaw who had asked Cardinal Law for a clarification of the Church's teaching on the doctrine *extra ecclesiam nulla salus*. It is Mother Teresa's feeling that your letter implied a 'walking away' from Father Feeney's teachings on their part.

"Several clarifications might prove helpful:

"1) The Sisters were asked to 'understand' the letter of the then Holy Office dated 8 August 1949. They were not asked to 'accept' its contents.

"2) The Sisters were asked to make a Profession of Faith. Nothing else was required.

"It would seem that the Congregation for the Doctrine of the Faith holds the doctrine to have been defined and consequently definitive. It is its theological interpretation and speculation which they see as problematical.

"In our discussions with the Congregation it seemed rather clear that proponents of a strict interpretation of the doctrine should be given the same latitude for teaching and discussion as those who would hold more liberal views.

"Summarily, Mother Teresa and her community in no manner abandoned Father Feeney's teachings. Consequently the Sisters do a good deal more than keep the memory of Father Feeney. They now actively proclaim his teachings as they did before the regularization.

"I do hope this information helps to clarify the status of these Sisters and their apostolate."

Even as the sisters of St. Ann's House were being regularized, their next-door neighbors, the men of the former St. Therese House, were progressing in the religious path they had chosen for themselves. On August 10, 1987, St. Therese House became St. Benedict Priory erected as a dependent Benedictine house of the Swiss-American Congregation. Its prior was Fr. Gabriel Gibbs, the former Bro. Gabriel. (He had been ordained a priest by Bishop Flanagan in 1976.) On April 18, 1993, the priory was elevated to abbatial status and Fr. Gabriel became Father Abbot.

The branch of St. Benedict Center headed by Bro. Francis in Richmond, N.H., has not been regularized. Nor has been the branch headed by Bro. Thomas Augustine in Still River. Does that mean they are somehow not Catholic?

In August, 1989, the Bishop of Worcester, then Timothy Harrington, received a letter from a gentleman inquiring as to whether it would be permissible to support the Richmond community financially. Answering on behalf of Bishop Harrington on August 10, Fr. Deery wrote, in part:

"It would seem permissible to support them financially even though their situation in the Church is not completely regular....Brother Francis and his community, though not officially regularized in the Church, are indeed very much Catholic."

Bro. Thomas Augustine cannot show a letter exactly like that, but he can point to an official statement concerning his branch of St. Benedict Center. One of the things his visibly flourishing community has done is picket a Planned Parenthood abortion mill in Worcester. In April, 1992, in a story about pickets at the killing facility, *The Catholic Free Press*, the Worcester diocesan newspaper, reported Bro. Thomas Augustine's community as having "broken away" from the Church. Bro. Thomas Augustine contacted the newspaper, and a "Clarification" was published by

182

*The Catholic Free Press* in its issue of April 17, 1992:

"In an article about pickets at the Planned Parenthood abortion clinic which appeared April 3, 1992 on Page One of The Catholic Free Press we stated that The Slaves of the Immaculate Heart of Mary is 'a group that has not been reconciled to the Catholic Church it broke away from.'

"This was an erroneous statement for which we apologize. The Slaves of the Immaculate Heart of Mary under Brother Thomas Augustine are Roman Catholics. They have not broken away from the Roman Catholic Church.

"However, in clarifying their status, Msgr. Lawrence A. Deery, vicar for canonical affairs in the Diocese of Worcester, stated that 'The Slaves of the Immaculate Heart of Mary are not in good and regular standing with the Roman Catholic Church although they are, indeed, Catholics.'"

Chapter Eleven

It is really incorrect to speak of today's English-language Mass as having been translated from the Latin. That is because the International Committee for English in the Liturgy (ICEL) did not make a true translation. Rather, when ICEL's Advisory Committee, the small body which did the actual work, turned its attention to the various parts of the Mass back in the sixties, its members sometimes made things up.

For instance, when they came to the Nicene Creed they did not translate *credo*. The translation of that Latin word is "I believe." The Advisory Committee made it up that *credo* means "we believe."This change of meaning is significant because if the Church intended her children to say "I believe" instead of "we believe," it must have been on account of formerly understanding that no man can truly attest to what another believes. An individual can only affirm his own belief with certainty. We simply do not know—we *cannot* know—what is in the hearts of our neighbors standing next to us in the pew.

For example, if Rev. Mother Helen McLaughlin, Superior General of the Society of the Sacred Heart and president of the International Union of Superiors of Women's Orders, were standing there in 1991, no one would know that the world's head nun did not mean it if she was heard to affirm the belief that Christ "shall come again with glory to judge both the living and the dead." No one would, unless aware that in an official letter sent that year to the 4,500 members of her order, Rev. Mother wrote: "With all those who fear death because they dread judgment, I would like to share a conviction: God does not wait for us to judge us. That would not be very polite nor worthy of a God who is Love. God waits to embrace us."

The real point about Rev. Mother's true conviction is less that we ought to say "I believe" instead of "we believe," than that Catholics nowadays—they include Catholics in very high places, like the top nun in the entire world—are liable to believe, or disbelieve, most anything. To quite a degree, this is sanctioned.

An example of the sanctioning is the letter we have seen from the diocesan official in Worcester to the archdiocesan official in Boston, the one in which it is reported: "In our discussion with the Congregation [for the Doctrine of the Faith], it seemed rather clear that proponents of a strict interpretation of the doctrine [*extra ecclesiam nulla salus*] should be given the same latitude for teaching and discussion as those who would hold more liberal views." In other words, the official position was that Catholics were free to believe in the doctrine as did Fr. Feeney, or not believe in it at all. If this is how Catholics are to believe (we probably should say "believe"), many are bound to end by believing nothing, or nothing that was once believed by everyone who called himself Catholic. When that point is reached—Who would argue it is not fast approaching?—there will still be buildings known as Catholic churches dotting the suburbs, but what goes on in them under the direction of a presider and the parish liturgy committee will have no more meaning for most than an Episcopalian service. It may look good. It could even be impressive. It may provide some emotional uplift. But it will have no meaning. The Real Presence may still be there, objectively speaking, but for those who no longer believe it will have become a Real Absence.

That the Faith could fall into such a state is what Fr. Feeney feared when he wrote to Pius XII in 1949, telling the pope that if he did not act decisively and soon to safeguard doctrinal orthodoxy, in ten more years it would be too late to save the Church in the U.S. Poor Fr. Feeney. He most probably could not imagine that in thirty more years the Church would be past recovery everywhere, including Rome, as witness the presence in the Eternal City of Rev. Mother, the president of the International Union of Superiors of Women's Orders.

Pius did something for doctrinal orthodoxy when in his 1950 encyclical *Humani Generis* he condemned those who "reduce to a meaningless formula" the dogma *extra ecclesiam nulla salus*. He may also be seen as taking the part of Fr. Feeney insofar as he never rewarded Richard Cushing with a red hat. But why did the pope not do more, as Fr. Feeney beseeched him? Why did he not, for instance, publicly repudiate "Letter of the Holy Office to the Archbishop of Boston" if he really did not approve certain of its paragraphs, as we have hypothesized?

These concluding pages of our book are meant to be devoted to a closer examination than we have so far made of the dogma *extra ecclesiam nulla salus* and the position of the Slaves of the Immaculate Heart of Mary regarding it. However, it seems in order to consider, as briefly as possible, the situation of the Church at the time the controversy surrounding St. Benedict Center was at its height and the pope's help was most needed. This was touched on in Chapter Nine, but a little longer look at the situation may shed some light on why more help from Pius was not forthcoming.

As we take that look, let us remember a couple of things. First, Pius knew the U.S. better than any predecessor. He had traveled in the country before assuming the Chair of Peter. As Fr. Feeney said when writing to him, he was "closer to the American mind" than had been any other pope. Accordingly, he probably had a sharper appreciation than they of the difficulty the Faith faced in trying to take root in liberal-democratic soil, and none of them had thought the chance of it to be very great. In a sense, the Church had written off the U.S. and would do so until in fact the spirit of Americanism, the spirit of a Church that wanted "to be different from that which is in the rest of the world" (as Leo XIII put it in *Testem Benevolentiae*) infested the Church in the rest of the world.

Next, we want to bear in mind that the head of any large organization is never free to do everything exactly as he might like. Even an absolute monarch, such as the pope as head of the government of the Church, operates under constraints. The very functioning of the government, its structure, the character of its personnel, and so forth, impose some. Others are imposed from without. When it comes to the government of the Church, the latter will vary from age to age, from papacy to papacy, but the constraints under which Pius labored were such as no other pope had ever had to contend since the fourth century, not even such a one as Pius VII when he was hauled off to France and made captive by Napoleon I. In truth the circumstances with which he contended were the very ones that made possible Americanism's infestation of the Church outside America.

They did not everywhere prevail at the beginning of Pius' papacy in 1939. Besides the outbreak of Europe-wide war in September, the most notable development of that year was the conclusion of three years of civil conflict in Spain. At ceremonies in Madrid to mark the victory of the military and political forces he led, General Francisco Franco declared: "We Spaniards must be under no illusion. The Jewish spirit, which was responsible for the alliance of large-scale capital with Marxism and was the driving force behind so many anti-Spanish revolutionary agreements, will not be got rid of in a day."

General Franco's statement is here quoted because in a message of his own, broadcast to the Spanish people by radio, Pius XII hailed the recent victory and spoke of the subversive forces named by the general in his speech. "The persistent propaganda and the unremitting efforts of the enemies of Jesus Christ," the pope said, "lead one to believe that they sought to make Spain a supreme example of the powers of destruction at their disposal and which are disseminated over the whole earth.... The wise people of Spain, with that generosity and frankness that are the two characteristics of a soul's nobility, rose decisively in defense of the ideals of the Faith and of Christian life...and aided by God...they were able to resist the onslaught of those who, deceived by what they believed to be a humanitarian ideal for the relief of the lowly, were in reality fighting for atheism."

The significance of Pius' remarks lies in the fact that although atheism's powers of destruction were disseminated over the whole earth by 1939, they did not everywhere threaten the interests of the Church as they would after the alliance between Western liberalism and its own most extreme expression, Communism, triumphed in World War II. From Central Europe to distant China, fifteen nations fell to formally atheistic Communist rule in the years after the war, and the Church was mercilessly persecuted in each of those lands. In the West, practical atheism reigned everywhere with but few exceptions. These exceptions were such as the Republic of Ireland, which did not figure greatly on the world stage. There were also Spain and Portugal, but their leaders, Franco and Salazar, were now treated as "fascist" outcasts. On the other side of the Atlantic, in Catholic Latin America, there was only one nation with real international standing in those years. That was Argentina. Its constitution required that the president of the republic be Catholic, and the president of the moment, General Juan Peron, and his glamorous and able wife, Evita, would keep the country from going Communist. Their government, however, was not a truly Catholic one and before the end of the forties tensions between Church and state reached the breaking point and the general was in fact eventually excommunicated. There was little overt persecution of the Church in all the countries where liberalism and its practical atheism held sway. There was something worse: official indifference to religion. That was worse because the Faith can and often has flourished under persecution, but never where there is indifference—not in the long run.

In summary, in some places where the life of the Faith had been vibrant in 1939, as in Poland and Hungary and Croatia, the countries' primates now languished in prison. In other places, as in the U.S., prelates were perfectly free, except to try to influence public policy. Such rigid separation of Church and state was harmful because Christianity is an exoteric religion. Its precepts and beliefs are meant to be publicly, socially *lived* and that is best and easiest done with the sanction and support of law as well as custom. Finally, it needs to be mentioned that in Italy itself Christian Democrats were in power, but it was by no means certain that they would remain so. Besides, though its hold on power would eventually prove durable, Christian Democracy was a very thin reed to cling to, as events in the early nineties finally showed.

So, here was the situation faced by Pius: Quite simply, he was the first pope since the conversion of Emperor Constantine who could rely on no secular power anywhere—no "sword" as the expression once was—to help advance the Church's spiritual as well as temporal interests. Defending those interests without that power was *the* problem of Pius' papacy. It consumed his time and energies.

It was compounded by the sorry state into which the episcopacy had already fallen, especially in the liberal West. The majority of ordinary Catholic laymen in Europe, and even in the U.S. before the outcome of the "Boston Heresy Case," still believed that outside the Church there is no salvation, but it was learned after Vatican II that Pius had thought to convene a general council whose purpose would be to consider and deal with the worldwide crisis then confronting the Church. After surveying the views of the world's bishops, however, he decided against a council, foreseeing that its outcome would be what was in fact produced by Vatican II: a liberal Church in a liberal world, a Church that has moved in two generations from general belief in *extra ecclesiam nulla salus* to belief, as expressed by the president of the International Union of Superiors of

Women's Orders in 1991, that Heaven awaits *everybody*. There is no judgment. Hell may exist, but no one goes there.

Would the Church have come to this state, or come to it so soon, had Pius acted more energetically to safeguard doctrinal orthodoxy? But how could he act more energetically? Let us remember, after surveying the world's bishops, he saw he was surrounded by revolutionaries. How could he be sure that anything he attempted would actually be enacted and enforced by subordinates as he intended? A successor of his, Paul VI, once complained to Dietrich von Hildebrand and his wife, Alice, that the Jesuits who translated his papal documents from Latin into English willfully mistranslated him. The present writer heard that directly from Dr. von Hildebrand's mouth. He and his wife had heard it from the pope in private audience. As for Pius, we have already considered the possiblity that "Letter of the Holy Office to the Archbishop of Boston" was "doctored." Was it not possible, or even likely, that anything else he tried beyond what he actually did to bolster *extra ecclesiam nulla salus* and Fr. Feeney (publish *Humani Generis* and deny a red hat to Cushing) would prove futile? Was it not the more likely because the "Boston Heresy Case" was being played out in the very bastion of post-war liberalism, the U.S. of A., where the life of the Church was never truly sound and orthodoxy never universal?

All of this assumes that Pius' condemnation of those who "reduce to a meaningless formula" the teaching that outside the Church there is no salvation reflected his real belief and that "Letter of the Holy Office" did not. Assuming it, however, we may see why the Pope did no more than he did. The "Boston Heresy Case" was *supremely* important to those caught up in it. Indeed, we can say it became their life, but with entire Catholic nations going Communist and most of the rest of the world gone liberal, with no more Christendom left (not even vestigially), with no power ready to assist Peter anymore, with a college of bishops upon whom he could not rely, not even to the point of daring to summon them to a general council, with millions of souls at stake, with only so much time and energy at his own disposal, with all that balanced against the welfare of a single priest in a corner of the Catholic world that was not very major in that world, was it not reasonable for the pope to do as he did and to attempt no more than that—again assuming that he meant what was said in *Humani Generis* and not what was said in "Letter of the Holy Office"?

If he did, he surely also hoped and prayed for what he must have believed in faith: that under attack as it was, the truth that outside the Church there is no salvation would again one day prevail. If he did, was there ever a time when he thought that when the truth again prevailed, especially in unCatholic America, the solitary priest in Boston—who now would certainly suffer—would be owed something by the Church? Did Fr. Feeney become a martyr *in pettore* to the pope? Who can say? Who can believe, except in faith, that the truth will again prevail? After all, within years of Pius' death, the Church, somewhat in the manner recommended by critics of American action in Vietnam (Declare victory and withdraw), would "open the windows" to a world whose liberalism she had theretofore resolutely condemned.

Even before he began preaching *extra ecclesiam nulla salus*, Fr. Feeney's lecturing at St. Benedict Center and his spiritual direction of its students left him without much time for writing. After he began preaching, he had still less. His once formidable energy also started to flag as his never-robust health began to decline toward the end of the fifties. Thus the time came when the formerly prolific poet and essayist wrote nothing at all. As a consequence—it is a somewhat ironic one—we have nothing today written by Fr. Feeney himself on the subject of *extra ecclesiam nulla salus*, though he be known as the dogma's foremost champion in recent time. All we have directly from him are his thoughts on the subject, and the related one of baptism, as expressed in the lectures collected in *Bread of Life*.

Our remaining pages will be devoted to consideration of those thoughts, and also ones expressed in Raymond Karam's essay, "Reply to a Liberal," written in close consultation with Fr. Feeney, and others gleaned from Sr. Catherine's book, *Gate of Heaven*, and Bro. Thomas Mary Sennott's *They Fought the Good Fight*. We shall conclude with the present writer making his own brief statement on *extra ecclesiam nulla salus* as he understands and believes the dogma.

It will be recalled that the "Liberal" to whom Karam replied in his essay was Rev. Philip J. Donnelly, S.J., professor of theology at the Jesuit seminary in Weston. Fr. Donnelly had prepared a paper for use at Boston College, "Some Observations on the Question of Salvation Outside the Church." The paper was prepared following the stir caused by another article Karam wrote, one published in the December, 1948, issue of St. Benedict Center's quarterly, *From the Housetops*. In the introduction to his "Reply," Karam says of Fr. Donnelly's paper: "A weaker defense of a theological opinion could not be found, nor a more perfect expression of liberalism."

An objective reading of Fr. Donnelly's paper would lead most anyone to concur with Karam's assessment. The Jesuit ignores the authorities Karam had quoted in his article of December, 1948, and cites in defense of his own position—"*extra ecclesiam nulla salus* must not be understood in the sense that salvation is impossible for any one who does not believe explicitly in the Catholic Church, and does not accept all the revealed truths proposed by her for belief"—two contemporary theologians, a Frenchman named Caperan and an Italian, another Jesuit, named Lombardi, neither of sufficiently large reputation to be known today by theologians querried by the present writer.

Beyond that, Fr. Donnelly quotes from an allocution of Ven. Pope Pius IX in 1854 and from an encyclical published by that pope in 1863. He also cites allocutions delivered by Pope Pius XI in 1927, 1930 and 1938 as they were reported in *L'Osservatore Romano*. The anonymous editor of Fr. Donnelly's paper additionally appended a sentence from a speech given by Pope Pius XII, as it was reported by the *New York Times*. Of the last quote, Karam asks: "Is this the way a Catholic is expected to know the revealed and defined truths of his Faith? Since when does a teacher of Dogmatic Theology have to depend on the good pleasure and honesty of newspapers in order to know what is the Catholic Faith and what he is supposed to teach? And what about the generations of Catholics who lived before the September 6th, 1948 issue of the *New York Times*? Was it impossible for them to have known the unadulterated Catholic truth? Does Father Donnelly prepare his course in Dogmatic Theology dependently on how a newspaper quotes or misquotes some radio address of the Pope?"

Fair questions.

Karam organizes his "Reply" into three parts and a Conclusion. The first part is an "Answer to Five Minor Points." The second part is entitled, "Outside the Church There Is No Salvation," and it is divided into six sections. The third part, "Baptism," has three sections and four subsections. Inasmuch as "Reply" took up the entirety of the Spring, 1949, issue of *Housetops* and the reprint of it runs to 61 pages in Bro. Thomas Mary Sennott's *They Fought the Good Fight*, it obviously cannot but be summarized here. In fact, we are largely going to overlook what Karam had to say about baptism, turning mostly to Sr. Catherine's book and one of Fr. Feeney's lectures for the position on this sacrament that was finally staked out at St. Benedict Center.

Of the "Five Minor Points" Karam answers in the first part of "Reply," we are going to look mainly at the fourth. As to the others, the first is that "It seems to be a habit of liberal theologians to give more weight to the opinions of theologians of their own type than to the infallible definitions of the Church. Some of them never quote the Scriptures and the Councils; others do, usually by way of pious preamble. Father Donnelly...uses only one statement from a Council of the Church. This long statement turns out to be wholly to his disadvantage." Karam also mentions, in relation to this point and others, the French liberal Jesuit theologian, J. Bainvel. The latter was author of a book of some influence, *Is There Salvation Outside the Catholic Church?*

The second point with which Karam deals is this: "Liberal theologians give the impression that the dogma that 'Outside the Church there is no Salvation' is still a question under debate. Father Donnelly says that 'at present there is no work in English that covers adequately the question of salvation outside the Church.' How can a dogma, after twenty centuries of

190

Christianity, be still a 'question' under discussion and debate? Not only is the teaching of the Church very clear on this point, but Pope after Pope has infallibly defined the same dogma."

Karam's third point is that "All liberalism is essentially skeptical. The liberals have studied Descartes, Hume, Kant, Einstein to such an extent that they have become skeptics and relativists themselves." Pointing to Bainvel, Karam shows how the liberal introduces skepticism into Catholic belief by being inconsistent. "He says that it is against the teaching of the Church to say that a person can be saved by good faith alone, or by belonging to the soul of the Church, or by belonging to the invisible Church. It is absolutely necessary for salvation, Father Bainvel says, that a man believe in the truths of the Church and belong to her body, and *visibly*. Moreover, he goes on, some theologians say that the Church is necessary for salvation by a necessity of precept so that a person totally ignorant of its existence could be saved without belonging to it. This, he says, is against the teaching of the Church, and we must hold that the Church is necessary for salvation by a necessity of means, so that without it salvation is *absolutely* impossible. BUT, he adds, good faith and invincible ignorance can easily excuse a man so that he could attain salvation without joining the Catholic Church, without knowing about the Church, and without believing in its truths!

"Now, I ask Father Bainvel, what is the use of asserting a dogma of the Faith if a BUT is going to undo it? Or why should the Church take so much care in defining a dogma if her intention is to say the very opposite of what she states in the definition? This we know is not the intention of the Church, but is, rather, the practice of the liberal theologian, which practice breeds skepticism and doubt."

We said we would look mainly to the fourth point of the five with which Karam deals in Part One of "Reply." To allow for that, we shall here pass to the fifth point, and then return to the fourth. Here is some of what Karam says concerning point five:

"Every Catholic knows that, along with the Holy Scriptures and the infallible pronouncements of the Popes, the greatest authorities in theological and dogmatic questions are the earliest teachers of Catholic truth. The authority of the Fathers is so powerful that all the Councils refer to their works in order to determine beyond question the body of truth contained in the Deposit of Faith. [All the Councils prior to Vatican II, it would have to be said today.]

"Liberal theologians, however, impressed by the methods of modern scholarship, depart from the traditional way, and seek the latest work on a subject....It is very noticeable that in Father Donnelly's paper the earliest authority quoted is the Council of Trent of 1547. He immediately passes on, without further explanation, to the nineteenth and twentieth centuries. Futhermore, although Father Donnelly quotes (or rather misquotes) some recent Popes, the two works which are the basis of his paper, as he attests at the beginning, are 1) a 'classic work by Caperan' (1934), and 2) 'the more recent work by Father Riccardo Lombardi' (1945). It is evident, from these data, how much support Father Donnelly was able to find in the tradition of the Church as preserved in the works of the Fathers and the Doctors."

As to the fourth point in Part One of "Reply," Karam sums it up thus: "One of the most common ways in which liberals confuse people on the teachings of the Church (and a very dishonest way, as everyone must admit) is to claim to quote a Pope or a Council, and then, by mistranslating the text and leaving out the most important words and clauses, misrepresent it completely."

As an example of that, Karam takes a passage from an allocution given by Ven. Pope Pius IX, *Singulari Quadam*, a passage of which both Bainvel and Donnelly make use: "'But at the same time it is to be held equally certain that those who labor under ignorance of the true religion, if their ignorance is invincible, will not be held guilty *of this* in the eyes of the Lord. (*Sed tamen pro certo pariter habendum est, qui verae religionis ignorantia laborent, si ea sit invincibilis, nulla ipsos obstringi* **huiusce rei** *culpa ante oculos Domini.*)'

"Father Bainvel translates this statement (I am quoting from an authorized English translation of his book, *Is There Salvation Outside the Catholic Church?*): ' It may be equally held as certain that ignorance of the true faith, if it be invincible, *excuses one from all fault* in the eyes of the Saviour.'

"This is more than a mistranslation."

In moving to Fr. Donnelly's use of *Singulari Quadam*, Karam first observes: "After saying that those who are invincibly ignorant of the Catholic Faith will not be held guilty *of this* in the eyes of God, Pius IX says: 'But now who would claim to himself to be able to designate limits to such an ignorance *according to the nature and variety of peoples*, regions, temperaments, and so many other things? (*Nunc vero quis tantum sibi arroget, ut huiusmodi ignorantiae designare limites queat* **juxta** *populorum, regionum, ingeniorum aliarumque rerum tam multarum raionem et varietem*?)'

"Father Donnelly renders the above passage of Pius IX in this way: 'Who would dare claim to be able to assign limits to such ignorance when he reflects on the diversity he sees among peoples, etc.' What the Holy Father is warning us *not* to do is exactly what Father Donnelly is doing, namely, he is intimating that anyone can easily judge that there are many more people who are invincibly ignorant than we would think there are, by reflecting on the diversity that can be seen among peoples, regions, temperaments, etc. Pope IX is warning us, on the contrary, not to judge of the invincible ignorance of people according to such superficial and sociological norms as diversity of the peoples and customs. What do the liberals do? They make it their main concern to *reflect* on this very diversity and to judge of the invincible ignorance of people *according to this consideration*. When a Pope warns them not to take sociology and other rational studies as a norm to decide theological or dogmatic questions, they misconstrue his utterances and proceed to become experts on sociological and scientific problems, and they misinterpret Catholic dogmas in accordance with their secular studies!"

Karam now goes to another, apparently willful, mistranslation. "Father Donnelly claims that Pope Pius IX says: 'For God, who sees distinctly, who searches into and knows the mind, spirit, habits and thoughts of all men, would never of His supreme goodness and mercy permit anyone *to be punished eternally* unless he had incurred the guilt of voluntary sin.'

"It is true that this passage is taken from an encyclical which is not infallible. But how can a professor of dogmatic theology have so little concern for the truth and so much less concern for the orthodoxy of a Pope as to claim that the Vicar of Christ could have made a statement like that? To say that God would never permit anyone *to be punished eternally* unless he had incurred the guilt of voluntary sin is nothing short of Pelagianism. It took all the strength and militancy of St. Augustine to destroy this heresy, and here it appears once more in our century, in the utterances of liberal professors of theology who try to hide behind a Pope by misquoting him.

"If God cannot *punish eternally* a human being who has not incurred the guilt of voluntary sin, how then, for example, can He punish eternally babies who die unbaptized? Did these babies incur 'the guilt of voluntary sin?' Or would Father Donnelly assert that they are not punished eternally, but are rewarded with the Beatific Vision? Or would he say that they are sent to Limbo, but that Limbo is not a place of eternal punishment but of reward? Is the teaching of the Church obscure on this, too? Or is it not rather one more instance of the way liberal theologians confuse Catholics by misquoting a passage and never giving an explanation?

[It must be noted that since Karam wrote in 1949, the teaching of the Church on unbaptized babies has become terribly obscured, somewhat as the teaching *extra ecclesiam nulla salus* was then on its way to becoming. In fact, the notion that unbaptized babies go to Heaven is now widespread among conservative Catholics and even some who call themselves traditional, as well as avowed liberals. It is even reflected in the new so-called *Catechism of the Catholic Church*. Doubtless this has come about in part because of the horror of "legal" abortion. I.e. persons accustomed to thinking sentimentally do not wish to believe that the millions of "innocent" babies being sacrificed on the altar of liberal democracy will enjoy less than a heavenly reward. Some even speak of the babies as "martyrs," forgetting that since the Fall, no human has been so innocent

193

except Our Lady. Of course the notion also arises out of our passage in two generations from *some* orthodoxy to the prevalent "cafeteria"-style Catholicism and actual widespread unbelief.]

"What Pius IX says is that 'God, who sees distinctly, who searches into and knows the mind, spirit, habits and thoughts of all men, would never of His supreme goodness and mercy permit anyone to be *punished with eternal torments (aeternis puniri supplicis)* who has not incurred the guilt of voluntary sin.' What is due in justice to original sin is punishment and not reward, but it is the punishment of loss, the loss of the Beatific Vision *(poena damni)*; and what is due to personal sin is the punishment of the senses, the fire of hell *(poena sensus)*. But the punishment of loss can be and actually is inflicted on those who die free from personal sin but unbaptized, hence still under the sway of original sin.

"Thus Innocent III said: 'The penalty of original sin is the loss of the vision of God; the penalty of actual sin is the torment of everlasting hell.' And St Bonaventure says: 'The punishment of being deprived of the sight of God and the loss of heavenly glory affects both adults and children who are unbaptized. The children are punished with the others, but by the mildest punishment because they deserve only the punishment of loss but not the punishment of the senses.'"

Fr. Donnelly made use of two other texts, the one taken from the Council of Trent and one from Pius IXs encyclical, *Quanto Conficiamur.* Karam contends that the Jesuit does not mistranslate them, but gives them a wrong interpretation by emphasizing some words in such a way as to lend false meaning to the passage. He shows how this is accomplished a few pages later, not in Part One.

We turn now to Part Two, "Outside the Church There Is No Salvation." In its first section, "Explicit Faith in the Catholic Church and in Her Teachings is Necessary for Salvation," Karam draws from various authorities, beginning with Holy Scripture (Mk. 16, 16 and St. Paul's Second Epistle to the Thessalonians, I, 7-10 and II, 8-11). He then passes to St. Thomas Aquinas, the Church's official teacher of Catholic Doctrine, and after that St. Alphonsus Liguori and St. Robert Bellarmine. Three popes are also cited in this section: Innocent XI, Ven. Pius IX and Pius XI. Karam also observes that the Council of Constance condemned the 41st proposition of Protestant "reformer" John Wycliff that it is not necessary for salvation to believe in the supremacy of the Roman Church.

Karam's citation of Innocent XI is from the pope's condemnation of certain errors on moral questions, *Errores varii de rebus moralibus*, specifically the proposition that "A man is capable *(capax)* of absolution, however much he may labor in ignorance of the mysteries of the faith, and even though through negligence, be it even culpable, he does not know the Mystery of the Most Holy Trinity and of the Incarnation of Our Lord Jesus Christ."

As for Pius XI, three of whose allocutions were partially quoted by Fr. Donnelly, Karam goes to the pontiff's encyclical, *Mortalium Animos*, for this: "Moreover, when the only Begotten Son of God commanded His legates to teach all nations, *He then bound all men with the duty to believe* what was announced to them by 'witnesses preordained by God.' He attached to His command the sanction,' He that believeth and is baptized shall be saved; but he that believeth not shall be condemned.' Now this double commandment of Christ, which must be observed, *to teach and to believe so as to attain eternal salvation*, cannot even be understood if the Church does not propose the evangelical doctrine entire and clear and if in the teaching of it, it is not free from all danger of error."

Of Ven. Pius IX, "whose utterances have been so pitilessly mutilated and mistranslated by the liberals of our day," Karam cites passages from two texts cited by Donnelly. The first is from the pope's allocution *Singulari Quadam*: "It is necessary that you inculcate this salutary teaching in the souls of those who exaggerate the power of human reason to such a point that they dare, by its power, to investigate and explain the mysteries themselves, than which nothing is more foolish, nothing more insane. Strive to call them back from such a perversity of mind, explaining indeed that nothing was granted to men by God's Providence more excellent than the authority of the divine faith, that this faith is to us like a torch in the darkness, that it is the leader that we follow to Life, that it is *absolutely necessary for salvation*, since 'without faith it is impossible to please God,' and 'he that believeth not shall be condemned' (Mk. 16, 16)."

The second document of Ven. Pius IX with which Karam deals is the pope's encyclical *Quanto Conficiamur*. He says: "In connection with the question of the necessity of the Catholic Faith for salvation, let me point out the fact that Fr. Donnelly and the other liberals quote texts without seeing that they can be easily turned against them. Thus the Encyclical *Quanto Conficiamur* by Pius IX is universally quoted by the liberals to support their doctrine that a man totally ignorant of the Catholic Faith can be saved. But what does Pius IX say?

"'It is known to Us and to you that those who labor under invincible ignorance of our holy religion, and who, zealously observing the natural law and its precepts engraven by God in the hearts of all, and who, prepared to obey God, lead an honest and upright life, are able, *by the powerful workings of God's light and grace*, to attain eternal life.'

"This means that God, in His mercy, will find a way of enabling the man who is invincibly ignorant of the Church and who follows the natural law to achieve his salvation. But Pius IX nowhere says that this can be done without the Catholic Faith. On the contrary, he explicitly says, a few lines later, that it is a 'Catholic dogma that no one can be saved outside the Catholic Church.' Thus, God will find the way to enable that man to save his soul, and this way will be the Catholic Faith and the Catholic Church.

"What is more, in the very sentence which the liberals quote to support their false doctrine, Pius IX says that God will enable that man to attain eternal life, not by keeping him in his ignorance of the Faith, but *by the workings of His light and grace*. God must give sanctifying grace to a person before that person can be saved, and He never gives sanctifying grace apart from or even before the Catholic Faith. Thus to say that God gives *His light* to a person is the same as to say that He gives His Faith to that person. Thus we speak of the 'light of Faith.'

"As a matter of fact, St. Thomas teaches not only that faith and light go together, but that light is the effect of the Catholic faith. In his *Commentary on St. John*, Chapter 12, St. Thomas says: 'Illumination therefore is the effect of faith: "That whosoever believeth in Me may not remain in darkness." "May not remain in darkness," namely, the darkness of ignorance, of infidelity and of perpetual damnation...And nevertheless unless they are converted to Christ they shall be led to the darkness of perpetual damnation. "He that believeth not the Son, the wrath of God abideth on him."'"

In the second section of Part Two, Karam addresses the question, "Are There Two Kinds of Membership in the Church?" The question arises out of Fr. Bainvel's declared position that "we can be members of the Church in two ways, externally (visibly) and internally (invisibly)." Later, the Jesuit theologian claims (this is all in his book, *Is There Salvation Outside the Church?*), "This distinction between union with the Church in *act* and union in *desire* dates far back into Christian antiquity." He goes further, maintaining that membership in the Church can be *unconscious*. "Souls affiliated with the Church *unconsciously* are united to her by invisible ties, for they are affiliated with her internally, by an *implicit desire*, which God is pleased to regard as equivalent to external membership."

Karam says of Bainvel's position, "This is the end of all Christianity and all sanity." It is also, merely five decades after Karam wrote, something that is taught and believed nearly everywhere in Catholicism. Against it, Karam enlists writing by St. Peter Canisius, Pius XI and St. Robert Bellarmine.

Here is St. Peter Canisius, Universal Doctor of the Church, in his *Catechism* (so different from the new so-called *Catechism of the Catholic Church*): "Who is to be called a Christian? He who confesses the salutary doctrine of Jesus Christ, true God and true Man, *in His Church*. Hence, he who is truly a Christian condemns and detests thoroughly all cults and sects which are found outside the doctrine and Church of Christ, everywhere, and among all peoples, as for example, the Jewish, the Mohammedan, and the heretical cults and sects; and he firmly assents to the same doctrine of Christ."

For Pius XI on the question of membership in the Church, Karam again turns to *Mortalium Animos*: "No one is found in the one Church of

Christ, and no one perseveres in it, unless he acknowledges and accepts obediently the supreme authority of St. Peter and his legitimate successors."

There are two passages from St. Robert Bellarmine. In the one, he says that "the one and true Church is the congregation of men bound together by the profession of the same Christian faith, and by the communion of the same Sacraments, under the rule of the legitimate pastors, and especially of the one Vicar of Christ on earth, the Roman Pontiff."

In the other passage, St. Robert Bellarmine says: "The Church is a society, not of Angels, nor of souls, but of men. But it cannot be called a society of men, unless it consist in external and visible signs; for it is not a society unless they who are called members acknowledge themselves to be so, but men cannot acknowledge themselves to be members unless the bonds of the society be external and visible. And this is confirmed by those customs of all human societies; for in an army, in a city, in a kingdom, and other similar societies men would not be enrolled otherwise than by visible signs. Whence Augustine in Book 19 *Against Fautus*, Chapter 11, says: 'Men cannot assemble in the name of any religion, whether it be true or false, unless they be bound together by some fellowship of visible signs or sacraments.'"

Karam next looks to the question, "Can a Person Who Remains Separated from the Church Be Saved?" He does so because Fr. Donnelly contended: "He [Ven. Pius IX] likewise teaches in the same place that only those who are 'contumaciter' and 'pertinaciter' divided from the Church cannot be saved as long as this condition exists."

Answering, Raymond Karam makes the following argument, in part: "In saying this, Father Donnelly gives us the impression that those who know the Catholic Church and the Catholic Faith can remain outside the Church either innocently and with a good excuse, or obstinately and without excuse, and that only the latter cannot attain eternal salvation. This is against Catholic doctrine. *No* one can refuse to enter the Church and be saved. When Pope Pius IX mentions those who obstinately remain separated from the Church, he does not contrast them with those who innocently remain separated, but with those who never heard about the Catholic Faith. What he says is that *those who are ignorant of the Church* because they never heard of it, if they have faithfully kept the natural law implanted in their hearts by God, can, with His help, come to the knowledge of the Catholic Church, in which alone they can be saved. But, on the other hand, *those who know* about the Catholic Church and refuse to enter her will perish. It is to emphasize the heinousness of their refusal that Pope Pius IX calls it contumacious and obstinate, not to distinguish between it and some other hypothetical kind of refusal which would *not* be obstinate."

Concluding this section of Part Two of "Reply," Karam asserts: "Liberalism is a blasphemy against the Incarnation of the Son of God. If there are other ways than the Catholic Church [to reach Heaven], whether they be easier or harder, the result is that Christ's Incarnation and death were in vain. Our liberal teachers of doctrine have stopped teaching Christ Crucified, and they are teaching the natural law, morality, good faith, sincerity and the like. St. Paul warned us against such blasphemy: 'If justice be by the law, then Christ died in vain.' (Gal, 2,21.) And again, 'And I, brethren, if I yet preach circumcision, why do I yet suffer persecution? Then is the scandal of the cross made void.' (Gal. 5,11)"

In the next section of Part Two of "Reply," Karam answers the question, "Are Protestants Formal Heretics?" He says it is "closely connected with this question of obstinately refusing to join the Catholic Church." Fr. Donnelly, in his paper, wrote of "that spirit of hostility manifested in the scarcely veiled assumption that Protestants are to be convicted of bad faith, and henceforth to be treated as formal heretics..."

Referring to those lines, Karam asks, "Does Father Donnelly mean to say that a Protestant who refuses to believe in the truths of the Catholic Faith and to acknowledge the infallibility and supremacy of the Church is only in *material* heresy"? Basing himself on St. Augustine and St. Thomas Aquinas, Karam makes the point that "only a faithful Catholic who obeys the Church and is ready to correct his opinions according to her admonitions can be in error in this sense, without being a heretic. This we call *material* heresy. A man who is in material heresy does not intend to contradict the authority and teachings of the Church. On the other hand, a man who does not intend in the least to follow the teachings of the Catholic Church and to be corrected by her cannot be called a material heretic. It is clear, therefore, that Protestants are not material heretics. Are they, then, *formal* heretics? What is a formal heretic?

"St. Augustine says: 'A heretic is one who either devises or follows false and new opinions.' It is not necessary to tell Father Donnelly that the teachings and opinions of Protestants fall under this last designation, and that Protestants, therefore, hold heresy *formally*. Of course, if Father Donnelly is referring to those millions of former Protestants who are neither baptized nor call themselves Christians, then we would agree that they are not formal heretics, but pagans. In either case, however, heretic or pagan, they cannot be saved unless they come to the Holy, Roman, Catholic Church."

(Three different dictionaries consulted for the present writing define the term pagan as meaning "one who worships false gods." According to that definition, Karam may be faulted insofar as most of our contemporary ex-Protestants and liberal Catholics really worship nothing. Not even belief in the national gods of freedom, democracy and progress runs very deep anymore. That is the case today, if it was not quite so when Karam wrote, and it makes the Christian's mission of evangelization harder than ever. Certainly it must be harder than it was for the original Apostles. They lived in a truly pagan world. We live in a secular one. They were persecuted. We are surrounded by indifference. The ancient pagans felt their false belief to be imperiled by the Good News, as it was. Today's secularist couldn't care less about what the Christian has to say. In a word, the man who already believed in some god, even a false one, had to be easier to convert than is the individual who believes in nothing, or nothing but himself—which belief invariably ends in the same thing: belief in nothing.)

Section five of Part Two of "Reply" explores "Pope Pius IX's Real Teaching with Regard to the Salvation of Non-Catholics." This section is important. The reason that is so is because Ven. Pius IX, as the author of the famous *Syllabus of Errors* (a liberal would call it notorious), is seen in the twentieth century to be the very incarnation of papal reaction, "rigid" orthodoxy, and so forth. Accordingly, the liberal contention that eternal salvation can be attained outside the Catholic Church and without obedience to the authority of the pope is much fortified if this supreme pontiff can be shown as concurring with it.

It is what Fr. Donnelly aimed to show when he wrote, for instance: "Pius IX likewise forbids unconditionally any manifestation by Catholics of a spirit of enmity toward those outside the Catholic Church. 'But let the children of the Catholic Church *in no way whatsoever* be hostile to those who are not one with us in faith and love.'"

Quoting those lines, Raymond Karam asks: "Does this mean, as Father Donnelly wants to give us the impression, that Pope Pius IX is asking Catholics not to show those who are outside the church any indignation on matters of doctrine, and not to tell them that they must become Catholics if they wish to be saved? Father Donnelly claims that this is the meaning of Piux IX in the above quotation. Let us point out that had Father Donnelly completed the sentence of the Pope, the message revealed would have been a *completely contrary one.*

"Here is the full quotation:

"'But let the children of the Catholic Church in no way be hostile to those who are not joined with us in the bonds of the same faith and of charity, yea rather, let them always strive to attend upon them and to help them in all the duties of Christian charity, whether they be poor or sick or afflicted with any other calamities, and *above all let them strive to snatch them away from the darkness in which they lie miserably, and lead them back to the Catholic truth and to the most loving Mother, the Church*, who never ceases to extend Her maternal arms lovingly to them and to call them back to her bosom, *so that being grounded and made firm in faith, hope and charity, and being "fruitful in every good work"* (Col. 1,10), *they may attain eternal salvation.'*

"Can a more deliberate misrepresentation of a Pope's utterance be found than Father Donnelly's?

"Again: we could also ask Father Donnelly not to take the trouble of underlining sentences in his quotations, because they always turn to his disadvantage. For example, in one of the passages which Father Donnelly quotes from Pius IX, the emphasized phrase proves our point, and not Father Donnelly's! This is the passage: 'But let us, so long as here on earth we are weighed down by this mortal body which dulls the soul, hold firmly to our Catholic doctrine: "one God, one faith, one baptism"; *to try and probe deeper is criminal...*'

"What does this mean? To try and probe deeper than *what* is criminal? Deeper than the Catholic doctrine: 'one God, one faith, one baptism'! Who is probing deeper than this doctrine? Is it the man who confesses *one God, one faith*, (the Catholic Faith), and *one baptism* (the gate to the Catholic Church), as the necessary means for salvation? Is it not, rather, the liberal, who goes around dispensing the name of *faith* to any arbitrary and false opinion and the name of *baptism* to any feeling or sentiment, however anti-Christian?"

"Concerning the Question of Ignorance" is the sixth and last section of Part Two of "Reply". It is a question that can never be discussed without consideration of what bonds exist, or should, between the Catholic faithful and those who are outside the Church.

As the interfaith movement of the 1940s developed into the post-Vatican II ecumenical one, liberals felt ever freer to advance the once unthinkable notion that in charity and for the sake of unity between Catholics and their "separated brethren" (as schismatics and heretics came to be called), no effort should be made to convert the latter. That would not be "loving." What was needed was to emphasize everything that Catholics had in common with non-Catholic Christians. That was at the beginning. Later, it became everything in common with Jews, who also became "separated brethren." Today, on the basis of our "common humanity," the liberals' ecumenical quotient embraces everybody of whatever "religious tradition" or "faith system"—and those of none. During the passage of the decades, the liberals' argument became easier for them to make as Catholic belief at an ever accelerating rate ran out of the dogma *extra ecclesiam nulla salus*. After all, if membership in the Catholic Church is not necessary for salvation, there really is no reason to try to convert anyone.

On their side, the "Feeneyites" continued to preach the dogma that was once universally believed by all who were Catholic but which itself has become probably unthinkable for most, and certainly unpreachable in the mainstream of the Church. They still uphold it, and they do so—according to them—for the sake of love and unity. If you truly love someone, they say, you will want him to be able to spend eternity with and in God, and the only chance he has of that is by uniting himself to the

Catholic Church. You must tell him that.

Pope Pius XI agreed. It is why Karam again quoted *Mortalium Animos* in the last section of Part Two of "Reply": "When the question of promoting unity among Christians is under consideration many are easily deceived by the semblance of good. 'Is it not right,' it is said repeatedly, 'indeed is it not the duty of all who call upon Christ's name to cease mutual recriminations and join together in ties of mutual charity? For who would dare to say that he loves Christ when he will not strive to his utmost to attain that which Christ prayed for to His Father when He asked that His disciples might *be one*? And did not Christ Himself wish His disciples to bear the sign and be distinguished by the characteristic that they love one another: *By this shall all men know that you are my disciples, if you have love for one another*?

"'Would,' they add, 'that all Christians were one, that they might drive out the evil of irreligion which every day spreads more widely and threatens to overturn the Gospel.'"

Pope Pius XI answers liberal arguments like those thus: "All remember how John, the very Apostle of Charity, who in his Gospel seems to have opened the secrets of the Most Sacred Heart of Jesus and who always inculcated in the minds of his disciples the new commandment, *Love ye one another*, and wholly forbade them to have relations with those who did not profess entire and uncorrupted the teachings of Christ. *If any man cometh to you and bring not this doctrine, receive him not into your house nor say to him, God speed you.* Since charity is founded in whole and sincere faith, the disciples of Christ must be united by the bond of unity in faith and by it as the chief bond."

As have other heterodox, including, most notoriously, Peter Abelard in the 12th century, Fr. Donnelly in his paper tried to claim that Christ's words from the Cross, "Father, forgive them for they know not what they do," somehow proclaim the innocence of His crucifiers on the grounds they were ignorant, they knew not what they were doing.

Karam cites three of the Church's greatest teachers in refutation of the claim. They are St. Bernard of Clairvaux, St. Alphonsus Liguori and St. John Chrysostom.

The citation of St. Bernard is from Chapter 4 of his *Epistle to Hugh of St. Victor:* "Perhaps he who asserts that one cannot sin through ignorance never prays for his ignorances, but rather laughs at the prophet who prays and says, 'The sins of my youth and my ignorances do not remember' (Ps. 24,7). Perhaps he even reproves God Who requires satisfaction for the *sin of ignorance*, 'and do one of those things which by the law of the Lord are forbidden, and being guilty of sin, understand his iniquity, he shall offer of the flocks a ram without blemish to the priest. according to the measure and estimation of the sin, and the priest shall pray for him, because he did it ignorantly; and it shall be forgiven him, because by mistake he trespassed against the Lord.' (Lev. 5,17-19.)

"If ignorance is never a sin, why is it said in the *Epistle to the Hebrews* that the high priest entered alone once a year into the second tabernacle not without blood, which he offers for his own and the people's *ignorance*? (Heb. 9,7.) If the sin of ignorance is no sin, therefore Saul did not sin, who persecuted the Church of God, because he did this indeed ignorantly, remaining in incredulity. Therefore he did well in that he was a blasphemer, and a persecutor, and contumeillious—in that he was breathing threats and slaughter against the disciples of Jesus—thereby being more abundantly a zealous imitator of the traditions of his fathers (Gal. 1,13-14)! If ignorance is never a sin, then he should not have said, 'I obtained the *mercy* of God' (I Tim. 1,13), but, rather, 'I received my reward,' for certainly if ignorance renders a man free from sin, then in addition emulation makes him worthy of reward.

"*If*, I say, *one never sins through ignorance*, what then do we hold against those who killed the Apostles, since indeed they did not know that to kill them was evil, but, rather, by doing this, they thought they were doing a service to God? (Jn. 16,2.) *Then also in vain did our Saviour on the Cross pray for those who crucified Him*, since indeed as He Himself testifies, they were ignorant of what they were doing (Lk.23,24), and therefore they did not sin at all! For neither is it allowed in any way to suspect that the Lord Jesus was lying, Who openly bore witness that they did not know what they were doing, nor should one suspect that the Apostle, emulating his flesh, could have lied as a man when he said, 'For if they had known it, they would never have crucified the Lord of glory.' (I Cor. 2,8) Is it not sufficiently clear from these passages in what a great darkness of ignorance lies the man who does not know that one can sometimes sin through ignorance?"

Having cited St. Bernard, Karam asks: "Is ignorance never a sin? Why is it that people are ignorant of the Truth?" He then observes that St. Alphonsus Liguori, Doctor of the Church, asked the same question. St. Alphonsus also answered it: "But why is it, then, that all men have not known it [i.e. the Truth] and that even at this day so many are *ignorant* of it? This is the reason: 'The light is come into the world, and men loved darkness rather than the light' (Jn. 3,19). They have not known Him, and they do not know Him, because they do not *want* to know Him, loving rather the darkness of sin than the light of grace."

Of St. John Chrysostom, another Doctor of the Church, Karam cites this: "Thus see how, speaking of the Jews, Our Lord deprives them of all excuse: 'If I had not come and spoken to them, they would not have sin,' and Paul again, 'But I say: Have they not heard? Yes, verily, their sound hath gone forth into all the earth.' For there is excuse when there is no one to tell a man, but when the watchman sits there, having this as the business of his life, there is not excuse any longer...Whether you go among the

Indians you shall hear this, whether into Spain, or to the very ends of the earth, there is no one without the hearing, *except it be of his own neglect.*"

It was said in this book's Introduction that we would not spend a long time looking at the position developed by Fr. Feeney and the Slaves of the Immaculate Heart of Mary on the Sacrament of Baptism for the reason that it did not figure in the storm that broke over St. Benedict Center in 1949 and Fr. Feeney's "excommunication" in 1953. The storm and "excommunication" resulted from the priest and his associates upholding *extra ecclesiam nulla salus.* Yet, the subject of baptism and the position taken on it at St. Benedict Center must not be ignored. If it were, not merely might it appear that we wished to avoid a controversy of our own insofar as there are Catholics today who say that they believe in *extra ecclesiam nulla salus* as did Fr. Feeney, but do not agree he was right on baptism. It would also be to avoid a question of vital importance, one inextricably bound up with the very teaching that outside the Church there is no salvation—so inextricably it was the cause of their giving long and deep consideration at St. Benedict Center to the matter of baptism. That is, if there is no salvation outside the Church, how does a man become one of her members—one of her *visible* members, we must say, if we follow the popes, saints and Doctors of the Church cited by Karam? The simple answer was provided by Karam a short space ago. He said baptism is "the gate to the Catholic Church." But what exactly is baptism?

When a Catholic recites the Nicene Creed, he says, "I confess one baptism for the remission of sins." Most Catholics probably understand the words to mean that the Sacrament of Baptism, like that of holy orders, is not repeatable, that there is no need for it ever to be repeated because its reception stamps on our souls a character which is indelible. "Feeneyites" take the words also to mean that there are not three baptisms in the sense of the so-called baptisms of desire and blood in addition to the one baptism of water. This may sound like they are playing with words, but only if we have been catechized to believe the Nicene Creed's formula has only the single meaning, or that the meaning taught now always was, and provided we have been catechized at all in an age when there is so little catechesis. (At a time when children graduate from Catholic schools without knowing anything as basically Catholic as the prayers needed for recitation of the Rosary, it may be reasonably supposed that many younger members of the Church lack much sense of the meaning of the words relative to baptism, or relative to any other part of the Creed, when they recite them.)

Whatever, the "Feeneyite" position is that there is only one baptism in the sense that the sacrament is not repeatable and also inasmuch as the so-called baptisms of desire and blood are liberal inventions, albeit routinely taught ones after the notion of them was introduced in this country with the publication of the *Baltimore Catechism* in the 1880s. This was the position developed by the Slaves of the Immaculate Heart of Mary in the years immediately after Archbishop Cushing's interdict of St. Benedict Center and even before Fr. Feeney's "excommunication"—in which, again, the priest's position on baptism did not figure.

The mildest statement of the position to be found in the works of Sr Catherine and Fr. Feeney is in the former's book, *Gate of Heaven*. It comes in reference to the Gentile, Cornelius, whose baptism by St. Peter is related in the *Acts of the Apostles* (Chapter 10) and the Ethiopian eunuch whose baptism by St. Phillip is also told in *Acts of the Apostles* (Chapter 8). Sr. Catherine writes (the emphases are hers):

"Now, if it were enough for salvation to have baptism of desire, in the sense in which the liberals of our day hold baptism of desire, certainly this eunuch had it. He was of good will, he sincerely desired God, and he was holy. However, all this was not enough—no more than it was enough for Cornelius, who also possessed these virtues. It still was necessary for the eunuch to be born again, of water and the Holy Ghost. It was necessary for him to be baptized, and by *water. Baptism of desire is desire for Baptism of water.*"

(The reference, "born again of water and the Holy Ghost," is to Holy Scripture, specifically *John* III: 5: "Amen, amen I say to thee, unless a man be born again of water and the Holy Ghost, he cannot enter into the Kingdom of God." We have already seen a related verse, that of *Mark* XVI:16: "He that believeth and is baptized, shall be saved: but he that believeth not shall be condemned.")

In the lecture, "The Waters of Salvation," published in *Bread of Life*, Fr. Feeney's language in regard to baptism is much more muscular than Sr. Catherine's. He begins his remarks by referring to the so-called *Baltimore Catechism*. (We say "so-called" because, as Fr. Feeney makes clear, there are really numerous *Baltimore Catechisms*.) When he delivered his lecture, sometime around 1950, the work was normative in the religious education of Catholic children in the U.S. It has long since ceased to be. The fact reminds us of something that is forgot at the risk of our becoming mentally and spiritually confused: As the *Catechism of the Council of Trent* once was for the entire Church, as the so-called *Baltimore Catechism* once was for the Church in the U.S., as the champions of the new, so-called *Catechism of the Catholic Church* doubtless intend it to be, a catechism may be normative for a time, but no catechism is infallible. It can contain error.

Here is Fr. Feeney: "The Catholic Faith in the United States of America is always academically ascribed to the *Baltimore Catechism*.

"The *Baltimore Catechism* was confected at the Third Plenary Council of Baltimore, by a group of American Bishops under the control and influence of James Cardinal Gibbons, Archbishop of Baltimore. James Cardinal Gibbons was a Catholic prelate who did not hesitate to get up before a Methodist congregation, in a Methodist Church, and give a supposedly Catholic sermon while reading from a Protestant Bible!...

"Cardinal Gibbons' main ambition was to show that Catholicism was good Americanism. It is for that reason he went out of his way to take such metaphorical expressions in theology as 'Baptism of Desire' and 'Baptism of Blood' and put them side by side with *Baptism of Water*. As a consequence, every little Catholic child in a Catholic school, from the time of Cardinal Gibbons on, has been required to say, in answer to the question, 'how many kinds of Baptism are there?': 'There are three kinds of Baptism: Baptism of Water, Baptism of Desire, and Baptism of Blood.'

"That is heresy! There is only *one* Baptism, just as there is only one Lord and one Faith. (Eph. 4:5.) The Council of Vienne explicitly defines that this one Baptism, which is administered by water, is the one which must be faithfully confessed by all.

"The Council of Trent, in its second Canon on the subject of Baptism, declares, with the majestic authority of the Church: 'If anyone shall say that true and natural water is not of necessity in Baptism, and therefore shall turn those words of Our Lord, Jesus Christ, "unless one be born again of water and the Holy Spirit" (John 3:5), into some metaphor, *let him be anathema*.'

"Therefore, I repeat, metaphorical water is forbidden under pain of heresy. And what is 'Baptism of Desire,' as the Liberals teach it, but metaphorical water dishonestly substituting for the innocent requirement of Christ?

"The same heretical theology that turned Baptism of Water into *any dry desire one might have in the general direction of Heaven*, has also turned *one Lord* into *one's personal sincerity*, and one Faith into the *light of invincible ignorance*!

"And, by the way, speaking of the *Baltimore Catechism*, even its most ardent supporters are forced to admit that shortly after the publication of the *Baltimore Catechism*, various editions with word meanings, explanatory notes, and even with different arrangements, came forth—so that, by testimony of all Catholic theologians in America, there is a considerable diversity in the books that go by the name of the *Baltimore Catechism*. Yet the *Baltimore Catechism* is always referred to in a singular apostrophe, as though it had the dignity of the Gospel itself.

"A catechism is as good as the man who wrote it. If the *Baltimore Catechism* is so good, why do they revise it and revise it and revise it?

"The crucial point, then, at which heresy entered the Catholic Church in the United States and backwashed to the dying Faith of Europe and the rest of the world, was through the teaching of the doctrine known as Baptism of Desire in the *Baltimore Catechism*.

"As I have explained to you many times, neither 'Baptism of Desire,' nor 'Baptism of Blood' should truly be called *Baptism*. Neither is a sacrament of the Church. Neither was instituted by Jesus Christ. No one can receive any of the other sacraments by reason of having received these so-called 'Baptisms.' *Baptism of Water* is the initial requirement for the reception of all the other sacraments."

Immediately after this long passage of Fr. Feeney's lecture that we have quoted, he turns to the subject of justification. We want to quote that passage, also, because it will allow us to move to another, one where Fr. Feeney completes, as it were, the thought expressed by Sr. Catherine in *Gate of Heaven*.

"Did Jesus really mean *water* to be essential for the Baptism He instituted? He did. When He started His public life Jesus came down and stood in water, in the River Jordan, where John was baptizing. He wanted, thereby, to let us know what *Baptism* was to mean in the Catholic Church forevermore. *Baptizing* forever means *pouring water* on you, or *sprinkling with water*, or *dipping you in water*.

"As John the Baptist was baptizing Jesus, John said to Him, 'I ought to be baptized by thee, and comest thou to me?' Then Jesus said, 'Suffer it to be so now. For so it becometh us to fulfill all justice.' (Matt. 3:14,15.)

"Unfulfilled justice is the state of justification. Fulfilled justice is the state of salvation. What Jesus is saying to us, at His own baptism by John in the River Jordan, is that justification is now being turned into salvation with the aid of water.

"Jesus goes so far as to praise and belittle John the Baptist in terms of this very rite of Baptism. He says of John the Baptist, 'Amen I say to you, there hath not risen among them that are born of women a greater than John the Baptist: yet he that is the lesser in the Kingdom of Heaven is greater than he.' (Matt. 11:11.) John the Baptist's greatness came not from being born in the state of justification. It came from being admitted into the Kingdom of Christ in salvation."

Now we turn to the portion of his lecture where Fr. Feeney "completes" Sr. Catherine's thought. It is in the catechism-like question-and-answer passage.

"Why did the North American martyrs come over here, if unbaptized Indians could make perfect acts of love? The Indians poured scalding hot water on one of the North American martyrs, St. John de Brébeuf, by way of ridiculing the Baptism of Water he was preaching. Why did the Church allow this torture to be provoked, if the waters of Baptism are non-essential to Indian salvation?

"Q. What does 'Baptism of Desire' mean?

"A. It means the belief in the necessity of Baptism of Water for salvation, and a full intent to receive it.

"Q. Can 'Baptism of Desire' save you?

"A. Never.

"Q. Could 'Baptism of Desire' save you if you really believed it

206

could?

"A. It could not.

"Q. Could it possibly suffice for you to pass into a state of justification?

"A. It could.

"Q. If you got into the state of justification with the aid of 'Baptism of Desire,' and then failed to receive Baptism of Water, could you be saved?

"A. Never."

Fairly frequently in his lectures Fr. Feeney employed the question-and-answer style of ante-Vatican II catechesis. Here is another passage in this same lecture, "The Waters of Salvation," where he does so:

"Q. Can anyone now be saved without Baptism of Water?

"A. No one can be saved without Baptism of Water.

"Q. Are the souls of those who die in the state of justification saved, if they have not received Baptism of Water?

"A. No. They are not saved.

"Q. Where do these souls go if they die in the state of justification but have not received Baptism of Water?

"A. I do not know.

"Q. Do they go to Hell?

"A. No.

"Q. Do they go to Heaven?

"A. No.

"Q. Are there any such souls?

"A. I do not know! Neither do you!

"Q. What are we to say to those who believe there are such souls?

"A. We must say to them that they are making reason prevail over Faith, and the laws of probability over the Providence of God."

We have described Fr. Feeney's language as "muscular." The reader has now seen that for himself. He has seen the priest unequivocally brand as "heresy" the position that there is more than one baptism, Baptism of Water. However, Bro. Thomas Mary Sennott writes that it was no more than Fr. Feeney's opinion that the position is heretical. (He does not write that he ever actually heard Fr. Feeney say such, and other "Feeneyites" have contested him for writing as he did, but none in print.) This is what he says in his book, *They Fought the Good Fight*:

"The newspaper reporters would often ask Father Feeney 'what would you do if the Pope came out and defines that there is salvation outside the Church?' Father Feeney would reply, 'but the Pope couldn't do that.' 'Why not,' they would ask, 'he's the Pope, isn't he?' Father Feeney would say, 'God can't contradict Himself; the Holy Ghost would prevent him.' The reporters would fall silent, but I suspect remained unconvinced.

"Father Feeney's opinion on the absolute necessity of Baptism for salvation, which developed only after his condemnation, was never the subject of reporters' questions. But if a reporter had asked, 'what would you do if the Pope said that a catechumen who had faith and charity, but died before the reception of Baptism, could be saved?' Father Feeney, I am sure, would have answered, 'I would submit immediately.' Father Feeney always considered his position on Baptism of Desire an opinion, an opinion which he shared with some great saints, such as St. Augustine, but only an opinion. That is why he sent copies of *Bread of Life* in which the lecture 'The Waters of Salvation' is contained, to the Holy Father and to every Cardinal; he was submitting his opinion to the judgment of the Church."

Save for a letter of appreciation sent by a Spanish prelate, none of the world's cardinals reacted to *Bread of Life*. It should almost go without saying that there was no response from Pius XII. The odds that he even saw his copy of the book would be slim.

In regard to what Bro. Thomas Mary Sennott had to say, he also speaks to the question of so-called Baptism of Desire as it relates to the victims of abortion. It is a subject on which we have already touched, but Bro. Thomas Mary gives it new point.

"It might seem today that the subject of Baptism of Desire is a dead issue, but many, even good Catholics, are now saying that aborted babies can be saved by Baptism of Desire—the desire being on the part of the parents or of the Church. It seems to me that this will only encourage abortion. If a poor girl in trouble is wondering if she should have an abortion, and someone tells her that her baby will be saved by Baptism of Desire, this could push her over the brink. It certainly seems that there is an urgent need of an authoritative magisterial pronouncement on Baptism of Desire, and on the closely related problem of the Limbo of the Unregenerate. This would also present a perfect opportunity to deal with the unanswered questions raised by Father Feeney.

"Galileo had to wait for three hundred years for his eventual exoneration by the Church. The question of a geocentric versus a heliocentric universe, however, was not a particularly pressing matter. But the questions raised by Father Feeney couldn't be more urgent; they are a matter of eternal life or eternal death."

Indeed. So important are these questions, we may suppose that when the Church is one day again sufficiently herself to want to define truth instead of considering "signs of the times" and her own position in the "modern world" (whatever it will then be like) there will be another general council—Vatican III or perhaps Trent II—which will take up such matters, and settle them.

Even as we speak in this vein, there is a thought which wants expressing, one which will be novel to anyone unaccustomed to thinking in historical terms and that is certainly contrary to the spirit of the 20th century's closing years. It is this: Even as the expectation of apocalypse seems to have been widespread in what we call the "early years of the Church," so it is now. But is it possible that in fact this time in which we live will one day be seen as still figuring in the "early years of the Church"? Who can say for sure that it will not? What if today's widespread feeling of impending disaster signifies not that the world is about to end, but that we are entering into a new Dark Age, one with the technology intact? That would be a nightmare, but surely the new Dark Age would eventually end as did the first. What sort of world, and what sort of Church, would then emerge? In a word, what will the Church Militant look like 500, 1,000 or even 5,000 years from now? The question is not fanciful. The Church herself used to think in such historical terms. That was until just a few decades ago when she became absorbed in the question of her position in this fleeting "modern world." Again thinking the old way could at least serve as an antidote to the fear and pessimism prevalent today. It is almost incidental that it would help bring an end to the hankering for signs and wonders that produces, among other results, hundreds of false Marian apparitions, for men who live in expectation of a better future are men who live in faith. They do not need miracles and apparitions.

One thing that must be said about the "Feeneyites" who do not await a future magisterial pronouncement but are already settled in their mind that there is no saving baptism but baptism of water, their conviction leads them to insights approaching the mystical.

For instance, there is William Biersach. Formerly lapsed from the Faith and a university professor who teaches a course on the history of rock music, of all things (this is in Southern California), he is just coming on the scene as a Catholic commentator, and a quite brilliant one. Whether or not he considers himself a "Feeneyite" as such, he has clearly been influenced by thinking that went on at St. Benedict Center.

In the manuscript of his yet unpublished book, *While the Eyes of the Great are Elsewhere*, Biersach refers to Our Lord's teaching as expressed in *John* III:15 and says: "He was stating a simple but comprehensive requirement for entry into Heaven: water Baptism. Water is such a common and ordinary thing. Unlike the bread, wine, and oil of other Sacraments which are the result of Man's labor, water is something we already find on our planet as part of God's Creation. We cannot take credit for its manufacture. It is elemental, basic, primary, a fundamental component of life itself. And Jesus commands us to take a small amount of this remarkable and readily available substance, pour it on the head of the believer, and utter a few words while doing so. To think that such an unremarkable action can bring about a profound change in a human being—the erasure of Original Sin and incorporation into Jesus—boggles the mind. Its very simplicity is perhaps the biggest barrier against the inflated expectations of our self-assured intellects."

The present writer is unaware of anyone else making Biersach's point that God by Himself makes available the matter for the one sacrament necessary for the reception of others, whose matter is provided from the work of men. Since reception of the other sacraments—the ones that use bread, wine and oil—depends on our reception of baptism, Biersach's fingering the divine origin of its matter, and its alone, underlines its primacy.

Another " Feeneyite," an avowed one, is Michael Malone, who makes his home in Texas. At the present writing, Malone was working on a book in which he argues that the Immaculata herself, the Blessed Virgin Mary, received baptism. His point: If she who was conceived without sin and therefore did not require baptism received it anyway, God meant her reception of the sacrament as a sign of its necessity to all others. In a sense, Malone's reasoning in regard to the Mother of God receiving baptism parallels the historical teaching as to why the God-Man Himself received it from John the Baptist. He certainly did not require it, but His willingness to go down into the Jordan set us the supreme example.

Meditation on the writings of St. Maximilian Kolbe, writings which were not available in English a half-century ago, seem to have been very fruitful during recent years in the "Feeneyites"' consideration of baptism. The present writer confesses, however, that he has not plumbed the works of the great 20th-century Franciscan to the same depth. Accordingly, for me to attempt to outline any of this newest thinking would risk its misrepresentation. In any event, we said in the Introduction and again a few pages ago that we would not deal with the "Feeneyite" position on baptism at great length. All that remains to be said concerning it is that although the position, or "opinion" (as Bro. Thomas Mary Sennott has it) was developed by the time *Bread of Life* first appeared in 1952, it was not when Raymond Karam wrote "Reply to a Liberal" in consultation with Fr. Feeney in early 1949. In the essay, Karam allows for both so-called baptism of blood and baptism of desire. He does so, however, in terms so restrictive that they bear no resemblance to what is typically meant nowadays by baptism of blood and baptism of desire.

Thus, "Martyrdom [i.e. baptism of blood] can replace Baptism only in the case of a man who cannot receive the Sacrament of Baptism *because* he is dying for Christ." Similarly, and following the teaching of St. Thomas Aquinas that "If anyone has *perfect contrition* before the absolution of the priest, he obtains the remission of his sins," Karam says, "In the case of baptism, too, if the catechumen to be baptized can make an act of perfect charity, remission of his sins can precede the actual reception of baptism, provided explicit faith and an *explicit intent to receive baptism* are not lacking."

Yet, a few lines later, Karam asks, "But who can presume to affirm about any man that he has received sanctifying grace before the actual reception of a sacrament, seeing that it is impossible to know whether or not he was able to make a perfect act of love?"

As will be seen presently, Karam's question very much bears on the present writer's understanding of the dogma, *extra ecclesiam nulla salus*. Before we come to our statement of that understanding, there is one last matter to examine.

It was noted in Chapter Nine that "Letter of the Holy Office to the Archbishop of Boston" came to be cited in a footnote at Vatican II. It was in the Dogmatic Constitution on the Church (*Lumen Gentium*). It is interesting that Bro. Thomas Mary Sennott argues in his book, *They Fought the Good Fight*, that it is precisely in the light of *Lumen Gentium* that we can arrive at what he calls a "proper interpretation" of "Letter." He does not take a long time making his argument. Here it is in its entirety:

"The two paragraphs in the *Letter* which Father Feeney found especially objectionable were:

"'12. That one may obtain eternal salvation, it is not always required that he be incorporated into the Church actually as a member, but it is necessary that at least he be united to her by desire and longing.

"'13. However, this desire need not always be explicit, as it is in catechumens; but when a person is involved in invincible ignorance, God accepts also an implicit desire, so called because it is included in that good disposition of soul whereby a person wishes his will to be conformed to the will of God.'

"A reference to the 'Letter of the Holy Office to the Archbishop of Boston' appears in an official footnote to *Lumen Gentium* (2,16). The *Letter*, however, is not mentioned in the *relatio*, the official report which accompanied the *schema*, so it was evidently just appended by one of the *periti* who composed the *schema*. The relevant passage of *Lumen Gentium* reads:

"'Those also can attain to everlasting salvation who through no fault of their own do not know the gospel of Christ or His Church, yet sincerely seek God, and moved by grace strive by their deeds to do His will as it is known to them through the dictates of conscience.' (*The Documents of Vatican II*, Abbot, Fr. Walter M., S.J., (General Editor), America Press, New York, 1966, p.35; n.59 Cf. *Letter of Holy Office to the Archbishop of Boston*, Denz. 3869-72.)

"This passage of *Lumen Gentium* is similar to the *Letter* but with one significant difference. The phrase 'implicit desire' (*votum implicitum*) which was so objectionable to Father Feeney has been dropped. Abbot Jerome Theisen, O.S.B., comments on this omission:

"'The suppression of *votum implicitum* is probably due to disenchantment with the term, especially since it was used indiscriminately to describe the situation of both separated Christians and the "unevangelized" in their diverse relations to the Roman Catholic Church. '

(Theisen, Abbot Jerome, O.S.B., *The Ultimate Church and the Promise of Salvation*, St. John's University Press, Collegeville, Minnesota, 1976, p.57.)

"The relevant passage from *Lumen Gentium* continues:

"'...Nor does divine Providence deny the help necessary for salvation to those who without blame on their part, have not yet arrived at an explicit knowledge of God, but who strive to live a good life, thanks to His grace. Whatever goodness or truth is found among them is looked upon by the Church as a *preparation for the Gospel* [the emphasis is Bro. Thomas Mary's.] She regards such qualities as given by Him who enlightens all men so that they may finally have life.' (Abbot, *Op. cit.*, p.35.)

"So a person of goodwill who is involved in invincible ignorance and has an implicit desire to be joined to the Church, may indeed be saved, but *not where he is*. Whatever of truth or goodness is found in such a person is looked upon by the Church as a *preparation for the gospel*, and, as *Lumen Gentium* continues, it is to such persons that the Church 'to promote the glory of God and *procure the salvation of all such men* [another emphasis of Bro. Thomas Mary's], and mindful of the command of the Lord, "Preach the gospel to every creature" (Mk. 16:16)...painstakingly fosters her missionary work.'"

Our work is nearly done. The story of Fr. Feeney, Sr. Catherine, St. Benedict Center, the Slaves of the Immaculate Heart of Mary and their beliefs and teachings has been recounted. If it has not been done exhaustively, we said at the beginning that it would not be. It could not. A complete history would require two things: a bigger book, and access to documents sealed away in archives that may not be opened for a long time, if ever.

The reason for the continued secrecy is easy to understand. Consider merely the matter of Fr. Feeney's being ordered to Rome to appear at proceedings against him. He asked what charges were being brought against him and who was pressing them, information to which he was entitled under provisions of Canon Law. The information was not provided, but he was told to proceed to Rome anyway. He did not, and was "excommunicated" as a consequence.

Who made the decision not to provide him with the information to which he was entitled? Was it foreseen that he probably would seek the information, and that failing to be provided it, he probably would stay in Boston, thereby furnishing grounds for his "excommunication"? Those are the kind of questions that could only be answered if the archives were opened. The answers could be embarrassing even a half-century later—embarrassing or worse. Open archives could provide documentary evidence of a *policy* to suppress a dogma, *extra ecclesiam nulla salus*, whose proclamation was become inopportune but which could not be simply denied precisely because it is a dogma.

Be that as it may, all that here remains to be done is for the present writer, first, to offer the promised statement of his understanding of the dogma, this after two years of thinking about it starting from the days when research for these pages began, and then to wonder a little about the future.

As regards the dogma, God is the owner of His gifts, including the gift of salvation in eternity. That is clear. As the owner of His gifts, He may bestow them as He sees fit. That recognized, however, it surely ought equally to be seen that we must not presume that in any particular case He will make an exception to the terms He Himself sets for the receipt of His gift of salvation: "Unless a man be born again of water and the Holy Ghost, he cannot enter into the kingdom of Heaven" and "Unless a man eat My Flesh and drink My Blood he shall not have life in him."

A particular case may be a man of another religion whom we knew only from afar but who seemed virtuous in his life, the famous hypothetical ignorant native on a desert island, or a dear friend or family member who dies outside the Church. For each one, God leaves us free to pray what we may, including that the departed sought Truth, and found and accepted it before the end. However, once we start presuming on His mercy (which is what we do when we suppose He will make an exception), not merely do we become guilty of presumption. We also run the risk of ignoring Our Lord's last commandment to His followers: to make disciples of all the nations, which means everybody in the world. God forbid, we could even wind up believing in Karl Rahner's "anonymous Christian"—the man who is a follower of Christ without knowing it. Of course if someone falls into that belief, he will finally have no compelling reason for himself remaining a faithful member of the Church, which is to speak of one willing to practice all her precepts. *Unwillingness* to practice all her precepts is the condition of today's "cafeteria Catholic."

Further, God is not pleased when His commandments are ignored, including His last one. Anyone who ignores His commandments, including the last, will not be right in His eyes. And anyone who is not right in God's eyes, individuals, a society, a people, the people of God who are the Church—but become faithless by ignoring Him—simply cannot endure. They will have an end, and it will not be such a one as they would wish or imagined they could still have even as they became faithless and presumed on His mercy: rest in Him, saved, for eternity.

As for the future, we have said that no one can know how much time must pass before the Church's present disarray is put right; that before it is, ex-Christendom and all the rest of the world could even know another Dark Age, but one with the technology intact.

The notion of a possible new Dark Age is not original with this writer.

I once heard the late Malcolm Muggeridge express his fear of such a time befalling us. It was one afternoon in about 1968 when he stopped at *Triumph's* offices to visit the magazine's staff. Young as I was at the time, I still had good enough manners not to interrupt the older, wiser man during the minutes he dilated on what he called his "worst" fear. Had I interrupted, it would have been with the suggestion that the new Dark Age would perhaps be succeeded by a new Age of Faith.

Why should it not? The main thing necessary for it would be for some men in each generation to keep alive the Faith and its teachings as they once were. In the first Dark Age, the work was done mainly in monasteries, and in none more importantly than Benedictine ones. Truly, there is a real sense in which we can say that Christendom was born at Monte Cassino and had its cradle at Cluny. When it is reborn, will it be due to the idea of it having been preserved at places with names like Fontgombault, Le Barroux, Randol, Trior and Still River, Massachusetts?

When the Priory of St. Benedict in Still River was elevated to abbatial status on April 18, 1993, the Rt. Rev. Gabriel Gibbs was installed as the first abbot of the 37-member community. It was a milestone of a life in religion which effectively began when Father Abbot, as a young pre-med student at Harvard, started attending lectures at St. Benedict Center while it was still located in Cambridge.

In September, 1992, while visiting Still River to do research for the present book, this writer enjoyed the immense privilege of having Father Abbot lead me through my personal consecration to Jesus through the Immaculate Heart of Mary with the vow recommended by St. Louis de Montfort. This was at an altar where Fr. Feeney used to celebrate Mass, and Father Abbot spoke eloquently on his community's "Feeneyite" origin and the continuity of tradition.

Similar talk could be heard in a statement he made to Virginia Kimball, a reporter for the Lowell (Massachusetts) *Sun*. It appeared in the paper on April 20, 1993. At the new abbey, he said, they believe in "one faith, one baptism, under one Holy Father. I suppose you can describe us as being on the far right and others on the far left."

In another newspaper article, one published in the *Harvard Post* for April 16, 1993, Fr. Peter Connelly of the abbey was cited: "And even though they no longer hold sermons on Boston Common, members of the abbey have not lost sight of the dogma [*extra ecclesiam nulla salus*] that drew them together in the first place. 'To be open and accommodating,' says Father Peter, 'does not necessarily signify a lessening of zeal.'"

We have seen in this book other evidence that the "Feeneyites" have "not lost sight of the dogma," and also evidence that four decades after the "excommunication" of Fr. Feeney they increasingly are not expected to do so. (There is that letter from the Judicial Vicar of Worcester to the Secretary for Ministerial Personnel of the Archdiocese of Boston, the one written after the M.I.C.M. sisters of St. Ann's House were "regularized" and which said the "community in no manner abandoned Fr. Feeney's teachings. Consequently the sisters do a good deal more than keep the memory of Fr. Feeney. They now actively proclaim his teachings as they did before the regularization.")

Well, merely not to "lose sight" of the dogma is the same as keeping it alive. "Actively proclaiming" it amounts to still more. To be sure, most persons calling themselves Catholic today no longer believe that outside the Church there is no salvation. Thanks to the "excommunication" of Fr. Feeney, many would even say that such a belief is "heretical." That view may persist for as long as the Church's current disarray continues, and that may be for as long as a new Dark Age, if we have one. Our final questions are these: Can the Church's disarray ever be put right without her once again embracing and teaching undiluted the dogma being kept alive and even actively proclaimed at Still River? Would an end of the Church's disarray be the thing, possibly the only thing, that could preserve us altogether from a new Dark Age, or at least bring one to an end, by its ushering in a new Age of Faith?

If the answer to the first question is no, and the answer to the second yes, the Church and world owe much to Fr. Feeney, Sr. Catherine and those who have followed them, and will, at Still River and elsewhere.